COMMUNITY
TOURISM
DEVELOPMENT

Third Edition

A publication of the U of M Tourism Center

The Tourism Center is a collaboration of University of Minnesota Extension and the College of Food, Agricultural and Natural Resource Sciences

Cynthia C. Messer, 2010
Community Tourism Development

Third Edition

Editor: Mary E. Vitcenda

Original graphic design: John A. Molstad

Third Edition graphic design: Gleason Printing

ISBN 9781888440515

For more information on the Tourism Center, visit www.tourism.umn.edu/

For more information on University of Minnesota Extension, visit www.extension.umn.edu/

Extension Store Item #: 08665

First printing December 2010, second printing July 2012 by Gleason Printing, Minneapolis, MN

IN PARTNERSHIP ...

UNIVERSITY OF MINNESOTA
EXTENSION
Driven to Discover℠

College of Food, Agricultural
and Natural Resource Sciences

UNIVERSITY OF MINNESOTA

Community Tourism Development

Project Director:	Cynthia C. Messer, M.A. Extension Educator and Professor University of Minnesota Tourism Center
University of Minnesota Contributors:	Kent Gustafson, M.A., Extension Educator and Professor Daniel Erkkila, Ph.D., Extension Educator and Professor Adeel Ahmed, M.P.P., Extension Educator Neil Linscheid, M.P.P., Extension Educator Ryan Pesch, M.U.R.P., Extension Educator John Bennett, M.A., Extension Educator Dave Wilsey, Ph.D., Extension Educator Mary E. Vitcenda, Extension Educational Materials Coordinator
Other Contributors:	David Bergman, Explore Minnesota Tourism Jim Zons, EZ New Media Wendy L. Oden, M.T.A., Tourism Consultant

A special thank you to the many communities, organizations and individuals who shared their stories, experiences and wisdom within these pages.

Some materials drawn from Rural Tourism Development published in 1991 by the University of Minnesota Tourism Center. Authors: Barbara Koth, Glenn Kreag, John Sem.

Funding:	University of Minnesota Extension Center for Community Vitality Carlson Tourism, Travel and Hospitality Endowed Chair
Front cover photos:	Riverboat, church, courthouse—© Cynthia C. Messer Canoeists, Visitors Expected sign—© Explore Minnesota Tourism
Title Page Photo:	Bentonsport, Iowa street—© Cynthia C. Messer

The University of Minnesota Tourism Center is a collaboration of University of Minnesota Extension and the College of Food, Agricultural and Natural Resource Sciences. The mission of the Tourism Center is to prepare and support the industry for success and sustainability.

For more information, visit the University of Minnesota Tourism Center website.

www.tourism.umn.edu

Contents

See the accompanying CD-ROM for interactive work and assessment sheets for use with this manual.

Preface

In the past several decades, tourism has evolved as a major economic development priority for many communities. Increasing consumer demand for educational and participatory travel experiences has resulted in a variety of specialty niche markets such as nature-based tourism, cultural-heritage tourism, and agritourism. Today, more and more communities seek to link strategic tourism planning with sustainable development. To address these trends and needs, the University of Minnesota Tourism Center developed *Community Tourism Development.*

This is the third edition of this manual and reflects updated data and changes that have emerged since the previous edition. This edition includes an updated CD-ROM of the work and assessment sheets that allows the user to input local data for easier use; new, streamlined binding; and new or updated case studies.

We designed *Community Tourism Development* to provide organizations and individuals with a development process and materials to help communities plan, initiate, and expand tourism as a means of long-term economic development. The development concepts are applicable to communities of all sizes and at various stages of tourism development.

This manual first evolved from the National Rural Tourism Development Project initiated by the University of Minnesota Tourism Center in 1991. Since then, *Community Tourism Development* and the previous *Rural Tourism Development* manual have been used by tourism, economic, and community development professionals, by community-based volunteers, and by educators and university faculty to help communities implement effective tourism programs. It has also been integrated into academic courses studying tourism and community development.

An important element of this manual is the incorporation of case studies and examples. Researchers have followed tourism development in four communities first profiled in 1991, and their stories of tourism development over the years are included. These communities are Dahlonega, Georgia; San Luis, Colorado; Sandpoint, Idaho; and the Villages of Van Buren, Iowa. Each community realized successes and challenges with its tourism programs, and lessons learned are shared in the case studies included in this manual.

We found the communities at various stages of a destination's life cycle. Each community has experienced benefits from tourism, but also faces different yet all too common issues relating to unplanned tourism growth—traffic congestion, lack of political support, lack of organizational funding, unrealized economic benefits for local people, and so on. This underscores how important it is for communities to engage in tourism visioning and planning at the outset of developing a local tourism industry, since potential impacts are often not visibly present until decades later, when changing course is often difficult and costly.

Purpose

This manual is intended to help communities expand their economic development potential by developing their travel and tourism industry. It is designed for community groups working on tourism development and for others interested in expanding their knowledge and skills in community tourism development.

Whether you are in a rural or urban setting, this material will help you:

- Identify important community and tourism development values to guide your tourism development effort;
- Revitalize your community's economy through tourism;
- Launch a community-based tourism effort through a strategic planning process; and
- Maintain a quality community tourism industry through development of attractions, services, marketing, and organization.

Using this Manual

This manual provides knowledge and tools to help your community launch or improve tourism efforts. Ideally, a community seeking to develop tourism will work through the process as laid out in the manual—taking the time and effort to develop a comprehensive community tourism plan and implementation strategy. However, because communities are in different stages of tourism development and have differing needs, the materials can also be used by communities looking to boost their existing tourism efforts. The manual is laid out so that chapters and worksheets can be used as needed.

The materials and worksheets provide directions and explanations for working through the tourism development process. However, some elements of the process will be enhanced by working with a skilled facilitator. This may be especially true if your community has mixed feelings about tourism, strong personalities, or concerns about objectivity. Throughout the manual, we offer suggestions on working with facilitators.

Work and assessment sheets are located at the end of each chapter and on the CD-ROM. The forms on the CD enable local data to be entered electronically and/or printed for easier use. They have been designed for use by individuals or by a group working on specific elements of tourism development. When completed, the worksheets can provide a comprehensive view of your community's tourism development efforts and opportunities. This information will provide the basis for business and marketing plans. It can also be used to encourage local and regional leaders, generate community and media support, and create benchmark information for future development and evaluation.

Timeline

Community Tourism Development provides a wide variety of tools to help your community develop and improve its tourism program. Communities just starting a tourism program can expect to take up to two years to complete all the recommended worksheets and activities. Some communities may already have an active tourism program and choose to implement only parts of the process. The following chart provides an approximation of the timing and sequence of an effective tourism development effort. This will help you keep track of the progress your community is making. The chart suggests a timeline and provides room for you to make assignments to carry out the process. If your community has completed part of the process, skip the corresponding steps. Remember, however, that no matter where your community is in the process, follow-through, evaluation, and commitment are needed for success.

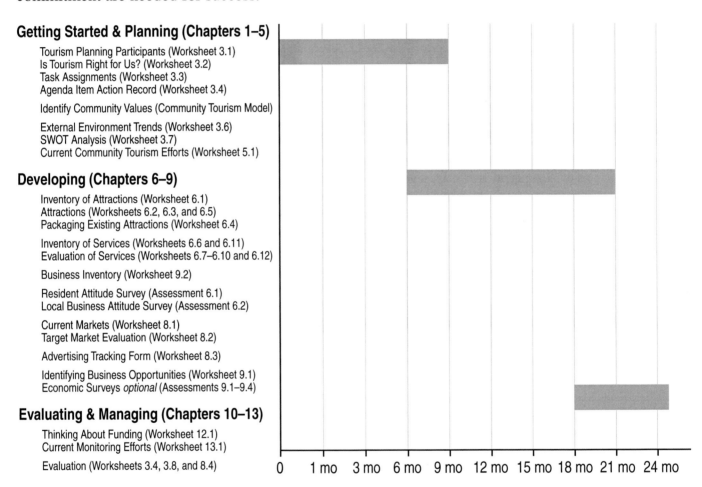

Getting Started & Planning (Chapters 1–5)

Tourism Planning Participants (Worksheet 3.1)
Is Tourism Right for Us? (Worksheet 3.2)
Task Assignments (Worksheet 3.3)
Agenda Item Action Record (Worksheet 3.4)

Identify Community Values (Community Tourism Model)

External Environment Trends (Worksheet 3.6)
SWOT Analysis (Worksheet 3.7)
Current Community Tourism Efforts (Worksheet 5.1)

Developing (Chapters 6–9)

Inventory of Attractions (Worksheet 6.1)
Attractions (Worksheets 6.2, 6.3, and 6.5)
Packaging Existing Attractions (Worksheet 6.4)

Inventory of Services (Worksheets 6.6 and 6.11)
Evaluation of Services (Worksheets 6.7–6.10 and 6.12)

Business Inventory (Worksheet 9.2)

Resident Attitude Survey (Assessment 6.1)
Local Business Attitude Survey (Assessment 6.2)

Current Markets (Worksheet 8.1)
Target Market Evaluation (Worksheet 8.2)

Advertising Tracking Form (Worksheet 8.3)

Identifying Business Opportunities (Worksheet 9.1)
Economic Surveys *optional* (Assessments 9.1–9.4)

Evaluating & Managing (Chapters 10–13)

Thinking About Funding (Worksheet 12.1)
Current Monitoring Efforts (Worksheet 13.1)

Evaluation (Worksheets 3.4, 3.8, and 8.4)

0   1 mo   3 mo   6 mo   9 mo   12 mo   15 mo   18 mo   21 mo   24 mo

Editor's Note

The names of two key tourism organizations have changed since the second edition, and we have updated the names accordingly throughout the manual. They are:

United Nations World Tourism Organization (UNWTO), formerly called simply the World Tourism Organization. Website: http://www.unwto.org/

United States Travel Association or U.S. Travel Association (USTA), formerly called the Travel Industry Association (TIA). Website: http://www.ustravel.org/

Chapter 1
The Community Tourism Model

Small, often rural, communities have a rich heritage and unique tourism resources to share with visitors from around the world. Many also have a desire to diversify their economy. Increasingly, communities are viewing tourism as an economic development strategy.

Tourism can provide many benefits to a community. It can create new jobs, foster an entrepreneurial base, generate local tax revenue, stimulate capital investment, facilitate infrastructure improvements, protect cultural and natural resources, and build community pride.

Developing tourism, however, is not an easy task. The tourism industry is very competitive. Communities must not only vie for visitors with neighboring communities, but also compete with national and international destinations made more competitive by low airfares.

Communities interested in developing tourism should do so with the same kind of long-term vision, commitment to work with a variety of groups, and strategic planning that is often used when luring other types of industries to town. This manual will help you develop your tourism program through an organized process based on a community tourism model.

WHAT'S IN THIS CHAPTER?

- What is Tourism?
- What is Community?
- The Community Tourism Model
- A Value System for Community Tourism
- Sustainable Tourism Development

What is Tourism?

Tourism has many definitions. Some, often created to measure economic outputs, limit tourism to activity that occurs within 50 miles from home. Others refer to activity that includes at least one overnight stay away from home. Some measure only visitors from out of state, while others use geographic boundaries such as county lines. Table 1.1 shows travel and tourism definitions used by the United Nations World Tourism Organization (UNWTO), a global intergovernmental tourism group.

Table 1.1: United Nations World Tourism Organization Definitions

Tourism: the activities of persons traveling to and staying in places outside their usual environment for not more than one consecutive year for leisure, business, and other purposes.

Domestic tourism: residents of the given country traveling within their own country.

Inbound tourism: nonresidents traveling in the given country.

Outbound tourism: residents traveling in another country.

Internal tourism: domestic tourism plus inbound tourism.

National tourism: domestic tourism plus outbound tourism.

International tourism: inbound tourism plus outbound tourism.

Tourist: a visitor who stays at least one night in a collective or private accommodation in the country visited.

Visitor: a person traveling to and staying in places outside his or her usual environment for not more than one consecutive year for leisure, business, and other purposes.

Same-day visitor: a visitor who does not spend the night in a collective or private accommodation in the country visited (includes cruise passengers).

Domestic visitor: a person residing in a country who travels to a place within the country, outside his or her usual environment, for a period not exceeding 12 months and whose main purpose of visit is other than the exercise of an activity remunerated from within the place visited. Includes tourists plus same-day visitors.

International visitors: persons who travel to a country other than that in which they have their usual residence but outside their usual environment for a period not exceeding 12 months and whose main purpose of visit is other than the exercise of an activity remunerated from within the country visited.

International visitors: tourists plus same-day visitors.

Source: United Nations World Tourism Organization. (1992). *WTO definitions, recommendations on tourism statistics*. Madrid, Spain: UNWTO.

Figure 1.1: Types of Travelers

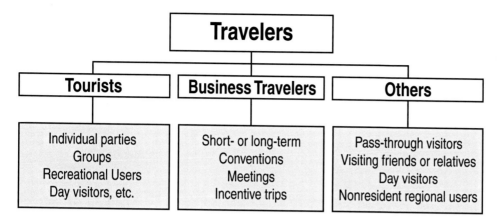

This manual will work from a common dictionary definition of tourism:

The practice of traveling for recreation; the guidance or management of tourists as a business or governmental function; the economic activities associated with and dependent upon tourists.

Travelers are people who travel to a community for any purpose (Figure 1.1). **Tourists** are people traveling for recreation and leisure. It may be useful to think of tourists as visitors or guests. These terms have neutral connotations for most people, and describe the type of relationship the tourist will have with a community.

In this manual we will focus on tourists. However, it's important to consider other travelers because they, too, have needs and wants that offer the community opportunities to benefit economically, and they may return as tourists. Your community may even find that nontourist travelers are a viable market.

As part of your community's tourism effort, you will need to learn about those visiting your community. If you understand their motivations, you can direct development and marketing efforts to satisfying their needs and wants.

McIntosh and Goeldner list four basic categories of travel motives:

Physical - motives related to physical rest, relaxation, participation in recreational sports, or health

Cultural - motives related to a desire to know about the culture of an area, including food, music, art, folklore, and religion

Interpersonal - motives that include a desire to meet new people, visit family and friends, or escape from daily routine

Targeting the Travel Market

The Marshall, Minnesota, Convention and Visitor Bureau focuses marketing efforts on a travel market rather than a tourist market. Bureau director Linda Erb says, "Our efforts are user driven. We asked, 'Why do people come here?' and then targeted those audiences." Marshall targets business travelers, sports groups, same-day surgery visitors, and students and parents from the state university.

Make a list of the different visitors to your community.

Status and Prestige - motives that include personal development, ego satisfaction, and pursuit of hobbies, knowledge, or education

Most people are motivated to travel by more than one reason. For example, a tourist seeking relaxation and recreation may also be interested in a cultural experience.

You Are a Tourist!

When you hear the word "tourist," you probably think of someone from far away who is sightseeing. Actually, many tourists are residents of the state in which they are traveling. In fact, many people spend much of their lives being tourists.

The last time you left town on a business trip or to play, enjoy a recreational activity in a nearby community, or spend a holiday with your relatives, you were part of the travel and tourism economy. The last time you drove more than a few miles out of town, you were a visitor. The last time you stepped on an airplane, you officially entered Touristland—a place you did not leave until you returned to the borders of your home community.

In 1997, nearly 70 percent of domestic travel in the United States consisted of trips lasting fewer than three nights; more than half of all travel by U.S. residents occurred over a weekend. More than half of all person-trips were made within a 300-mile radius of travelers' homes, and more than one-third were made within a 150-mile radius. Whatever technical definition is used, it is clear that the travel and tourism industry consists of a large number of people traveling within their own region.

Source: Adapted from South Carolina Sea Grant Consortium. (1991). *Coastal heritage* 6(3); and U.S. Travel Association of America. (1997). *National travel survey.* Washington, D.C.: USTA.

What is Community?

Many definitions address the concept of community in relation to tourism. They often relate to a group of people with a common interest or geographic boundary. Hart defines community as "a group of people who live and interact in a specific geographic area."

The geographic area is best defined by the location of people affected by tourism who have come together due to shared interests, concerns, and goals, rather than by political boundaries. The community may be as small as a neighborhood, or as large as a state or region. The term *community* does not imply that all members agree on things. In fact, most communities consist of a diverse group of individuals who often have many shared interests and concerns but also opposing viewpoints.

A community tourism industry may be defined as a collection of businesses that creates sales of goods and services to tourists. Figure 1.2 shows the relationship between tourists and the community. Tourists spend money, both at businesses that are primarily tourist-oriented (e.g., lodging, attractions) and at those primarily oriented to residents (e.g., gas, food, recreation). Businesses spend money on supplies, wages, and taxes. Employees spend tourist-related wages on everyday needs. Thus, to maximize the economic benefit of tourism, communities need to encourage local ownership of businesses and purchase of locally produced goods and services.

Figure 1.2: Tourism and Your Community

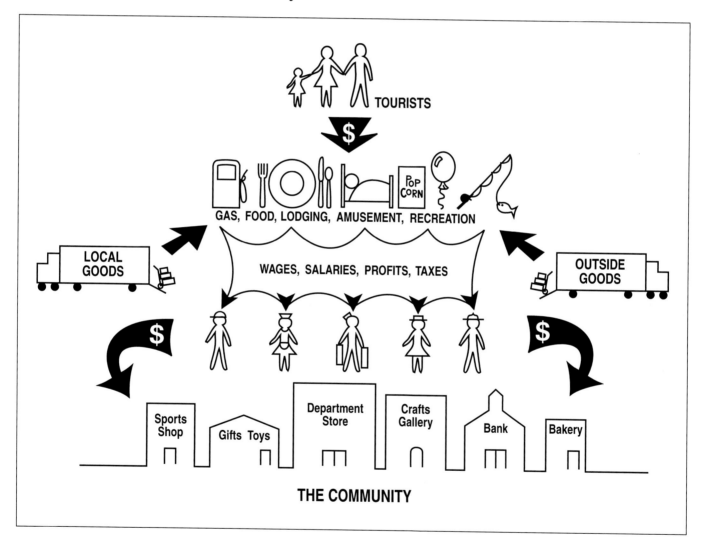

The Community Tourism Model

The community tourism model (Figure 1.3) shows the basic relationships between the tourism industry and the community. It is based on five elements needed to produce a successful tourism program. Each element has associated steps your community should take to create a successful tourism and travel industry.

Figure 1.3: Community Tourism Model

Community Values

- Explore the importance of community values in creating an effective tourism program.
- Learn methods of identifying community values.
- Maintain community values as tourism develops.

Attractions

- Identify activities, cultural resources, arts resources, historic resources, natural resources, and developments that can attract visitors to your community.
- Develop and manage attractions.

Services

- Identify public services that help visitors enjoy your community.
- Develop and expand small businesses that sell the visitor goods and services.
- Help your community diversify and strengthen its economy by creating new jobs and revenue sources.

Marketing

- Identify visitor needs.
- Select target groups of people to invite to the community.
- Select marketing methods to communicate with these groups.
- Evaluate and adjust your marketing methods to maximize effectiveness.

Tourism Organization

- Organize local individuals and groups to develop and coordinate tourism efforts.
- Identify local resources and power groups.
- Search for stable funding for tourism development.

It is the community's responsibility to create, encourage, and develop a tourism industry and/or to limit its growth. In most cases, communities that take an active approach to defining and guiding their tourism industry, and that maintain control of the impact of tourism on residents, will have more positive outcomes than those that do not.

A Value System for Community Tourism

For the tourism industry to stay in harmony with the larger community, it needs to understand the values and goals of the community, and help preserve and enhance those values and goals by embedding them in its own goal setting and planning. This allows tourism to develop in a nonconfrontational atmosphere. Tourism can be an expression of the life, geography, history, and culture of the community, not a foreign invader.

Key values for tourism development are:

- *Commitment to Assessing True Benefits and Costs*
Accurate assessment of tourism's benefits and costs (social, economic, and environmental) can help your community avoid problems and maintain support for growth.

- *Diversification*
Tourism should be a diversification tool, not a substitute for other local industry. A community's ability to weather hard times is enhanced when there are several sources of economic activity.

- *Quality*
Healthy tourism communities provide quality products and services. Tourism development must be balanced to sustain the quality of the experience over time. Overuse can deteriorate the tourism product and result in loss of visitors.

- *Shared Benefits and Control*
Businesses and community residents must share the benefits of tourism and the control of future tourism development. Communities can encourage local control through business development and expansion programs and active involvement in tourism planning.

- *Authenticity*
Authenticity is the lifestyle of a community that emerges in response to its physical and social nature, its significant historic and economic events, and the special qualities of the people who live there. Authentic attractions reflect the basic fabric of the community and focus on attributes that make a community unique.

The community tourism model (Figure 1.3) shows how community values are embedded into the tourism industry. The industry works with the community to identify and express important community values. Community values thus become the standard against which businesses and tourism organizations judge tourism development proposals. Once community values have been identified and expressed, a three-way "checks and balances" situation is created among the community, the tourism organization, and individual tourism businesses. Each of these three will watch to ensure that community values guide tourism growth.

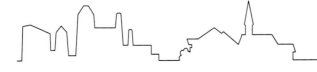

To see how some other communities have addressed values, you may want to review a film in DVD format "Weaving Tourism into Community: Four Stories over Time," produced in 2010. The film is available from University of Minnesota Extension, item #08662. The film revisits four communities first profiled in 1991 as part of the National Rural Tourism Development Project: Dahlonega, Georgia; Sandpoint, Idaho; San Luis, Colorado; and the Villages of Van Buren, Iowa. These four communities' were selected in 1991 from more than 190 because they demonstrated how key values play out in real communities. The University of Minnesota Tourism Center has followed tourism development efforts in these communities over the years. Each segment of the film is approximately 12 minutes long, with local leaders describing their communities' successes and challenges in their own words. It may be helpful to view the film early in your tourism planning. Updated written case studies of these communities are also included in Appendix A of this manual. To learn more about the film, visit the Tourism Center website at www.tourism.umn.edu.

Sustainable Tourism Development

Tourism is dependent on the very resources it seeks to use. Therefore, sustainability should be a fundamental consideration in tourism development.

The concept of sustainability was first popularized by *Our Common Future,* published by the United Nations World Commission on Environment and Development in 1987. The concept was further advanced in 1992 at the Earth Summit in Rio de Janeiro. Agenda 21 for the Travel and Tourism Industry, which evolved from the Earth Summit, is a commitment to make travel and tourism a model industry for sustainable development.

The UNWTO defines sustainable tourism as follows:

> Sustainable tourism development meets the needs of present tourists and host regions while protecting and enhancing opportunities for the future. It is envisaged as leading to management of all resources in such a way that economic, social, and aesthetic needs can be fulfilled while maintaining cultural integrity, essential ecological processes, biological diversity, and life support systems.

Source: United Nations World Trade Organization. (1998). *Guide for local authorities on developing sustainable tourism.* Madrid, Spain: UNWTO.

Tourism depends in large part on attractions and activities that are related to the natural environment and cultural heritage of the region. With good planning and management, tourism can help conserve and enhance these resources. This in turn influences customer satisfaction, which helps a destination remain popular and marketable. A true partnership of the tourism industry, the local community, and the public sector will help ensure economic and sociocultural benefits are maximized for all. This builds local support and commitment to maintaining a viable tourism industry.

This manual takes the concept of sustainable tourism development as the foundation for all efforts. It will help those working to develop tourism at the community level to integrate the principles of sustainable tourism development into local efforts.

References

Hart, M. (1999). *Guide to sustainable community indicators* (2nd ed.) (p.14). North Hanover, MA: Hart Environmental Data.

Innskeep, E. (1998). *Guide for local authorities on developing sustainable tourism* (p.21). Madrid, Spain: United Nations World Tourism Organization.

McIntosh, R.W., & Goeldner, C.R. (1990). *Tourism principles, practices, philosophies* (6th ed.) (pp. 131-132). New York, NY: John Wiley & Sons.

Chapter 2
Tourism Basics

The travel and tourism industry in the United States has grown tremendously over the past several decades. Domestic and international expenditures increased from $350 billion in 1989 to $525 billion in 2003 and to more than $704 billion in 2009. Today, travel and tourism comprise one of the nation's largest service export industries and it is the third-largest private employer in the United States after health and business services.

This rapid growth has raised the awareness of this industry at the same time many communities are experiencing diminished economic competitiveness and dependence on too few sources of income. Communities large and small are increasingly looking at tourism as a source of income and jobs.

Expectations of quality by visitors are rapidly increasing. This calls for investments to improve attractions, and makes effective customer relations and personal attention critical. Marketing messages must now be tailored and delivered specifically to targeted groups interested in a particular product in order to be effective.

Technology advances, particularly the Internet and new media marketing techniques, are also revolutionizing tourism. They have altered the way travel and tourism products are distributed and have expanded competition to a global scale. Many destinations are looking for a bigger piece of the tourism pie, while at the same time struggling with growth that, if not appropriately managed, may change the characteristics that draw tourists in the first place.

WHAT'S IN THIS CHAPTER?

- **Components of Tourism**
- **Tourism as a System**
- **Benefits and Costs of Tourism**
- **Tourism as an Economic Development Tool**
- **Obstacles to Tourism Development**
- **Tourism Area Life Cycle**

Components of Tourism

Tourism has three components: community, industry, and the tourist market.

The *community* is the heart of tourism. It supplies the location in which tourism occurs, leadership and organization for tourism development, the labor force, and public services such as roads and utilities, and hospitality.

The second component, *industry,* consists of attractions and events that draw tourists to the community, the businesses that meet their needs, and the organizations, chambers, and businesses that do promotion, planning, and market research.

The third component, the *tourist market,* consists of visitors who pay for transportation, food, lodging, personal services, and entertainment. Markets can be defined by geography, by psychographics (lifestyles, activities, interests, and opinions), or by demographics. Each market has behavior and income characteristics that influence whether it will be drawn to your community's tourism product.

Tourism as a System

Tourism is not so much an industry as it is a system of interrelated industries all serving a common market. It includes parts of a variety of economic groups, such as transportation, accommodations, food and beverage services, attractions, public services, and distribution channels. As a result, the travel and tourism industry's economic strength is difficult to track using the conventional Systems of Economic Classification (SEC) used in most countries.

Privately owned businesses that offer accommodations, tour and travel services, and attractions are the parts of the system most frequently identified as the "tourism industry." Government and nonprofit entities often manage attractions such as museums, national parks, historical sites, and wildlife preserves. Transportation, infrastructure, and other public services used by tourists are usually the responsibility of government agencies or public or private utility companies, and are also used by local residents. The marketing, information, and promotional aspects of tourism often involve the public and private sector working together. Table 2.1 shows the range of tourist-related activities in which the private, public, and nonprofit sectors may be involved.

The most successful tourism communities are those that have created a network of public-private relationships. A successful travel and tourism experience depends on collaboration among groups that otherwise might not work together. A break in one link of the chain affects the delivery of the total product and thus the entire travel experience.

Table 2.1: Sectors Involved in Tourism Development

	Private	Public	Nonprofit
Attractions	Theme parks, wave pools, theaters, shopping malls, recreation outfitters, entertainment, sports arenas, events and festivals, craft shops	Parks, preserves, lakes, monuments, playgrounds, zoos, outdoor theaters, recreation areas, museums, historic sites	Performing arts, museums, historic sites, conservation areas, botanical gardens, festivals, theaters
Services	Hotels, motels, restaurants, shops, tours, taxis, travel agents	Local bus transport, public rest rooms, visitor information, police, fire, medical	Guided tours, museum shops, tea rooms, artist co-ops
Transportation	Scheduled bus lines, airlines, trains, car services, gas stations, car & boat rentals, cruise lines, taxis	Airports, ferries, public transit systems	Shuttle buses
Atmosphere (Environmental & Social)	Downtown revitalization, ownership pride, beautification projects, hospitality training	Maintenance of parks, road access, parking, waste disposal, cleanup projects, signage, public awareness	Garden displays, local beautification, historic preservation, employee and volunteer training
Communication Promotion	Guidebooks, maps, brochures, magazines, directories, advertising, PR, incentives	Directional signage, information centers, community maps & brochures, advertising, PR	Brochures, information centers, maps, guidebooks, advertising, PR, interpretation
Research	Business and visitor surveys, ticket counts, license plate checks, sales conversions	Visitor center counts, surveys, image studies, attendance records, impact studies	Suggestion boxes, ticket counts, surveys, impact studies

Adapted from Texas Agricultural Extension Service. 1999. *Developing tourism in your community*. College Station, TX: Texas Agricultural Extension Service.

It is helpful to define key roles and responsibilities of the public and private sectors when pursuing tourism development. Table 2.2 identifies some of the most common areas of responsibility for each of these sectors.

Table 2.2: Roles and Responsibilities in Tourism Development

Public Sector	Private Sector
Adopt sustainable development principles	Adopt sustainable development principles
Include tourism in comprehensive growth and land use plans	Include nontraditional groups in planning meetings (public sector, nongovernment organizations, residents)
Establish policy and regulations affecting tourism; create financial incentives for development	Facilitate comprehensive tourism planning
Conduct research on environmental, social, and economic impacts	Establish an effective tourism organization; assess local attractions and services
Develop standards and regulations for impact	Incorporate environmental standards into management assessments decisions
Develop public infrastructure necessary for tourism (roads, police, fire, medical, etc.)	Encourage citizen input and participation in local tourism projects
Establish conservation and protected areas	Provide capital for business development
Implement/enforce zoning, building regulations	Conduct hospitality training for businesses
Develop public educational awareness programs	Facilitate collaboration and partnerships
Facilitate collaboration among public land management agencies and private sector	Provide education and training opportunities for local residents and youth
Maintain accurate tourism statistics	Conduct market research, monitor visitor trends
Ensure tourism interests are represented at key environmental and economic planning meetings	Implement effective marketing and promotion strategies
Establish a tourism advisory council	

Worldwide Travel & Tourism Facts

- As of mid-2010, estimates were that the travel and tourism industry generates (directly and indirectly) US$5,751 billion annually, equal to 9.2 percent of the world's gross domestic product (GDP).
- In 2010, travel and tourism represented more than 235 million jobs, or 1 in every 12 jobs worldwide.
- Travel and tourism accounts for US$802.3 billion dollars (9.4 percent) of capital investment and 3.8 percent of all government expenditures.
- By 2014, travel and tourism is projected to generate US$9,557.5 billion annually. Increases in employment are estimated at 1.5 percent annually to more than 259 million jobs worldwide by 2014.
- International arrivals are expected to reach over 1.56 billion by the year 2020. Of these, 1.2 billion will be intraregional and 0.4 billion will be long-haul travelers.

Sources: World Travel & Tourism Council. (2010). *Economic data search tool*. London, England. Retrieved August 6, 2010, from www.wttc.org. United Nations World Tourism Organization. *Tourism 2020 vision*. Madrid, Spain.

U.S. Tourism Facts

- In 2009, the United States hosted 41.9 million visitors. Those visitors spent over $121 billion—an average of $4,500 per person per trip.
- In 2009, total travel expenditures within the United States by both domestic and international travelers totaled US$704.4 billion. This is an average of $1.93 billion a day, or $80.4 million per hour.
- Americans earned $186.3 billion in payroll income from tourism in 2009.
- Travel and tourism generated $113 billion in tax revenues for federal, state and local governments in 2009, or 3.2 percent of all taxes collected nationally.
- Travel is the third largest private employer in the United States after health and business services.
- The travel and tourism industry ranks as the first-, second-, or third-largest employer in 29 of the 50 states.
- Leisure travel accounts for the majority (77 percent) of all U.S. domestic travel.
- Auto travel, including travel by truck and recreational vehicle, accounts for the majority (76 percent) of travel in the United States.

Sources: United States Travel Association. (2010). *Travel facts*. Washington, D.C. Retrieved Aug. 6, 2010, from www.ustravel.org.

Benefits and Costs of Tourism

Tourism can generate jobs and income and contribute substantially to the economic health and vitality of a community. But, like all development activity, tourism also generates social, economic, and environmental benefits and costs. Communities often tend to focus on only one type of impact that development might generate. Accurate assessments of both benefits and costs can help communities avoid problems and maintain community support for continued growth.

Changes viewed as positive by one group can be viewed negatively by others, polarizing the community. Planning allows communities to put the whole range of impacts on the table, assess who will and will not benefit, and facilitate a compromise that results in mutual benefit.

Tip

Trade-offs and compromise are necessary. Consider potential impacts and community values in decision making and planning.

Economic Impacts

Economic impacts are the ones most often referred to when a community begins to consider tourism development. Focus is on the income and jobs that might be stimulated by tourism. Often the emphasis is on direct sales to tourists by front-line tourism-related businesses. A more appropriate economic assessment also considers the many businesses that do not interact directly with tourists, but sell products and services to the front-line providers. This relationship is further discussed as the "multiplier effect" below.

Economic costs associated with tourism are real and should not be overlooked. Tourism is a highly complex and sophisticated industry and it requires a financial commitment in order to be successful. In addition, tourism development can inflate housing and other living costs, making it difficult for long-term residents to remain in the community. An overabundance of outside owners and investment can cause revenue generated by tourists to leave the community, minimizing economic benefits for residents.

Social Impacts

Social impacts from tourism are inevitable due to the very nature of the host-guest relationship. Tourists interact with residents during the purchase and use of tourism goods and services, through shared use of attractions and facilities, and through encounters within the community. Positive impacts can include renewed interest in cultural traditions, increased community pride, upgrades to services and facilities used by residents, and increased peace and understanding.

Negative impacts become more apparent over time as tourist visitation increases. In the early stages of development, community residents are often excited about positive economic changes. As time progresses, social and environmental impacts become more apparent and residents may become less tolerant and even resentful of tourists. The extent and types of social impacts experienced within a community depend upon the intensity and speed with which tourism development occurs. Integration of community values, planning, and good tourism management can help reduce negative impacts.

Doxey identified four stages, coinciding with succeeding stages of tourist facility development, at which sociocultural impacts are likely to occur (Figure 2.1). At the "euphoria" stage, which corresponds to the initial/discovery stage of tourism in an area, residents support tourism and are eager to open their community to visitors. As growth in tourism development begins to slow, apathy sets in. The novelty of drawing visitors has worn off; the social structure of the community is changing due to inmigration. Unequal distributions of economic benefits are now apparent and residents become skeptical. As tourism development continues, irritation sets in. Social and environmental impacts are apparent. Tourism is occurring in environmentally sensitive areas, prices and inflation have risen faster than tourist-related income, lifestyles in the community have changed, and residents feel a loss of community character.

Figure 2.1: Doxey's Irridex (Adapted)

Initial phase. Residents welcome visitors and investment. Little complaining or control.

Euphoria

Visitor-resident contact more commercial. Planning focuses on marketing.

Apathy

Saturation point. Resident misgivings about tourism. Increasing infrastructure seen as solution.

Annoyance

Open hostility to tourism, planning remedial. Increased promotion to offset image decline.

Antagonism

As negative impacts continue to grow, residents begin to blame tourists rather than unplanned and uncontrolled development, and antagonism sets in. By now, the type of visitors drawn to the community has probably changed and no longer represents the kind of tourism residents wanted. The antagonism is probably not physical, but is demonstrated in how locals treat visitors, complaints about tourist behavior, and a call for limitation of tourism.

Environmental Impacts

Environmental impacts associated with tourism development can relate to either the natural or the built environment. All development usually involves some form of physical transformation or change that can impact the environment. This is especially true of tourism development because of the close relationship between tourism and the environment.

The tourism-environment relationship consists of three key aspects:

- The natural, physical environment often serves as attractions for tourists.
- Tourist facilities and infrastructure are one aspect of the built environment.
- Tourism development and visitor use create environmental impacts.

Tourism can generate positive environmental impacts—for example, increased environmental awareness, greater appreciation for conservation of natural areas, added incentive for community cleanup and beautification projects, and improved local infrastructure that can reduce existing pollution and enhance overall environmental quality.

Unplanned tourism can create many negative environmental impacts. Architectural pollution can be caused by resort development and infrastructure designs that are not integrated into the surrounding natural environment. Ribbon development and sprawl can occur as tourist facilities are constructed farther away from initial activity centers. Infrastructure overload and traffic congestion can result from development that occurs too rapidly or from major fluctuations in seasonal demand. Finally, excessive use can damage the natural environment as much as pollution and litter left by tourists.

Minimizing Negative Impacts

Sustainable tourism balances economic, social, and environmental needs while minimizing negative impacts. The goal is to maximize the benefits and reduce the costs that tourism, like any industry, can bring to a community. This process requires attention to the various stages in the development process at which changes begin to occur, and the development of strategies to help prevent or minimize the costs.

Tip

Planning is the key to maximizing benefits and reducing costs.

Table 2.3 lists common economic, social, and environmental impacts that communities might face as a result of hosting visitors and strategies that can help mitigate costs.

Table 2.3: Impacts of Tourism

Economic Impacts of Tourism

Benefits
- Brings new money into the community
- Helps diversify and stabilize the local economy
- Attracts additional businesses and services to support tourism industry
- May be a catalyst for other industries and bring capital investment to area
- Creates local jobs and new business opportunities
- Increases expansion and retention of existing businesses
- Contributes to the state and local tax base
- Helps support local businesses that might not survive on resident income alone

Costs
- Imposes organizational and operational costs to develop
- Places demands on public infrastructure that may exceed what the local tax base can support
- May inflate property values and the price of goods and services
- Requires customer service training of employees, business owners, and community residents
- May be cyclical and impacted by forces outside the community's control
- Reduces local economic benefits if developers come from outside the community
- May cause economic and employment distortions if development is not geographically balanced

Techniques to Minimize Costs
- Use tourism development as a supplement to, not a substitute for, other sources of economic activity
- Use local capital, goods, services, labor, and expertise whenever possible
- Involve both public and private sectors in development process
- Provide financial incentives and training to foster local business ownership
- Implement tourism awareness programs for local businesses
- Establish programs to ensure affordable housing for residents

Social Impacts of Tourism

Benefits
- Supports development of community facilities and other local improvements
- May enhance community's "sense of place" through cultural/historic celebration
- Encourages civic involvement and community pride
- May help maintain cultural identity of minority populations that are dying out
- May facilitate renewed interest in traditional lifestyles among younger residents
- Provides cultural exchange between hosts and guests
- Promotes peace and understanding

Costs
- May introduce lifestyles, ideas, and behaviors that conflict with those of residents
- May create crowding, congestion, and increased crime
- May encourage "trinketization" of local arts and crafts
- Brings residents competition for services and recreation opportunities
- May create conflict among residents if benefits are unequally distributed
- May produce a "demonstration effect" (Imitation of visitors' behaviors and spending patterns), resulting in loss of cultural pride
- May create racial tension and resentment between hosts and guests

(Continued)

Table 2.3: (Continued)

Techniques to Minimize Costs
- Inform residents about both the benefits and costs of tourism
- Establish quality controls to maintain authenticity of handicrafts and cultural activities
- Plan tourism based on goals, values, and priorities identified by residents
- Ensure residents have convenient access to tourist attractions, facilities, and services
- Strictly control drugs, crime, and prostitution
- Use selective, target marketing to draw the right kinds of tourists
- Educate and train local residents to work at all levels of tourism
- Have ongoing public awareness programs about tourism

Environmental Impacts of Tourism

Benefits
- Fosters conservation and preservation of natural, cultural, and historical resources
- Increases local environmental awareness
- May encourage community beautification, revitalization, and environmental quality
- May improve local urban/rural landscapes through facilities development
- May simulate improvements in infrastructure (airports, roads, water, waste, sewage)
- May be cleaner than other industries

Costs
- May cause environmental hazards due to poor land use planning and facility design
- May create land use problems, add to urban sprawl
- May degrade quality of natural and historic sites
- May increase water, air, and noise pollution
- May result in visual/architectural pollution
- May create solid waste problems
- May bring overcrowding and traffic congestion

Techniques to Minimize Costs
- Implement land use planning and zoning laws prior to tourism development
- Design hotels and tourist facilities to reflect local architectural styles
- Set standards for water, sewage, and power supplies that encourage conservation
- Establish guidelines for local carrying capacity and limits of acceptable change
- Implement visitor use and management plans for cultural, historic, and natural attractions
- Organize proper building, park, and landscaping maintenance for public areas
- Establish conservation/protected areas to prevent growth in ecologically sensitive areas
- Execute environmental public awareness programs for visitors and residents

Sources: 1) Adapted from Richardson, S.L. (1991). *Colorado community tourism action guide*. Boulder, CO: University of Colorado. 2) Inskeep, E. (1991). *Tourism planning: An integrated and sustainable development approach*. New York, NY: Van Nostrand Reinhold. 3) McIntosh, R.W., & Goeldner, C.R. (1990). *Tourism principles, practices, philosophies* (6th ed.). New York, NY: John Wiley & Sons. 4) Gartner, W.C. (1996). *Tourism development: Principles, policies, practices*. New York, NY: Van Nostrand Reinhold.

Tourism as an Economic Development Tool

Tourism can be a valuable economic development tool. However, like any long-term economic strategy, it requires substantial commitment from local leaders, residents, and businesses. Communities unwilling to make adequate commitments of effort and funds to develop a competitive tourism industry should not use tourism as an economic development strategy.

Tourism as a Diversification Strategy

Tourism, like any industry, should not be the only source of local economic activity. It should be viewed as a strategy for diversifying economic development, not as a substitute for other industry. Economic diversity helps improve communities' options for developing a variety of attractions and services. It also helps communities weather economic downturns.

As a diversification tool, tourism has many advantages over other types of industry. The ambience and scenic appeal of a community naturally draws visitors. The local labor force is in place. There is little initial need for increased public services. Tourism is considered a "clean" industry, and its potential is untapped in many areas.

The Multiplier Effect

Economists use the term *multiplier* to refer to the primary (direct) and secondary (indirect and induced) effects that new spending or purchases have on an economy (Figure 2.2). In the context of tourism, it recognizes the fact that each tourist dollar filters throughout the community in many ways.

Tourists spend money on a variety of things, including accommodations, transportation, attractions, and other services. That spending translates into *direct effects* on a business and economy in the form of income that pays taxes and wages. Because businesses themselves are not just sellers but also buyers of goods and services, these direct tourism business receipts are further spent by firms in the form of investments or purchase of goods and services. A hotel, for example, purchases cleaning material for laundry and upkeep. This subsequent round of spending creates *indirect effects* by contributing to wages and employment in other businesses.

Figure 2.2: The Multiplier Effect in Tourism

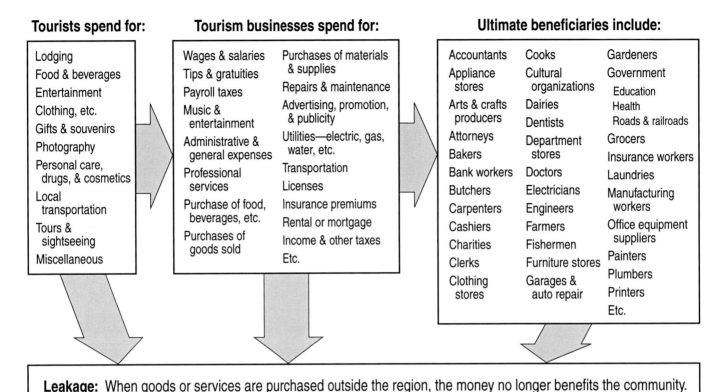

Tourists spend for:

- Lodging
- Food & beverages
- Entertainment
- Clothing, etc.
- Gifts & souvenirs
- Photography
- Personal care, drugs, & cosmetics
- Local transportation
- Tours & sightseeing
- Miscellaneous

Tourism businesses spend for:

- Wages & salaries
- Tips & gratuities
- Payroll taxes
- Music & entertainment
- Administrative & general expenses
- Professional services
- Purchase of food, beverages, etc.
- Purchases of goods sold

- Purchases of materials & supplies
- Repairs & maintenance
- Advertising, promotion, & publicity
- Utilities—electric, gas, water, etc.
- Transportation
- Licenses
- Insurance premiums
- Rental or mortgage
- Income & other taxes
- Etc.

Ultimate beneficiaries include:

- Accountants
- Appliance stores
- Arts & crafts producers
- Attorneys
- Bakers
- Bank workers
- Butchers
- Carpenters
- Cashiers
- Charities
- Clerks
- Clothing stores

- Cooks
- Cultural organizations
- Dairies
- Dentists
- Department stores
- Doctors
- Electricians
- Engineers
- Farmers
- Fishermen
- Furniture stores
- Garages & auto repair

- Gardeners
- Government
    - Education
    - Health
    - Roads & railroads
- Grocers
- Insurance workers
- Laundries
- Manufacturing workers
- Office equipment suppliers
- Painters
- Plumbers
- Printers
- Etc.

Leakage: When goods or services are purchased outside the region, the money no longer benefits the community.

Adapted from World Tourism Organization

As incomes rise and wages are paid throughout the economy due to the direct and indirect effects of tourism spending, some of the increased personal income is spent within the community, creating what are known as *induced effects*. Induced effects may also include government expenditures produced by tax revenues generated by travel and tourism spending.

TIP

Tourism spending creates direct, indirect, and induced effects in the community. Purchasing local goods and services benefits the community.

Primary and secondary benefits are related to the capability of a community to provide locally produced goods and services that are competitively priced, a qualified local work force, and a strong local entrepreneurial base with access to capital. When communities are unable to provide the inputs needed by businesses (e.g., a strong secondary business support system), local businesses are forced to purchase goods and hire employees from outside their own community. Income that leaves the local economy is lost. In economic development this is commonly known as *leakage*. Revenue that would otherwise benefit a community by purchasing local goods or hiring local people leaks out of the region in order to keep local businesses operating.

Multipliers attempt to quantify direct, indirect, and induced impacts from a single dollar spent in an economy. Multipliers can describe a number of variables such as income, sales, or employment. Transaction (sales) multipliers are most common. For example, a sales multiplier of 2.1 means that for every $1.00 spent by a tourist (direct effect) another $1.10 is generated in indirect sales to the local economy ($1.00 + $1.10 = $2.10). Tourism sales multipliers commonly range from just over 1.0 to 3.0.

The multiplier is a function of the geographic size, population, mix of industries, and self-sufficiency of the region. This means that every community will have a different multiplier effect from tourism spending. It will depend on how big the region is and how well the local economy can provide inputs (goods, services, labor) to existing businesses. Consequently, multipliers are generally no more transferable than, say, weather. However, urban areas generally see higher multiplier effects than rural regions because they are more likely to be able to provide labor and other inputs for themselves to existing businesses.

Obstacles to Tourism Development

Many communities, particularly smaller destinations and rural areas, face extraordinary challenges in developing an effective tourism program. Key obstacles may include a low population base, limited financial resources, heavy reliance on natural resource–based economies, and shortages of other important resources. These obstacles are often complicated by long-entrenched work styles that may not be ideal in terms of cooperation and leadership. Table 2.4 lists some common obstacles your community might face when trying to develop a tourism program.

Table 2.5 highlights some key strategies that can help your community achieve success. Careful planning and development of authentic attractions and sensitivity to social and environmental concerns are important if a community is to safeguard its resources. Community character, values, and quality of life are important local resources, and care should be taken to protect these assets.

Tip

Identify which obstacles in Table 2.4 your community might face. Then look at Table 2.5 to identify strategies your community can use to achieve success.

Table 2.4: Obstacles to Tourism Development

Obstacle	Description
Reliance on Natural Resource–Based Economy	Industrial sector work forces are seldom prepared for the service orientation and customer contact needs of the tourism industry.
Small Population Base	The community may lack the organizational and professional skills required for developing strong visitor attractions. Local leaders and volunteers may be overworked.
Limited Financial Resources	Smaller communities often lack access to financial resources needed to develop tourism facilities, services, and staff.
Transportation Isolation	Many small communities lack access to major airports, highways, and public transportation. Visitors find it difficult and expensive to visit.
Underdeveloped Resources	Many communities have natural and cultural resources to draw tourists, but limited funding and lack of knowledge about tourist needs prevent adequate development.
Industry Misperceptions	Residents believe they have no control over tourism development and fear that increased visitors will change the local character and reduce quality of life.
Neighboring Competition	Small communities often have a history of competing with their neighbors and don't realize that tourism is more successful if larger geographic areas work together.
Inadequate Leadership	Local leaders are often overworked and overstressed due to high out-migration, limited resources, and economic struggles. Tourism development requires dedicated leaders and followers.
Sustainability Issues	Many communities struggle to balance the public's concern for environmental protection with development. Divergent viewpoints cause polarization and impede progress.
Strategic Planning	Small communities often have not initiated planning for community development. Lack of comprehensive growth plans and tourism planning increases failure due to poor product development and delivery.
Failure to Work Together	Local firms that do business with travelers often do not understand that they are part of the tourism industry. Failure to work together as an industry reduces the effectiveness of a community tourism effort.
Lack of Information	Many small communities lack information on local tourism impacts, visitors, and local businesses, making it difficult to plan for tourism or develop appropriate communication strategies.

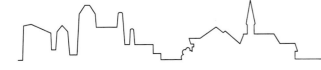

Table 2.5: Strategies for Success

Success Strategy	Description
Tourism Organization	Don't try to "dabble" at tourism or expect the industry to "just happen." Adopt a serious, consistent, systematic approach with a community tourism organization and dedicated paid or volunteer staff.
Product Development	Tourism is a dynamic industry. Constantly change to provide more interesting and extensive attractions and services to meet travelers' expectations.
Target Marketing	Use specialized marketing strategies targeted to specific groups of travelers. Profile customers accurately to maximize your marketing budget.
Customer Service Management	Customer service is paramount to successful tourism programs. Use hospitality training programs to improve front-line service and stress service quality in local businesses.
"Big Picture" Perspective	Recognize that neighboring towns are allies, not competitors. Small destinations compete with national and international attractions for tourists, so regional products are more competitive.
Selling "Experiences"	Many tourism businesses sell their physical features when crafting marketing messages. You will be more successful if you focus on marketing the "experience" of travel.
Collaboration	Join forces with other communities through effective collaboration to maximize your marketing potential and improve your ability to provide the attraction and service base needed to draw visitors.
Maintaining Competitiveness	Staying abreast of change and understanding the impacts and opportunities that will result can help you distinguish yourself by capitalizing on new travel trends.
Public-Private Partnerships	As the industry becomes better understood, it has become clear that governments must play a much greater role in tourism development. Create and participate in effective public-private partnerships that define roles and responsibilities.
Growth Management	If you define local carrying capacity limits, you will be better able to manage tourism growth and balance visitor needs with maintaining quality of life.

2

Tourism Area Life Cycle

Tourism development is a process. It generally begins with initial discovery by small numbers of tourists. This leads to increased economic activity by the community in providing facilities and services. If tourist growth continues, the community enters a stage of institutionalized development, in which tourism becomes a formal business activity. Along the way, thoughtful planning and monitoring are needed to ensure that tourism development meets the needs of the community as well as the visitors.

One model that has been widely accepted as a conceptual framework for planning, developing and managing tourism is R.W. Butler's Tourism Area Life Cycle model. Butler breaks the life cycle of tourism development into six stages (Figure 2.3). *Exploration* is the initial discovery of the destination, when small numbers of tourists visit. During *involvement*, visitation increases and the community becomes involved with small facilities and businesses catering to tourists. *Development* brings more tourists and more extensive facility construction for attractions and services.

At the *consolidation* stage, the early influx of tourists levels off. If significant negative sociocultural and environmental impacts occurred during the development stage, the host community begins to recognize impacts.

At this point, according to Butler, the destination can enter *stagnation, decline, or rejuvenation*. With stagnation, no new growth in arrivals indicates physical capacity has been reached or tourists have lost interest. Decline occurs when tourists move to newer, undiscovered destinations. The third option, rejuvenation, takes place when the community invests in new development or changes product offerings to accommodate new tourist markets.

While progress through Butler's cycle is not inevitable, communities need to be aware of the evolutionary nature of tourism development in order to maintain the vitality of their local tourism industry over time. Ongoing planning, monitoring, and management should help guide tourism growth.

Figure 2.3: Tourism Area Life Cycle

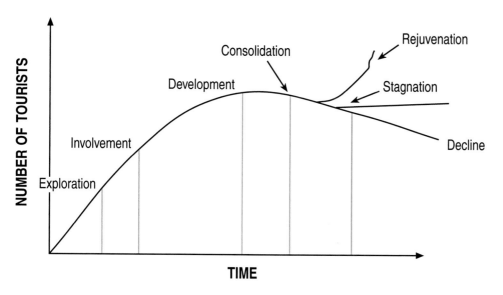

References

Butler, R.W. (1980). The concept of a tourist area cycle of evolution: Implications for management resources. *Canadian Geographer, 24(1),* 70.

Doxey, G. (1976). When enough's enough: The natives are restless in Old Niagara. *Heritage Canada, 2(2),* 26-270.

Chapter 3
Planning: Why and How

Planning is necessary for tourism to develop in a way that is beneficial, sustainable, and not detrimental to the environment, culture, or community.

Integrate tourism planning into your overall community planning. According to Gunn, "Many communities view tourism as a separate layer that is simply added to a community. Engaging in tourism from this viewpoint is always disappointing because it fails to integrate tourism into the social and economic life of the community."

Tourism may already be partially included in your local or regional recreation, land use, or economic development plans. If this is the case, you may work with the planning authority to expand tourism's role. If not, tourism planning may catalyze further planning in your community.

WHAT'S IN THIS CHAPTER?

• Local Involvement
• The Community Tourism Planning Process

Local Involvement

Tourism touches all aspects of a community—businesses, government services, the natural environment, and residents. Efforts to involve representatives of these various elements in discussions and decisions will help create positive attitudes and a healthy tourism industry that is in harmony with community values.

All residents should be invited to participate in fundamental tourism development decisions. Residents will be more inclined to support tourism if they are involved in initial discussions and have opportunities to voice their opinions. They will also be more willing to volunteer for tourist-related activities (recreation, information sharing, interpretation) and events (festivals, celebrations, sports) later on.

The community tourism planning process described below provides a forum for local involvement. It emphasizes the inclusion of a variety of residents to:

- Articulate community values;
- Select broad tourism goals for the community;
- Generate local support for tourism development;
- Help achieve tourism goals; and
- Help monitor and evaluate tourism's success in meeting goals.

Figure 3.1 highlights the steps needed to successfully build and maintain community involvement.

Figure 3.1: Promoting Community Involvement

1. Decide who should be involved
- Assess current involvement. If lagging, actively solicit participation.
- List people and groups affected. Invite them all!
- Make the first meeting a well-publicized community event to draw a variety of participants who may stay on as volunteers.

2. Gather information
- Locate existing materials (current tourism efforts, information on who visits your community or region, etc.)
- Determine whether there is enough information available for both tourism and nontourism interests to make basic decisions about tourism.
- Gather additional information as needed (seek expert advice, conduct surveys, etc.)

3. Conduct community meetings
- Hold meetings to gather information, seek input, plan, or get feedback.
- Present proposals and opportunities in terms of both costs and benefits.
- Use group process techniques to elicit community values and ideas about tourism.
- Limit the agenda to one or two questions; solutions may take several meetings.
- Work toward consensus and establish priorities for actions.

4. Communicate and evaluate
- Distribute meeting results to the public via the media.
- Solicit ongoing citizen feedback; be open to unexpected responses.
- Continue meetings/consensus building until there is general agreement on goals.
- Evaluate local involvement on an ongoing basis; assess shifts in attitudes and goals that may require a new direction for tourism development.

The Community Tourism Planning Process

Planning usually begins with an initial idea that tourism development is a desired economic development strategy for the community. In communities with some tourism, development efforts often begin with an existing organization such as a chamber of commerce, retail association, or economic development group. The organization may provide initial leadership to planning efforts. Leadership may also come from tourism businesses, individuals, or elected officials.

Planning will help your community set goals for tourism and provide guidelines for development. Ideally, these will grow from more general community goals and objectives and answer the question "How can tourism contribute to community goals?" It is important to start with a sense of your community's vision.

Preliminary Steps

Identify Tourism

The first step in the tourism planning process is to identify tourism as a possible economic development strategy.

Identify Participants

After you have identified tourism as something you wish to explore for your community, identify key people who should be involved in or aware of planning activities. This group should represent the entire community. Community tourism development is often left to a small group of individuals who are directly involved in tourism-related businesses. Usually, these individuals mostly favor tourism development since their businesses and livelihoods depend on it. Many others are affected by tourism and should be included in decision making. These stakeholders are usually more cautious about tourism and more vocal about potential negative impacts.

Government agencies and elected officials are important partners for several reasons.

First, government is responsible for most of the infrastructure and services upon which tourism depends: water, sewer, law enforcement, emergency services, roads, and so on. Government participation will help ensure that infrastructure development, zoning, building policies, and regulations will facilitate tourism while meeting residents' needs.

Second, government helps plan and manage many tourist attractions and facilities, such as recreational areas, parks, community swimming pools, beaches, and golf courses. Springfield, Minnesota, for example, promotes the community water slide as one of its attractions. In Chisholm, Minnesota, the state owns and operates Ironworld Discovery Center, dedicated to preserving the history and heritage of Minnesota's Iron Range, where open pit mining flourished until the mid-1970s.

Nongovernment organizations (e.g., religious, arts, recreation, historic, environmental, professional, ethnic, and youth groups) represent the cultural aspects of a community that help make it unique. They also should participate in tourism planning. Many are already involved with visitors through events, festivals, or attractions. Local historical societies preserve, develop, and manage sites that attract visitors; youth organizations assist at county fairs; arts and ethnic organizations coordinate events. Nongovernment organizations also support specific causes such as environmental protection, youth training, and ethnic awareness development that can benefit tourism.

Because nearly all *businesses* are affected by visitors at some point, they too should have an opportunity to be involved in tourism planning. Small business operators may not have time to be actively involved in committee work, so you will need to identify other ways to include them. You can use simple methods such as asking for input on specific topics via mail or e-mail, or asking them to handle short-term, specific tasks. Being involved will help them more clearly see the benefits, support tourism development, and potentially lend creative new ideas to the process. Be sure to include media—local and regional newspapers, radio stations, and television stations. They are important in keeping the public informed, and can be key influencers of community opinion.

Table 3.1 shows the variety of traditional and nontraditioal community members and organizations that should be invited to participate in tourism planning. They are divided into those traditionally included in tourism and nontraditional stakeholders, who might easily be overlooked. Use the table as a guide to complete Worksheet 3.1 (found at the end of this chapter).

Table 3.1: Potential Participants for Community Tourism Planning

TRADITIONAL	NONTRADITIONAL
City, County, Government Officials	
Mayor or Chief Executive City Council City Manager County Commissioners County Extension Educators	Fire/Police Chief Natural Resource/Public Land Agencies Local Parks & Recreation Director Planning & Zoning Department Transportation Dept. & Public Utilities Other Local Political Leaders
Civic, Business, Nonprofit Organizations	
Chamber of Commerce Convention and Visitor Bureau Hotel/Restaurant Associations Downtown Business/Retail Associations Economic Development Officer Attractions Associations Business/Professional Clubs Event & Festival Organizations Fine & Performing Arts Councils	Historical Society/Preservation Groups Cultural Organizations Minority Groups/Indigenous Populations Environmental/Conservation Groups Rotary/Lions/Optimist/Kiwanis Civic Clubs American Legion/Veterans of Foreign Wars Junior Chamber Garden Clubs and Other Civic Groups Sports Clubs – Ski, Snowmobile, etc.
Local Businesses	
Hotel/Motel Managers Tourist Attraction Operators Restaurant/Food Service Managers Theater/Amusement Operators Outdoor Recreation Outfitters Retail/Shop Owners Taxi/Car Rental Operators Travel Agents	Service Station Owners Automotive Dealers Real Estate Agents Newspaper Editor or Columnist Radio/TV Station Managers Grocers/Pharmacists Banks or Financial Institutions Hospital/Medical/Insurance
Other Community Decision Influencers	
College & University Officials Local Tourism or Business Professors School Principals/Superintendent/Teachers	Church Leaders Religious Organizations Other Decision Influencers

Adapted from Texas Agricultural Extension Service. (1999). *Developing tourism in your community.*
College Station, TX: Texas Agricultural Extension Service, Texas A&M University.

Hold an Initial Meeting

Once you have identified potential participants, schedule a meeting to
explore the interest and support within your community for tourism
development. Send personal invitations to individuals and groups on
Worksheet 3.1. Publicize the meeting widely and be sure people

understand that it's open to all community members. Do all you can to ensure key community decision influencers are present.

Before the meeting, develop an agenda and select a facilitator. Objectivity and facilitation/moderation skills should be key criteria. A county extension educator, local college or university faculty member, or paid professional facilitator can help keep the discussion flowing and directed toward your goals. This individual can also help you develop the agenda.

The agenda should include:
- Introduction to tourism development:
    - What it is, who is involved, etc.;
    - Tourism as an economic diversification strategy;
    - Benefits and costs of tourism; and
    - Need for planning, community involvement.
- Open discussion:
    - Identification of current tourism efforts;
    - Quick identification of local assets; and
    - Decision to proceed or not to proceed.

Tourism is not appropriate for every community. As part of your meeting, use Worksheet 3.2 to help you decide whether your community should proceed with tourism development. If the assessment shows your community is not ready to make the long-term commitment and investment necessary for tourism to succeed, discuss what *is* needed. Is tourism an option in the future? Do you need more research and discussion to build interest, or is tourism simply not a preferred economic development strategy? Those interested in tourism development may want to explore community interest and perhaps even conduct the resident attitude survey (Assessment 6.1) before determining future actions.

If, on the other hand, there is sufficient support and interest among the key decision makers in the community to proceed, you are ready to form a planning committee.

Form a Tourism Planning Committee
Before establishing a new committee, identify entities already involved in tourism. You may choose to have an existing entity lead

the tourism development process. If it is a committee within a larger organization such as a chamber, you will develop the tourism planning effort under that umbrella and it will have to fit within the organization's goals and plan of work. At some point down the road, you may want to create a separate organization (see Chapter 5).

If you establish a separate committee, include representatives of key business, government, and nongovernment interests. Also include a representative from any organizations already involved in tourism to help avoid opposition or ill feelings. The committee may be appointed by government, the community, or a local organization, or it may be a self-determined group of interested parties. If it is a self-determined group, consider developing an organization early in the process.

The Planning Process

Figure 3.2 illustrates the flow of tourism planning. Planning is an ongoing process, not a one-time effort. Each step of the process should allow for modification or response to unforeseen circumstances. Monitoring and evaluating will help you refine your approach as needed to achieve the intended outcomes.

Figure 3.2: The Community Tourism Planning Process

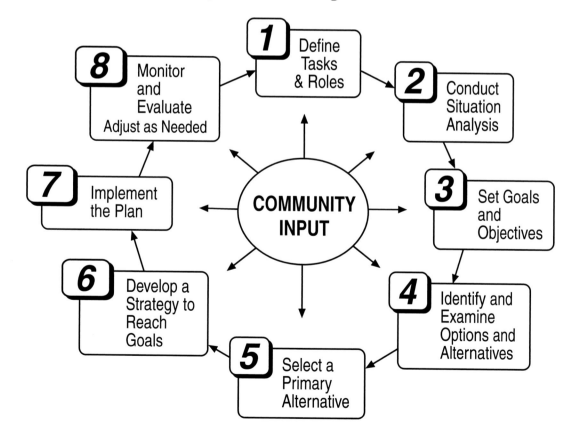

Step 1: *Define Tasks and Roles*

The committee should begin its work by deciding who will lead it and how tasks will be assigned and completed. Worksheet 3.3 can help you track assignments. Use Worksheet 3.4 to record agenda information and key decision and action steps for specific agenda items so future tourism leaders can tell what you've done. Worksheet 3.5 can help you keep track of your meetings.

You'll also need to establish a funding source for the planning process. In most communities, funding is provided through an existing organization such as the chamber of commerce or economic development group. Or, your committee may seek funds from local government or from regional or state granting resources. Chapter 12 provides more information on funding.

Next, determine your timeline. This will help you get active participation, generate community support, and show results. Communities just starting the process can expect to spend up to two years to create and begin implementing a tourism development plan. The sample timeline provided in the preface can help you.

Step 2: *Conduct a Situation Analysis*

The situation analysis is the research aspect of planning. It involves gathering information about community resources, current and potential target markets, and your competition. You need to inventory and objectively assess the quantity and quality of what you have to offer in order to focus tourism development effectively.

An important part of your situation analysis should be an overview of trends in external "environments" (Figure 3.3) that might influence your tourism development efforts. Use Worksheet 3.6 to organize your thoughts as you identify trends and potential effects.

You will also want to identify and consider tourism trends. For local tourism trends, consult regional and state tourism organizations. For international trends, consult the United Nations World Tourism Organization (UNWTO), World Travel and Tourism Council (WTTC) and United States Travel Association (USTA).

Assessments of existing attractions and services as well resident and business attitudes toward tourism are key parts of your situation analysis. Chapter 6 provides extensive help in conducting these assessments.

Figure 3.3: External Environments

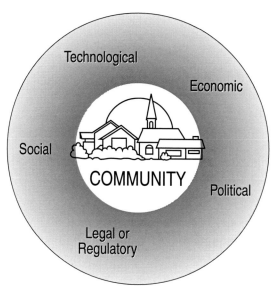

The situation analysis should also include a profile of the current visitor market, estimated numbers of tourists visiting your community, and the economic impact. Visitor profile information includes:

- An average of the total tourist visitation (preferably by season);
- Estimates of daily and total expenditures by visitors;
- Demographic information (age, education, income, residence); and
- Trip-specific information (activities, attractions visited, accommodations, purpose of trip, satisfaction levels).

Economic profiles are useful in determining what role tourism plays in the community's overall economy (e.g., jobs, personal income, number of businesses, tax revenues).

Key questions to ask at this stage include:

- How big a role does tourism currently play in our local economy?
- How does tourism compare with other sectors of the local economy in terms of jobs, income, businesses, and tax revenues generated?
- Who is already visiting our community and why?
- How many tourists are already coming per year?
- What are the key attractions that are drawing tourists?
- What are the characteristics of tourists who are coming?
- What are the current and future trends in travel and tourism?
- Who are our "potential customers," based on these trends?

Much of the information needed to develop visitor and economic profiles has probably already been collected and published. See Chapter 7 for suggestions for sources of such information.

The answers to these questions will provide a current snapshot of the importance of tourism to your community and a baseline to use later as you develop marketing strategies and monitor economic impacts.

Finally, identify the internal *strengths* and *weaknesses* and external *opportunities* and *threats* for the community. Assessing these elements, frequently identified by the acronym SWOT, will help you develop effective strategies that focus on strengths and opportunities while minimizing or overcoming weaknesses and threats.

Internal strengths are resources or capabilities that help achieve stated goals and are the basis for developing a competitive position. Internal weaknesses are deficiencies in resources or capabilities that may prevent you from achieving your goals and competing effectively for visitor markets. In some instances, a weakness may be the flip side of a strength.

Tip

It's a good idea to use an outside facilitator for your SWOT analysis. Contact your local Extension office or community college for assistance.

Opportunities are outside factors that may be beneficial to growth and help your community profit from tourism, while threats are uncontrollable outside factors that could negatively affect tourism. For example, terrorism may generate a surge in holidays at closer-to-home destinations, but it can also signal a need to upgrade facilities to meet increased customer concerns around security and safety.

Communities should not necessarily pursue all opportunities. A SWOT analysis can help identify a match of the community's strengths with compatible opportunities. This exercise can also help identify weaknesses that need to be addressed in order to be prepared for profitable opportunities.

To conduct a SWOT analysis, provide a copy of Worksheet 3.7 and a pencil to each participant. Follow the directions on the worksheet.

Step 3: *Set Goals and Objectives*

Next use the information gathered during the situation analysis to set specific, realistic, and achievable goals and objectives. Setting goals and objectives means stating clearly what tourism will bring to the community.

Goals are the broad statements about the community's vision for tourism. They establish long- and short-term targets you hope to achieve as a result of tourism development. Goals may relate to economic, social, or environmental needs. Some examples:

• To create long-term sustainability for natural, cultural, and social resources;

- To identify and create partnerships within the region;
- To create job opportunities and economic benefit; and
- To preserve local culture and indigenous arts.

These are then translated into objectives. Objectives explain how you will achieve the goals. They address the concerns and strengths inherent in the goals. Good objectives are clear, concise, measurable, and include a specific action within a set time frame.

Step 4: *Identify and Examine Options and Alternatives*

Prioritize your goals and objectives according to the internal and external factors you identified through the situation analysis. Then, using your goals and objectives as a guide, generate a list of options and alternatives for tourism development projects and strategies. This is the time for creative thinking and brainstorming. There is no single "right" alternative.

Next weigh alternatives according to the opportunities and potential for success they offer in achieving your goals. Consider resources, timelines, market trends, and community needs. In assessing each alternative, ask:

"Can it be done?"

"What are the consequences?"

Goals and objectives will evolve and become more focused as your involvement with tourism and tourism planning grows. For example, in the early stages of tourism development, goals may involve establishing organizational structures and collecting information. Selecting goals that produce short-term success might be an effective strategy for building community support early in your development program.

There are many methods to identify and prioritize goals. Using a group process that allows everyone in a group to have input can help build support for the alternative that is ultimately selected.

Step 5: *Select a Primary Alternative*

The primary alternative is simply the one(s) that you decide to move forward with. There is no "right" alternative.

Step 6: *Develop a Strategy to Reach Goals*

The selected alternative will now guide the development of strategies and specific actions to fulfill the goals and objectives. Worksheet 3.8 will help you develop actions and choose evaluation methods for each strategy. Complete as many of these worksheets as needed.

Step 7: *Implement the Plan*

Now that you have drafted a plan, it's time to implement it. Follow through with your planned strategies.

Crisis Planning

Your community should be prepared to deal with crises long before a strong tourism industry has been established. During the tourism development planning process, examine your community's existing crisis and disaster relief plans. Is the community prepared to manage the effects a serious crisis might have on tourism? Are the community's existing crisis management capabilities adequate to handle a crisis during peak seasons, when local population may be double or triple? Does the community's crisis communication plan include input from the tourism sector? As you plan to develop tourism, plan also to expand your community's crisis management capabilities accordingly.

Step 8: *Monitor and Evaluate*

Monitoring and evaluation of your efforts are critical. They allow you to measure how well you are meeting your goals, and to make adjustments if necessary. Evaluation will help you identify what is or isn't contributing to the progress of your tourism efforts.

Evaluation must be continual to be effective. Build evaluation measures into each effort from the beginning. Establish measures to evaluate quantity and quality of outputs, timelines, and the effectiveness of the selected alternative. Regular monitoring and evaluation enable you to identify weaknesses or problems so that corrections can be made before they become unmanageable. Regular monitoring also provides a basis for comparison, and for forecasting future trends.

Chapter 13 of this book contains advice on monitoring your tourism program and making adjustments to ensure that your goals are being met without compromising your values.

For More on Planning

Inskeep, E. (1991). *Tourism planning: An integrated and sustainable development approach.* New York, NY: Van Nostrand Reinhold.

Bryson, J. M., & Farnum, K. A. (1996). *Creating and implementing your strategic plan.* San Francisco, CA: Jossey-Bass Publishers.

Minnesota Planning. (1998). *Community-based planning.* St. Paul, MN. www.mnplan. state.mn.us.

References

Gunn, C. A. (1994). *Tourism planning: Basics, concepts, cases.* (3rd ed). Washington, D.C.: Taylor & Francis.

Worksheet 3.1: Tourism Planning Participants

Use this list to identify potential tourism planning participants for your initial meeting. Some may not participate in the initial meeting, but all should be kept informed of progress. Planning committee members may also be selected from this list. All groups may eventually be involved in your community tourism development efforts.

Group Represented	Contact Person(s)	Phone Number(s) E-mail Address(es)	Participant (P) or Keep Informed (I)
City Manager			
City/County Elected Officials			
City/County Planners			
Public Works Department			
Law Enforcement and Emergency Services			
Parks & Recreation Department			
Land Use Agencies			
Highway Department			
Local Chamber of Commerce			
Local Economic Development Agency			
Existing Tourism Organizations			
Regional Tourism Organizations			
Business / Retailers' Associations			
Tourism Businesses (lodging, restaurant etc.)			
Tourist Attractions			

Over ⟳

Group Represented	Contact Person(s)	Phone Number(s) E-mail Address(es)	Participant (P) or Keep Informed (I)
Festival/Event Organizers			
Museums			
Historical Society			
Theater Groups			
Artist/Craft Guilds			
Recreational or Sports Associations			
Agricultural Organizations			
Banking/Financial Leaders			
Conservation Groups			
Educational Leaders			
Clergy			
Youth Groups			
Civic Organizations			
Senior/Retiree Groups			
Ethnic/Minority Groups			
Local Media Newspaper Radio Cable TV			
Others _____			

Worksheet 3.2: *Is Tourism Right For Us?*

The questions below will help you decide if tourism is right for you. In some instances, it may be right, but at a later time.

1.   Why do we want to develop tourism?

2.   Do we already have tourism that we can build on?

3.   Is it compatible with lifestyle and other businesses?

4.   Do we have businesses that can supply the products and services to support tourism?

5.   Do we have an available local labor force, and training potential?

6.   Do we have public services and infrastructure to handle additional use?

7.   What resources do we have locally or regionally to assist us?

8.   Who/what will benefit from tourism in our community?

9.   Who/what will be hurt by tourism?

10.   The best thing about living in this community is:

11.   If I could change one thing about our community it would be:

12.   In 10 years I would like to see our community:

Worksheet 3.3: *Task Assignments*

Date: _____   Committee: _____

TASK:

Assigned to:

Action Steps: Date Completed:

1.

2.

3.

4.

5.

Self Evaluation: Please briefly describe the successes or challenges of accomplishing the task. Was adequate help available? Was a budget set (if needed)? What suggestions or recommendations do you have?

Worksheet 3.4: *Agenda Item Action Record*

Date: _____   Committee: _____

AGENDA ITEM:_____

Key discussion points:

Decision:

Action Steps:

Timeline:

Assigned to:

AGENDA ITEM: _____

Key discussion points:

Decision:

Action Steps:

Timeline:

Assigned to:

Worksheet 3.5: *Meeting Record*

Date: _____   Committee: _____

Attending:

Agenda:

( ) Minutes of last meeting read and approved
( )
( )
( )
( )
( )
( ) Agenda review

Summary of committee decisions:

1.

2.

3.

4.

5.

Action steps to be taken by next meeting and by whom:

1.

2.

3.

4.

5.

Next meeting date/time/location:

Worksheet 3.6: *External Environment Trends*

As part of your situation analysis, list trends in each of these "environments" and how they might affect your tourism development efforts. An example is given for each.

Economic Environment	Potential Effect
Low unemployment	*Labor shortage, increased wage and benefit expectations*

Political Environment	Potential Effect
Support for tourism	*Can influence other elected officials to support*

Social Environment	Potential Effect
Aging baby boomers	*More free time, discretionary dollars*

Legal or Regulatory	Potential Effect
Year-round schools	*Change in traditional vacation times, seasonal travel*

Technological	Potential Effect
Internet for reservations	*New markets, creative marketing, interactive options*

Facilitator Instructions:

The purpose of this tool is to help planning committee members identify organizational or community strengths, weaknesses, opportunities, and threats that might affect tourism planning and development.

Materials: copy of SWOT Analysis form and pencil for each person
flip chart and markers
tape

Time: Allow at least one hour for the exercise, including discussion.

Distribute copies of this SWOT analysis form and pencils to each participant. Divide into teams or pairs. Assign each one of the four categories (strengths, weaknesses, opportunities, or threats). Allow about 20 minutes for participants to list things in their categories that may affect the community's tourism efforts. While participants are working, post a piece of newsprint for each SWOT category on the wall. At the end of 20 minutes, ask participants to call out their responses. List them on the newsprint, consolidating similar responses as appropriate. When finished, discuss the findings and implications.

Definitions:

Strengths and weaknesses are *internal* elements that may affect performance. (e.g., human resources, leadership, funding, communications, or lack of vision)

Opportunities and threats are *external forces* that may impact the organizational or community goals (e.g., technology, suppliers, government regulations, changes in the market, customers, labor force, etc.)

For example, terrorism may generate a surge in holidays at closer-to-home destinations, but it can also signal a need to upgrade facilities to meet increased customer concerns around security and safety.

A community SWOT analysis is similar to a SWOT analysis for a business, and provides information that can be helpful in matching the community's resources and capabilities to the competitive environment.

Participant Instructions:

Please complete this form with your assigned group or partner. Be as specific and frank as possible. If you understate weaknesses or avoid identifying them, you can seriously flaw the planning process.

Definitions:

Strengths and weaknesses are internal elements that may affect your ability to reach your goals (e.g., human resources, leadership funding, communications, lack of vision).

Opportunities and threats are external forces that may affect your ability to reach your goals (e.g., technology, suppliers, government regulations, changes in the market, customers, or labor force).

Area Being Analyzed: ❑ Community ❑ Organization _____

Date: _____

(name)

STRENGTHS	Ways to Build on Strengths	WEAKNESSES	Ways to Overcome Weaknesses

OPPORTUNITIES	Ways to Take Advantage	THREATS	Ways to Overcome/Minimize

Implications for our community tourism planning/development:

_____

_____

_____

_____

_____

Worksheet 3.8: Action Plan

To achieve objectives and goals, you need to develop a strategy of specific actions. Make copies of this worksheet and use them to identify actions; the budget, staff, and time needed to accomplish them; and when they should begin and end. Finally, list the type(s) of evaluation methods you will use to measure your success. Once the action step is done and you have evaluated it, you can indicate the outcomes at the bottom. This can serve as a record of efforts and growth, and should be used in helping plan further actions.

GOAL:

OBJECTIVE:

ACTION	BUDGET	STAFF	TIME	BEGIN ----- END	EVALUATION METHOD(S)

OUTCOMES:

Chapter 4
Building Community Support

In tourism, community support is key to community involvement. You need to gain support of three distinct groups: government, residents, and businesses. Ongoing communication with each is required to maintain support for tourism. Open dialogue will enhance knowledge about tourism and provide a feedback loop for monitoring and evaluating progress.

Communication about what tourism is and how it can benefit your community may be a good starting place. Your state tourism office may have resources to assist you. The U.S. Travel Association (USTA) provides several online resources and research at www.ustravel.org that can help in building tourism awareness within communities. The PowerofTravel.org, a product of the USTA, includes resources on economic travel data, trends in international travel, and the non-economic benefits of travel.

WHAT'S IN THIS CHAPTER?

- Government Support
- Citizen Support
- Local Business Support
- Cooperation and Compromise

Government Support

Government plays an important role in tourism. In many cases, support by elected officials is a critical factor in success. City and county government may run the tourism organization. City officials may serve on the board of directors or advisory councils of tourism organizations. Involvement of government may range from minimal to full operation of tourism activities.

It is important for local government to understand the value of tourism to the community so it provides appropriate public services. Official endorsement and political support for the tourism industry by government officials are important for growth and development. Improved public facilities (streets, sidewalks, parks, lighting, rest rooms) and coordination with utility providers (water, sewer, power, solid waste) can boost tourism. Other public services (fire, police, medical) are necessary for increased visitation and special events.

A positive attitude on the part of government officials can ensure that tourism needs are considered in community planning and infrastructure development. Coordinated development helps guide growth and protect community values. Local government can also help stimulate tourism by developing financial packages for development projects and providing funding for marketing.

Five Ways to Encourage Government Support for Tourism

1. Invite local officials to sit on your tourism board or advisory council.

2. Work with your state tourism office and tourism associations on a "Tourism Day at the Capitol" to meet with legislators and educate them about tourism's economic impact.

3. Host National Tourism Week events and invite local officials, residents and media.

4. Ask the city council or mayor to declare a special tourism day locally each year.

5. Prepare a one-page fact sheet for local officials on tourism's positive impacts in your area. Update and present this to the city council each year with a thank you for officials' support.

Citizen Support

One of the tourism industry's most powerful marketing tools is word-of-mouth support from local citizens. But local support is not automatic; it must be developed and encouraged. Citizens need to know the scope of their tourism industry; how it affects their lives in terms of costs, benefits, and intangible quality-of-life factors; and the direction in which it is headed. They must be encouraged to promote tourism to their friends, relatives, acquaintances, and business associates.

Tourism places stress on public agencies by increasing demand for existing public services and creating needs for new ones. One way to prevent problems is to address issues relating to tourism development in the community's overall comprehensive growth plan. Planners and public agency personnel may need to be educated about the tourism industry and its reliance on public services.

Developing citizen support includes fostering pride in the community. Many elements blend together to create a positive image for tourism and for the community. Citizens need to feel positive about the various elements of their tourism industry (attractions, services, and marketing efforts) before they can express that feeling to others. Tourism leaders must constantly interact with local citizens to ensure that tourism development stays in line with community interests and values, and helps support and enhance the community's self-image.

A community can build citizen support for tourism in many ways. Local media, public forums, and speakers can be used to inform citizens about benefits and costs. Leaders and residents should be given opportunities to voice their ideas and concerns about tourism on an ongoing basis. Invite neutral third parties (university Extension staff, regional planning staff, professional meeting facilitators) to facilitate meetings in an unbiased manner. Ask the community at large to participate in identifying community goals for tourism. Group process methods are particularly useful for structuring the dialogue. Encourage credible research so that appropriate data about the tourism industry (visitor statistics, impact statements, and development issues) can be communicated on an ongoing basis.

A Tour of Success

Pierre, South Dakota (pop. 12,906), found "our best strategy was [instituting] a course on economic development, which included an expert leading the class on a bus tour to those South Dakota communities we felt were leading the way in economic development and tourism," says Ellen Lee, former executive director, Pierre Chamber of Commerce. "This course has been repeated... it is the best source for local assessment and visioning."

4

Five Ways to Find the 'Unity' in Community

1. Conduct local familiarization tours for residents and frontline employees before the tourist season. Inform participants about the important "hospitality-tourism" link.

2. Beautify your community and create ways to engage people via farmers' markets, festivals and other events celebrating local heritage and/or attractions.

3. Involve high school and college students by hosting job fairs and internships for hospitality careers. Hold contests involving youth in tourism-related projects such as photo contests.

4. Host a "Volunteer Appreciation" event and present awards to recognize and honor local citizens who participate in tourism projects. Recognize volunteers on your community website and in the local newspaper, too.

5. Hold a "Resident Appreciation Day" and ask local attractions, hotels, and restaurants to offer free admission or discount coupons to local residents.

Local Business Support

When tourism is developing, residents are often greatly concerned that "outsiders" will exploit their community and they will be unable to control tourism growth. They fear outsiders may take over attractions and natural resources, or manipulate and take over local government.

Workers fear that large corporations may dominate the community and become impersonal employers offering only minimum-wage jobs. Local businesses fear they will be pushed out of the community by larger franchise operations, unable to compete with the marketing means or buying power of national chains. The community may develop resentment toward outsiders who start up small tourism businesses that crowd out and change the established pattern in the community.

One way of reducing these concerns is to encourage local ownership and investment in tourism. Financial institutions in small communities usually don't have experience loaning to tourism businesses and are reluctant to make investments without means of evaluating the risk involved.

Training programs for community financial lenders on tourism business financing and management may help allay concerns.

As with other industrial development, local government programs can be set up to offer local investors/owners incentives such as reduced taxes, special utility rates, assistance in construction, and free or reduced cost of land. Government and financial institutions can team up to offer financing. Government backing or guarantees can make financial institutions more willing to make loans. Governments participating in such efforts should have staff or hire advisors to protect their community's interests and investments.

Five Ways to Gain Support of Local Businesses

1. Give a tourism presentation annually to local civic organizations like the Economic Development Authority, Rotary, Lions, etc.

2. Write a regular column for the local paper that informs the community about tourism impacts and highlights local tourism business strategies.

3. Host a community familiarization trip for staff and owners of tourism businesses at the beginning of each tourism season.

4. Offer tourism and customer service training to local students seeking part-time employment.

5. Visit local businesses and make them aware of tourism's economic impact.

> **Tips for Encouraging Local Involvement**
>
> ✔ Recognize that your community is composed of many different audiences that will be motivated to get involved for different reasons. Make your appeals based on their reasons.
>
> ✔ Involve your town's youth: Their energy and enthusiasm are contagious. Involve senior citizens: Their knowledge of community history and resources can be instrumental.
>
> ✔ Keep community residents informed. Select residents to contribute to a weekly newspaper column on positive community changes.
>
> ✔ Nothing generates more community spirit than the sense that things are being accomplished. Focus on projects that are doable and visible.
>
> ✔ Create ownership in projects by identifying different ways people can contribute. Some residents will want to give time and talent, others money, still others, materials and goods.
>
> ✔ Make participating a social opportunity. Get business done, but have fun.
>
> ✔ Work with businesses to get them involved. Will they sponsor an event? Can employees receive paid time off to assist with a project? Can staff be recognized for civic involvement?
>
> ✔ Reward participation in community improvement projects. Ask your newspaper if it will identify and feature a "Citizen of the Week."
>
> ✔ Reward outstanding resident hospitality. "Sidewalk Ambassador" and similar programs allow all residents to get involved and provide a means of rewarding outstanding hospitality.
>
> ✔ Recognize barriers to involvement and identify creative ways to overcome them. If parents want to attend planning meetings, can the local recreation department provide child care?
>
> ✔ Make the most of community festivals and special events. These are times to celebrate the uniqueness of your town—those qualities that make it a special place to live and for tourists to visit!

Source: Richardson, S. (1991). *Colorado community tourism action guide*. Colorado Center for Community Development. Denver, CO and Boulder, CO: University of Colorado.

Cooperation and Compromise

The road to community involvement is never ending and often bumpy. Navigating the many ups and downs of developing a successful community tourism program will be much easier if all participants commit to the journey with a spirit of cooperation and compromise.

There will be many times when individuals in your community may not agree on the best course of action. If they aren't willing to cooperate, and if necessary, compromise, community tourism efforts can get derailed. Viewpoints may be so polarized that it is not in the best interest of the community to continue to move forward with tourism

development at that particular point in time. A break may be needed before certain groups are willing to consider options and negotiate. If your community is experiencing such difficulties, you may want to complete Worksheet 4.1. This worksheet can help you determine what tactics might be used to avoid polarization or get your community back on track. Be aware that if you answer "yes" to most of the questions and community discussions are still not moving forward, it may be best get off the tourism bandwagon for a while. Communities unwilling to cooperate and compromise are simply not ready to travel down the tourism path!

If your community is polarized over certain issues, there are several action steps that may jump-start community cooperation. Complete the questions below to evaluate what methods you have already tried. Then, tally your responses in each column.

Action Strategy	YES	NO
• Have leaders of key groups met with an outside facilitator/moderator to explore ideas and strategies for cooperation or compromise?		
• Have the key opposing groups developed action steps for cooperation?		
• Have tourism officials identified problem groups or individuals and met with them privately to try to work out differences?		
• Has your community conducted a community opinion survey to determine areas of consensus and encourage cooperation?		
• Have key people from community groups met to identify common points of interest, rather than dwelling only on problem areas?		
• Has your community held an educational seminar to explore community problems and issues?		
• Has your community identified action steps to improve cooperation among community groups?		
• Has a respected community leader discussed cooperation problems with important community groups? *Direct intervention may solve conflicts.*		
• Has the issue been debated through local media or public forums? *Open debate may force the community to face cooperation problems.*		
• Have you identified groups willing to cooperate and taken action anyway on certain projects? *This may not solve the problem.*		
• Have respected community members met with groups to evaluate cooperation solutions? *This can promote more dissension.*		
• Have issues become so volatile that it is best for the community not to take any immediate action? *A cooling off period is needed.*		
Total Your Responses!		

Total your responses. A high score in the **"YES"** *column indicates your community has already made several attempts at cooperation. If groups are still polarized, it might not be the best time to move forward. If the score in either column is in the mid-range, try one of the action steps you haven't yet implemented. A high score in the* **"NO"** *column indicates that there are several action steps you might try. Pick one or two you think might work in your community, and see if that helps!*

Chapter 5
Organizing for Tourism Development

An important part of your community situation analysis is determining what organizations are or could be involved in developing tourism. It is important to identify and shape an organization to address the collective needs of the community's tourism industry. You will need to determine whether an organization already exists that can spearhead planning and development, or whether a new organization must be developed. This chapter will help you refocus or redefine efforts of an existing organization or provide guidance for forming a new one.

Through an organization, ideas are examined and tested, problems are identified and solved, efforts are coordinated, themes are developed, and cooperative activities are implemented to extend the abilities of a group of individuals or businesses to reach common goals. To be a leader and voice of the tourism industry, the organization must stay current on tourism issues and ensure that its interests and the greater community interests are harmonious. In order to succeed, it must:

- Have a clear vision;
- Establish a mission statement;
- Determine specific goals and objectives;
- Develop consistency in leadership;
- Provide adequate funding; and
- Conduct periodic evaluations.

WHAT'S IN THIS CHAPTER?

- **Existing Efforts**
- **Organizational Structure**
- **Leadership and Staffing**
- **Funding**
- **Evaluation**
- **Vision**

Existing Efforts

If your community already has a tourism organization, use it if possible. This recognizes the efforts of established "players" and prevents duplication of efforts. Many groups have a direct or indirect interest in tourism. Coordinating and cooperating with them builds support and helps avoid wasteful conflicts and misunderstandings later.

It's important you understand who the players are, and their interests and roles in tourism. Check to see if there is a group or groups in your community that will assume leadership for tourism planning and development. Table 5.1 and Worksheet 5.1 will help you identify the players and existing tourism development efforts.

Table 5.1: Groups Commonly Involved in Tourism

Government Bodies	Business Groups	Tourism Groups
City Council		Convention and Visitor Bureau
County Boards	Chamber of Commerce	
Planning Commission	Downtown Business Association	Local Tourist Bureaus/Board
Economic Development Agency	Resort/Hotel/Motel Association	Community Tourism Council
Regional Development Org.	Attractions Group	Tourist Promotional Boards (County/Regional)
Special Districts	Mall Merchants	Other Development Organizations
Parks and Recreation Department	Other Special Interest Groups	Historical Associations
County, State, National Parks, etc.		

Many communities and counties have a chamber of commerce and a tourist bureau (or convention and visitor bureau) with tourism responsibilities. Tourist bureaus are usually funded through lodging tax revenues. Chambers of commerce are usually funded by membership dues. When both groups have tourism responsibilities, tourist bureaus normally handle marketing (i.e., attracting visitors), while chambers provide member education and training and tourist information and services (e.g., visitor information centers). Political issues are often a joint effort. Festivals and events may be operated jointly or by either group.

There are many ways of dividing tourism work. Often the division of responsibilities responds to opportunities or requirements laid out by state or local laws and regulations, or by an organization's charter or bylaws. One method of coordinating activities is to have representation from the lead tourism organization on boards of smaller organizations, and vice versa.

Adapted from Alexander, P. (1987). *Developing a tourism organization*. East Lansing, MI: Cooperative Extension Service, Michigan State University; and Richardson, S. (1991). *Colorado community tourism action guide*. Boulder, CO: University of Colorado.

Organizational Structure

Base your tourism organization's structure on community needs, existing organizations, and options available in your state. Table 5.2 illustrates some of the most common tourism organization structures. There are many other modifications or combinations of these basic organization types. Consider your community's strengths and unique resources when creating your tourism organization. Spending time to research structure types and choose one that's right for your community is critical to the success of your organization.

An excellent resource for information on creating a tourism organization is the international association for convention and visitor bureaus known as Destination Marketing Association International (DMAI) at www.destinationmarketing.org.

Table 5.2: Common Tourism Organizational Structures

Structure	Descriptive Characteristics/Advantages
Chamber of Commerce Committees	Common structure Organization usually already exists Key members are often already interested in tourism As tourism develops, a separate organization may evolve
Voluntary Membership Tourism Groups	Can be used to jump-start tourism planning, but eventually paid staff must be allocated for program continuity May be useful if tourism region is larger than the focus of existing organizations May encompass two or more communities, a county, or a multicounty region Can be effective for policy, political, and marketing coordination Members may represent business, government, and citizen interest groups
Local Government Departments	Provides official recognition of tourism's importance to economy Provides paid staff to coordinate tourism efforts May support planning, development, marketing, and visitor information May limit involvement of local tourism/business community
Tourism Federation	Umbrella organization of trade groups (restaurant, hotel/motel, attractions, museums, retail, entertainment, etc.) Coordinates interests of groups Good for lobbying Effectiveness depends on strength of member groups Care should be taken so that no one group dominates policy or activities
Lodging/Room Tax Organizations	Formed to oversee expenditures of revenues from lodging taxes, the most common funding method for tourism mandated by laws or ordinances States differ on how a lodging tax district may be formed, who manages it, and how the monies can be spent A board of elected officials, lodging operators, and local tourism businesses determine expenditures Some states require funds be used only for marketing and promotion; others allow funding of development of tourism facilities and/or general community needs Most stable structure, since portion of tax revenue is allocated to staffing/programs

Figure 5.1 offers a sample organizational structure that uses volunteer committees to define and carry out tasks. Committees are effective because they can focus on specific areas of concern and can operate more informally and efficiently than large structures. Members usually elect to participate in committees that fit their interests and skills, so individual dedication and involvement is usually high. This structure also provides opportunities for committee members to explore additional areas of interest and so develop new skills. One challenge

of the committee structure, however, is member burnout. Recognition and new member recruitment are key to keeping the group motivated and refreshed.

Figure 5.1: Sample Tourism Organizational Structure

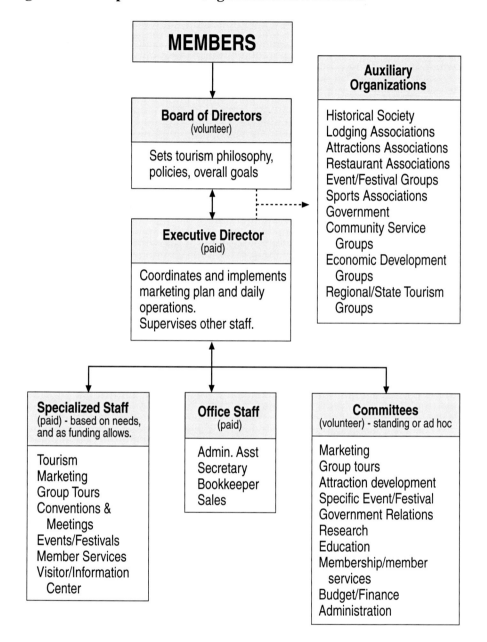

5

Leadership and Staffing

Regardless of the structure, your tourism organization must have strong leadership and adequate staffing to be effective. The leader will set the tone for the organization. He or she may also serve as facilitator for tourism planning efforts, and may train other members of the organization. Leaders often must take on the role of moderator when members' viewpoints do not coincide. The leader's primary job is to facilitate dialogue and empower the group by delegating tasks and authority. Effective leaders have many of the following characteristics:

- Responsibility;
- High standards;
- Knowledge;
- Communication skills;
- Ability to motivate others;
- Willingness to teach others;
- Trust; and
- Respect.

Most community tourism organizations depend on leadership from both volunteers and paid staff. Volunteers provide leadership in a number of roles, including serving on the organization's board of directors, chairing or participating on committees, and supporting the organization within the community. Paid staff report to the volunteer board of directors, conduct the daily business of the organization, and work closely with volunteers to carry out the organization's responsibilities.

Paid Staff

Paid professional staff, experienced in tourism development and marketing, bring expertise to the organization and can greatly increase productivity. Recruiting and hiring good professional staff is a worthwhile investment. Paid staff work closely with volunteers in all capacities.

The number of paid staff, and the roles they fill, vary greatly with the organization's structure and size. Small organizations may have only one or two paid staff, while larger organizations may have several employees with specialized responsibilities.

Generally, a tourism organization will hire an individual to provide the daily leadership for the organization and carry out the sales and marketing efforts. This individual, often called the executive director, serves as the head of staff and reports to the board of directors.

Some important factors to consider when creating staff positions:

- Roles of paid staff and volunteer leaders should be clearly delineated. Paid staff normally are responsible for identifying and recommending (but not making) policy decisions. Volunteer leaders normally are responsible for making policy decisions.

- Paid staff and volunteers work together to implement many programs. Paid staff should make the work of volunteers easier, but should not take over the volunteer's task. Volunteer leaders should not dump the job on the paid staff. The role of the paid staff will vary with each program. Both paid staff and volunteers must have a thorough understanding of the division of roles and responsibilities.

- Avoid the tendency to turn over organizational maintenance tasks (e.g., membership, bookkeeping, financial accounting) to paid staff. In minimally staffed organizations, volunteer leaders and paid staff should probably share organizational maintenance. The time paid staff spend on organizational maintenance tasks is time they don't spend on professional sales and marketing duties that increase the output of the organization.

- Paid staff provide the most benefit if they stay current in their field. It is important to encourage membership in professional associations and active participation in conferences, workshops, and professional meetings. This also provides visibility for the community and the organization.

When creating your tourism organization, seek assistance from state or regional convention and visitor bureau associations, the Destination Marketing Association International (DMAI) at www.destinationmarketing.org, or state offices of tourism and labor. They can help you develop job descriptions, and provide information in areas such as hiring, policies, and labor laws.

Volunteer Leaders

Volunteers are the backbone of any good community organization. Professional staff depend on volunteer leadership to provide program support, direction, and insight.

This leadership generally takes the form of a board of directors. There are many possible board structures; be sure to take time to do the research and choose the one that's best for your community.

Board members are appointed or elected for a term of office—often a multiyear term. Officers (president, vice-president, secretary, and treasurer) are elected from among board members. Many boards are set up so as to include representatives from the various tourism industry sectors (lodging, attractions, travel, transportation, festivals, etc.), community leadership, retail organizations, government, and other organizations. In selecting board members, seek individuals who are interested in the work of the organization and willing to commit time and support to its activities.

The earlier discussion of planning participants explained the diversity of traditional and nontraditional community stakeholders who may be involved or affected by tourism development and should be invited to the initial meeting to explore tourism development. These same groups and individuals may be potential members for your tourism organization's board.

It is important that all tourism groups are adequately represented on the tourism organization board. Take care to identify individuals who:

- Know the community or region;
- Understand tourism;
- Have skills or access to information needed by the committee;
- Can work productively in a group;
- Have time to regularly invest in committee work; and
- Want to be part of a community tourism program.

The board of directors traditionally has five primary functions:

1. Set organizational policies;
2. Hire and evaluate the executive director;
3. Approve programs and budgets;
4. Provide community access and political clout for the programs; and
5. Serve as advisors and disciples of programs and initiatives.

In addition to serving on a board of directors, volunteers are important for committee work. Committees can be permanent or ad hoc (temporary). Committee members serve as links to and advocates within the community. They also can work at events and help recruit, train, and mentor other volunteers.

The following strategies can help improve volunteer leadership.

- Clearly define the roles of officers, board members, and committee chairpersons in the bylaws. Misunderstandings about who does what reduce efficiency and can cause conflict.
- Have fixed terms of office. In most cases, volunteers should be asked to assume responsibilities for one to three years. Too many organizations stagnate because the same volunteers keep offices

and chairs indefinitely. Without specific terms, it can become difficult for officeholders to step down or for organization members to ask for a change.

- Reach out to new audiences for volunteers. Look for people who may be involved in "fringe" areas of tourism. Be willing to take risks. Don't wait for people to volunteer—ask for their help.

- Help volunteers learn roles before they take on the full responsibilities. Train volunteers on roles and responsibilities. Conduct training sessions for new leaders. Use "vice-," "assistant," "-elect," or "co-" leader positions to create orderly succession and allow volunteers to learn their roles before assuming leadership positions.

- Document specific tasks with logbooks or reports from previous leaders. This is especially useful for recurring activities or events. Include such information as people to contact, reservations to be made, contracts to be signed, deadline dates, prices paid, and rates charged.

- Whenever possible, encourage volunteer leaders to attend workshops for additional training. In addition to learning specific skills, participants will meet others with similar responsibilities, building useful networks and exchanging information.

Maintaining good volunteer leadership takes effort because most organizations need many volunteer leaders, and because volunteer leaders change frequently. For an in-depth discussion of volunteer management, see Chapter 11.

Profit or Nonprofit?

Tourism organizations can operate as for-profit or nonprofit entities. When forming your organization, seek qualified professional advice to help you consider the pros, cons, and legal implications of various business classification categories. For example, nonprofit status can be beneficial when applying for grant and foundation monies, but may set limitations on the business you can conduct "for profit."

Funding

Money is a critical component of most programs. Among the most important areas that require funding are operating the tourism organization, implementing its programs, and developing local attractions and services. Tourism organizations need money to market the area to tourists, to communicate with their members, for education and training, and to conduct special programs and events. Money is critical for developing the attractions and services that are the foundations for tourism industry growth.

Critical to your organization's success is the adoption of funding methods that will provide funds on a stable and ongoing basis. Without some stability in funding, planning and programs are uncertain and the image and productivity of the organization are often affected. Table 5.3 lists common methods for funding tourism organizations. For more information on funding, see Chapter 12.

Table 5.3: Methods of Funding Tourism Organizations

$ Method $	Potential Sources
Organization Dues/Fees	Local members, associate members, sponsors
Voluntary Contributions	Percentage of gross sales paid by tourism businesses; sometimes tied to "fair share" concept to pay for marketing
For-Profit Business Operations	Profits of businesses owned and/or operated by tourism organization as a means of funding
Retail Sales	Sales of souvenirs, T-shirts, books, crafts, beverages
Festivals & Events	Revenues from ticket sales, concessions, or leased space
Advertising Sales	Local or regional "lure" books, cooperative advertising
Donations & Gifts	In-kind contributions from local merchants and corporations
Grants & Matching Funds	Governmental agencies, foundations, corporations
Local Government	General fund revenues, special tax revenues, tourism/recreation user fees
Lodging or Food/Beverage Tax	City, county, regional, special district or statewide
Sales Tax/Special District Levies	Additional sales taxes, development districts, special trade zones with property tax; development, maintenance, or marketing levies or assessments

Evaluation

Organizations need to regularly evaluate their performance, programs, and outcomes. Measuring the impact of your efforts will help you focus on your goals. Evaluating your success in achieving those goals will help you determine effectiveness, identify problems, reevaluate goals, and formulate new plans and strategies. It is useful to examine how your organizational effort is allocated among primary goals, secondary goals (e.g., group maintenance), and nongoal-related work.

Following are a few evaluation methods that your organization can easily implement:

- Create annual reports not only to communicate the results of your efforts with others but also as a source of information for evaluation efforts.

- Ask project leaders for project completion reports. Written documentation is valuable for measuring success and as an aid for similar future projects.

- Survey attitudes and opinions of organization and community members. Measure both support and opposition to your goals and the methods used to achieve them. Ask for ideas, new goals, and suggestions for improvement.

- Ask program participants to evaluate the effectiveness and relevance of programs. This information can be used to improve the content and effectiveness of programs.

Effective Tourism Organizations

The U.S. Commerce Department lists five key functions needed for a tourism organization to succeed.

Communications

Tourism organizations must establish effective and efficient channels of communication to reach visitors, local residents, and internal members. The tourism organization is usually responsible for producing information about area attractions and services, as well as managing the local visitor center. Other forms of communication include informational signs, public meetings, and organized dissemination of information such as press releases or newsletters.

Promotion

Promotion is aimed at influencing people's decision to travel by increasing their awareness of your community. This is done directly (e.g., advertising) or through intermediaries such as travel agents and tour operators. Public relations is a means of promotion that builds awareness and goodwill. Tourism organizations engage in promotion to increase visitor numbers and maintain or increase tourism market share.

Education/Training

Quality and customer service are cornerstones of the tourism experience. Tourism organizations should be actively involved in educating and training local businesses and workers about providing a quality tourism experience. They may also educate residents about the value of tourism and its impact on the community.

Research/Data Collection

Tourism organizations should collect information about visitors. An understanding of who is coming to your town, why they are coming, and what they are doing is an important part of an effective promotional strategy. The most common types of research are visitor profile surveys and work force/economic surveys of local businesses. By collecting data over time, you can observe changes and trends that can guide decisions. Visitor satisfaction, attractions visited, image assessment, and evaluation of promotional activities should be continually tracked.

Budget/Finance

Budget and financing are critical to any tourism organization. Organizations must have solid methods of generating, receiving, and spending funds. Funds are needed for daily operations, promotional activities, research, education, and special projects such as capital improvements.

In summary, a community tourism organization acts as an administrative arm of the local tourism industry. It provides a forum for collaboration and a means of coordinating the many diverse players that are required for tourism to exist.

Adapted from Weaver. G. (1991). *Tourism USA: Guidelines for tourism development.* (pp.34-38). Columbia, MO: University of Missouri.

Vision

An organization must have a purpose that meets the needs of its members and challenges them to invest their time and money to accomplish that purpose. Stating that purpose by creating a vision of the future helps people understand what the organization is for, why it is needed, and what goals it hopes to accomplish.

The tourism organization's vision should be tied directly to the community's vision and fit with overall community attitudes and values. It should contain not only a direction for tourism development, but also desired outcomes for the community. Creating a vision is essentially packaging ideas and goals into concepts that are easy for the community to understand and to accept.

In setting your vision, balance long-term goals with short-term goals. Achieving short-term goals will build enthusiasm and support for the vision.

The vision focuses on results. There may be several methods employed to accomplish the desired results, and the methods may change to accommodate different situations. Still, the vision remains as the target toward which the community's tourism efforts are directed.

Review and revise your vision from time to time. If your organization is unable to achieve its vision, it must create a new vision, or it will no longer have a purpose. Changing conditions often necessitate a change of focus and vision. Stimulating and steering your organization toward clear visions of the future presents continual challenges, but helps focus your energies on the most important tasks.

5

It's important to communicate your vision to others. You can do this by publicizing it in the local media, printing it on your organization letterhead, or sending out a newsletter highlighting your vision and what the organization is doing.

"If you don't know where you are going, any road will take you there."

Sample Vision Statements

• Tourism will focus on eliminating usual seasonal unemployment by developing festivals and events during those periods.

• Tourism will target development of high-quality restaurants and accommodations to enhance opportunities for other business development.

• Tourism activities will be encouraged as a means of preserving and restoring historic downtown areas and neighborhoods.

• Tourism will create quality jobs that will allow youth to find meaningful careers and stay in the community.

List groups or businesses currently involved in tourism development or marketing in your community. Then identify what they are doing and the methods being used.

WHO	TYPE G,B,T*	WHAT THEY ARE DOING	METHODS USED
Example: Economic Development Officer	G	Working with community government to develop a tourism business on Main Street. Writing a grant for museum expansion.	Seeking financing packages, facilitating meetings with business owner and local back, government offices.
Chamber of Commerce	B	Community brochure, answer calls about community, sponsor annual Blueberry festival	Tourism committee Volunteers

* G = Government   B = Business   T = Tourism

Chapter 6
Assessing Your Tourism Potential

Communities do not all have equal potential for developing a successful tourism industry. Factors that influence success include quality, uniqueness, price, availability of attractions and visitor services, and demand for what you offer.

Before developing tourism, you must have a clear picture of your existing tourism product, your potential for developing new products that coincide with visitor demand, and local attitudes toward tourism growth. This chapter will help you develop that picture. It will help you come to some decision about the set of core elements that you will market and to identify your strongest assets and new areas that could be developed. The information you generate in this chapter will help you prioritize your tourism development goals and projects and develop feasibility studies and market plans. It will also help you decide whether your community serves a pass-through market, offers day trip or touring options, or is an overnight destination—roles that demand different development and marketing strategies.

If your community is just beginning its tourism involvement, start with the inventory of attractions and visitor services. If your community has an existing attractions inventory, make sure it is thorough and up to date. Even if you have been at this for several years, you still need to do the evaluation and packaging steps, since tourism trends, competition, and your community all change over time.

The idea behind the assessment process described in this chapter is simply to give you a picture of your tourism attraction base—to help you see what your community has to offer visitors as a first step to developing and marketing your attractions mix. Modify it as necessary to meet your community's needs.

WHAT'S IN THIS CHAPTER?

- **About Attractions**
- **Assessing Your Attractions**
- **Assessing Private Sector Services**
- **Assessing Resident Attitudes**
- **Assessing Business Attitudes**
- **Assessing Public Sector Facilities and Services**
- **Synthesis**

Before you start on this assessment process, identify the geographic area to be considered. In some cases, a single community will have enough attractions and services to go it alone as a destination. However, you also need to consider how nearby attractions and services relate to your set of attractions and services. The geographic area you assess should be large enough to have significant drawing power. Don't simply let political boundaries and attraction ownership determine the boundaries of the area being analyzed. Visitors do not consider these boundaries when seeking to satisfy their wants and needs. Try to view your geographic area from the consumer's viewpoint.

About Attractions

Attractions are the reason people visit an area—the places that provide things for visitors to see and do. They pull tourists to one place instead of another and focus tourist interest. Each area has unique attractions that can be developed and improved. Attractions may be publicly or privately operated.

Today's market requires that attention be given to creating multiple appeals. The more a community offers, the better its opportunities for tourism income. A concentration of quality attractions helps to hold visitors longer, and a longer stay translates to greater spending.

Types of Attractions

Places of *natural and scenic significance* are often a starting point when thinking about attractions. The landscape of a place, particularly topographic and aquatic features, sets the tone in creating options and constraints for visitors. It serves as a backdrop for tourist activities and is an important part of the product.

Natural resources can also be, with appropriate development, the setting for *outdoor recreational activities*. These may include the use of motorized equipment (e.g., snowmobiling, power boating), self-propelled activities (e.g., bicycling, canoeing, cross-country skiing), pursuits that consume resources (e.g., hunting, fishing), or appreciative activities (e.g., birding, nature photography). Spending for such activities can range from minimal amounts to thousands of dollars.

Figure 6.1: Types of Tourist Attractions

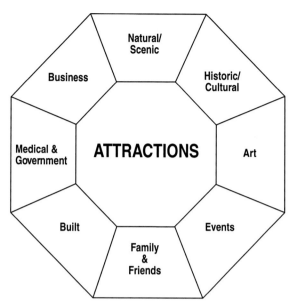

Source: Richardson, S. (1991). *Colorado Community Tourism Action Guide*. Colorado Center for Community Development, University of Colorado at Denver, and the Center of Recreation and Tourism Development, University of Colorado at Boulder.

Figure 6.1 provides a broad look at the many types of community features that can serve as tourist attractions.

Historic and cultural resources are obvious tourism assets. Contributions made by previous generations are what distinguish one place from another; the human drama of history brings locations and events alive. Whatever your area's past, sites can be preserved, restored, interpreted, and expanded to become part of a sightseeing circuit.

Art, as a subset of cultural features, can create a distinctive atmosphere. The use and display of locally produced works, including performances, can draw many tourists.

Events have become important attractions for many communities. Celebrations can be built around an unlimited number of themes, such as harvest time, foods, physical fitness, or music. Events can be the main draw, or reinforce other attractions. They can introduce new-comers to your town and its offerings, fill slack times of the year, distribute visitors over a longer season, or offer a changing product that draws repeat visitors. Such attractions are often intended for both local people and tourists.

Look at your community from a visitor's viewpoint to identify unique attractions.

Built attractions, such as amusement parks, zoos, and theme resorts, offer entertainment in a created environment. Also, don't neglect "experience" attractions related to the local economy, such as farmers markets and tours of plants, mines, cheese factories, or wineries.

Services and transportation modes also function as reasons to visit. For example, bed and breakfast inns are often an attraction as well as a lodging choice. Unique shopping—for example, the Appalachian crafts stores in Dillsboro, North Carolina—can be the primary attraction. Unusual means of transport, such as ferryboats, carriage rides, and excursion trains, or bicycle-only towns, can also draw visitors.

Visiting *family and friends* is still the number one reason people travel, so residents may be your community's most important asset. You can keep visitors in the area by providing both visitors and residents information about local attractions.

Your community's *businesses* and local industries can be attractions for business travel. Visits to local corporations, convention centers, or legal offices can be extended to include other area highlights. So can visits to *medical facilities and government agencies.* Travelers to these rely heavily on local hospitality services and amenities. By identifying and promoting other community attractions, you may expand their stay or encourage them to visit your community for leisure purposes.

Attraction Characteristics

Characteristics of attractions include quality, authenticity, uniqueness, drawing power, and activity options. It is the combination of these elements that sets attractions apart from one another. While some may be more important than others to different groups of visitors, they are all important to the community tourism development process.

High quality is a guiding value of tourism development. For attractions this means a pleasing and clean appearance; smooth, customer-driven operations and procedures; resource protection; and hospitality. Product quality benefits and protects both residents and visitors. Tourism thrives on word-of-mouth reports to family and friends. Failure to offer a high-quality experience dooms the attraction and community as a destination.

Authenticity is also a fundamental value. It means letting the distinctive regional flavor of a community shine through in a way that produces a true "sense of place." The demand for "authentic" travel experiences is high and increasing. A community that takes advantage of, showcases, and protects its natural setting promotes its authenticity. Small communities have a competitive advantage in that they are uniquely positioned to provide authentic tourist experiences that

reflect local character. As you consider how much to alter attractions for public accessibility, remember that the more authentic the attraction, the more likely it is to be integrated easily into the community and to have long-term market appeal.

> **Authentic vs. Built Attractions**
>
> There is a difference between a region that promotes a "wander the backroads" style of tourism (e.g., visiting artisans, historic churches, Amish settlements, trout streams) and one that offers an experience based more on constructed attractions such as racetracks and water slides. Both can offer a significant financial return and both are acceptable so long as the community agrees with the direction tourism is taking. The big difference is that in the former instance, tourism relies on dispersed attractions and captures regional uniqueness and authenticity, whereas in the latter case tourism is based on built facilities that might be replicated in any number of communities.

Because tourists have many choices, *uniqueness*—an attraction "edge" that sets your community apart from the competition—is also important. After conducting an attractions inventory and sorting for authenticity, many towns find they have multiple options for attracting tourists. The challenge is to choose one dominant attraction mix that represents your town's uniqueness. Communities that identify their special appeal, or niche, have a greater chance of success.

Drawing power is measured in terms of the number of tourists who will travel a specified distance to visit your community and whether they will return for repeat visits. It depends on variables such as proximity to major population centers, ease of access, number of people traveling through the area, competition, attractions, and strength of promotional campaigns. It is usually measured in terms of the point of origin of the visitors—local community, county, state, national, or international. If time and money allow, obtain this information from feasibility or market studies. Otherwise, compile it from secondary data sources (e.g., attendance and average growth rates), comparisons with nearby attractions, and best guesses.

Activity options are another important characteristic of attractions. When listing existing and potential attractions, the first impulse is to concentrate on buildings, sites, and facilities. But it's important also to remember the activities that give visitors things to do. For example, natural resources can be the basis for outdoor recreation, historical sites can offer reenactments of past events, art galleries can host workshops, and Main Street can be the start and finish for a bike race. Ask: "Is there something for tourists to do?" and "Can the activity or

Enhancing Drawing Power

Passamaquoddy Bay and Fundy Isles (population 35,000) is a region of small towns with populations ranging from 200 to 5,000 encompassing the coastal area of Maine and New Brunswick. It traditionally saw only "pass-through" tourists. In an international effort to increase length of stay, the tourism planning group developed The Quoddy Loop, a recommended highway/ferry route along rugged coastlines and forested areas. The tourism product emphasized is appreciative, low-key sightseeing: wildlife viewing; bird and whale watching; visiting lighthouses, parks, and wildlife refuges; hiking the many coastal and inland trails; canoeing on local rivers; relaxing on the beach; and visiting a working fishing village in the "Down East" tradition.

attraction be periodically changed through expansion or seasonal shifts so that visitors will consider a repeat visit?"

Classification of Attractions

Thinking about attractions in terms of quality, authenticity, uniqueness, drawing power, and activity options immediately suggests that all attractions are not created equal. Some have more potential than others to draw tourists. A common classification scheme divides them into primary and secondary attractions.

Primary attractions are attractions that influence a traveler's decision about where to go. They are often the main reason for visiting an area, and are intricately linked to the image of the destination as promoted in marketing campaigns.

Secondary attractions are those that enhance the tourist experience, but are not part of the major destination selection process.

For example, the savanna game parks of Kenya, the lush tropical beaches of Tahiti, and the art museums of Italy are primary attractions. Corresponding secondary attractions might be a well-known Kenyan handicrafts market, traditional dance performances in Tahiti, and Italian cuisine.

Sorting your attractions into primary and secondary ones helps to focus development energies and attention, and feeds critical information into the marketing process. It helps you develop core groups of attractions that work well together and that can be collectively marketed to keep the visitor in your community longer.

Attractions Packaging

Few attractions can stand alone in today's marketplace. Most travelers have limited vacation time, so they try to combine as many activities as possible into one destination visit. The drawing power of attractions tends to be stronger if there is a complementary set of features — that is, an "attraction package."

This principle is demonstrated by the clustering of attractions and activities in Orlando, Florida. Walt Disney World is a primary attraction, but there are also several other major theme parks, water parks, and museums that attract visitors. Clustering allows them to benefit from each other and encourages longer stays. The clustered competition, in fact, increases the volume of business.

Developing a Secondary Attraction

St. Marys, Georgia (population 8,500), is a fishing village located on the meandering St. Marys River close enough to the Atlantic Ocean to catch the salt air. Salt marshes and barrier islands, and the recreation they offer, are a backdrop to historic churches and homes, a trolley car, streets lined with giant live oaks, and the ruins of a sugar mill. Some 38 sites in the historic district were marked with raised letters and braille for sight-impaired visitors: the Braille Trail tapped into a growing target market, gained significant media attention, and increased community awareness of the needs of persons with disabilities.

The fundamental idea in selecting a core group of attractions is to identify those that work together to present a strong, concise image, or those that complement one another, thus increasing their capacity to draw the visitor.

A community attractions package is the sum of all the attractions. It consists of:

- The relationship of attractions to each other (positive, neutral, negative);
- Market considerations (traveler spending potential, compatibility); and
- Community image opportunities (identity, theme).

Once you have identified a primary set of attractions, you can combine them with complementary secondary attractions to develop specialized "packages." Many communities develop several different packages (or itineraries) that can be marketed to different special interest markets. The more diverse your attractions mix, the more success you have for repeat visitation.

Note that regardless of the attraction package, the natural setting is always part of the attraction mix. It can be a primary draw or simply a backdrop for tourism activities. Similarly, many attraction packages include a festival component. Festivals tend to celebrate the strong features of a community, drawing in new visitors to sample the community's other attractions. No matter how strong the attraction package is, adding festivals to the mix can bring added benefit and help sway the visitor's decision to come to your community.

Seasonality

Seasonality affects all attractions. It is defined in many different ways. It can refer to climatic changes that affect demand for various activities such as downhill skiing or water sports. It can also refer to events, including traditional or religious holidays (e.g., Thanksgiving), vacation patterns (e.g., summer or spring break from school), or sports seasons. Attractions may experience a high and low season (referring to the number of visitors at different times of the year) or peak and off-peak times (referring to the number of visitors in a particular month, week, or even time of day).

One of the primary ways communities can reduce seasonal fluctuation in their local tourism industry is to develop a variety of diverse attrac-

Building on Natural Resources

Teton Valley, Idaho (population 3,412), is an exemplary tourism community bordering natural resource areas. An agricultural valley and mountains provide four-season recreation: hiking, backpacking, bicycling, horseback riding, all-terrain vehicle use, fishing, boating, snowmobiling, and skiing. Second, tourism projects, such as the start-up of Hot Air Balloon and High Country Cowboy Poetry festivals, ski resort expansion, and conversion of abandoned tracks to a scenic rail line, have enhanced recreational opportunities. Services to help the visitor enjoy the outdoors include dude ranches, backcountry outfitters, hunting/fishing lodges, and retail stores provide equipment, guide service, or simply the opportunity to enjoy the scenery.

6

History and Culture

Natchez, Mississippi (population 18,500), builds its tourism around a strong image of the traditional South. The town's wealth of resources includes more than 30 antebellum homes open for tours, horse-drawn carriages, paddle-wheel riverboat excursions, black gospel choir performances about the African-American experience, and a theatrical production about the Old South, all set in the community's five National Historic Districts. The Victorian Christmas—a month-long series of events such as candlelight tours, Santa's arrival by riverboat, high teas, decorated mansions, and shopping promotions—was created to fill a typically slow month; in the first year December hotel occupancy increased 10 percent. Additional black history initiatives seek to both enhance the tourism product and improve community solidarity.

tions or develop new activities at existing attractions. A good example can be seen in the trend among ski resorts, formerly thought of as just winter destinations, to offer summer and springtime activities such as mountain biking, horseback riding, and jazz festivals. Many communities have created special festivals or events around various seasons to spread tourist visitation more evenly throughout the year. The Winter Carnival in St. Paul, Minnesota, is a successful example of using an event to generate tourism in a low season.

Attractions and lodging establishments often use lower rates or value-added features to encourage visitation during off-peak times or low seasons. Regardless of the strategy used, communities need to evaluate their tourist attractions in terms of seasonality to gain a more accurate perspective of the potential economic return of tourism development and to balance visitation.

Assessing Your Attractions

Multiple attractions in an area can complement and enhance each other, or compete and detract from each other. The intense competition among communities to capture tourist traffic makes it necessary to look at all options in order to create a distinctive product that will hold its own in the marketplace. This section will help you identify and evaluate the full range of existing and potential attractions in your community.

Worksheets are included both in the following pages and on the CD-ROM included with this manual.

Inventory

Begin your evaluation by completing a checklist of attractions by category (Worksheet 6.1). As you inventory attractions, you may want to identify their location on a map. This may also be a good time to note details such as hours, entrance fees, etc. If possible, those inventorying and assessing attractions should visit each site. Identify existing sites and facilities, but also consider potential attractions that could be developed. Don't overlook any possibilities that could be an attraction with proper development and packaging.

For example:

- Guinness & Co. in Dublin, Ireland, offers self-guided tours of its Storehouse, where visitors learn about the brewing process for varieties of the famous Irish beer. Visitors also can taste Guin-

TIP

Different teams can be used to divide the inventory and assessment work to lend greater perspective.

TIP

Take pictures of different sites and facilities during the assessment.

ness from the "keg line," and with the assistance of official tasters, learn how to savor the beer just like real connoisseurs.

- Walnut Grove, Minnesota (see Community Spotlight, page 162), draws on the fame of former resident Laura Ingalls Wilder, author of *Little House on the Prairie,* with an annual pageant, museum, and dugout site attractions.

(see Community Spotlight, page 162)

To complete Worksheet 6.1:

1. Check each category that represents an existing attraction for your community. If you have more than one of any item, indicate the number. If you don't know the number, simply check the box. Note facility conditions, problems, or other useful information in the "Description" column.

2. Check categories that could be a potential attraction. Indicate the time frame in which you think each could be developed, based on your perspective of community support and knowledge of the potential site. Generally, attractions that require little physical infrastructure or capital investment (e.g., a walking or historical tour) can be developed in a relatively short time frame—perhaps a year. More complex projects such as a paved bicycle trail, or projects requiring significant infrastructure or new facilities, will take longer.

Evaluate

The next step is to evaluate attractions.

Existing Attractions

Use Worksheet 6.2 as follows to evaluate existing attractions:

1. Copy your list of existing attractions from Worksheet 6.1 to the left column of Worksheet 6.2. (Make copies of the worksheet if you need more room.)

2. Give each attraction a score for each category under "Tourism Development Assessment Criteria" based on the scales on the bottom of the worksheet. As you score each attraction, ask yourself:

> *Quality:* Is the attraction in good, visitor-friendly condition? How does it rate in the areas of appearance, operations, hospitality, and resource protection?

> *Authenticity:* Does the attraction reflect the cultural or economic heritage of the community? Does it reflect the community's "sense of place?"

Tip

Use a portable file box to collect promotional materials about each attraction. This will provide insight into how the attraction is currently marketed and may suggest ideas for packaging.

Community Spotlight

Inventory of Attractions

Houston County, Minnesota, volunteers spent nearly six months gathering detailed information about attractions in their county. This information was entered into a spreadsheet, placed in binders, and distributed to a variety of establishments including chambers, libraries, historical society sites, lodging facilities, and local government offices. This inventory has become a well-used, easily maintained, and helpful tool for promoting the whole county. It also enhanced residents' sense of pride about how much the county has to offer.

6

Tip

Include youth and seniors in your assessment team. Different committees or teams can be used to divide the inventory and assessment work.

Uniqueness: Is the attraction unique within a 150- to 300-mile market area?

Drawing Power: What geographic area do/will customers come from?

Activities: Does the attraction offer a varied and changing set of activities?

Note that low scores do not necessarily mean the attraction has no visitor potential. If it could be a central component of the attraction mix, it may just need improvement.

3. Add the scores for each attraction and divide by 5 to get an average rating for the attraction's overall tourism development potential. Write this number in the "Average Rating" column.

4. In the next series of columns, identify the market(s) from which visitors currently come. Shade in each of the boxes according to the scale at the bottom of the page. Use the same technique to indicate which months the attraction is open or used.

Potential Attractions

Now use Worksheet 6.3 to evaluate your community's potential attractions as follows:

1. Review Worksheet 6.1. List items you identified as potential attractions under the appropriate time frame category on Worksheet 6.3.

2. Evaluate each potential attraction according to the criteria under "Potential Tourism Development Evaluation Criteria." Again, score each category from 1 to 4 using the scales at the bottom of the page and referring to the questions above for authenticity, uniqueness, and drawing power. For infrastructure and support services needed and project viability, ask yourself:

    Infrastructure and Support Services: Are there adequate infrastructure, support services, and visitor services nearby to accommodate development of the potential attraction?

    Project Viability: What is the project's overall viability? Is there sufficient community support for development of the attraction? Are other necessary resources and adequate funds in place?

3. Add the scores and divide by 5 to get an average rating for the attraction's overall development potential. Write the score in the space provided. In the adjacent column, make notes regarding possible visitor types to which it would appeal. Also note any key problems or concerns in this space.

4. Rank potential attractions in terms of their overall potential for success.

Package

With the inventory and evaluation complete, your next job is to select from the options listed the "package" or "mix" with the greatest chance of success. This exercise is best done with a group to get a variety of perspectives.

Existing Attractions

Start by reviewing your evaluation of existing attractions (Worksheet 6.2). Then use Worksheet 6.4 to classify and package your existing attractions as follows:

1. Divide the attractions you have evaluated into primary (those that initially draw the tourist) and secondary (those that enhance the visitor experience) attractions. List them in the space provided in Section A of Worksheet 6.4.

2. Answer the questions in Section B of the worksheet.

3. Using the information in Sections A and B, choose three primary attractions that have the potential for drawing the most visitors and list them in Section C. Review your list of secondary attractions and see how you might group them with your three primary ones to develop an "attraction package." Use your best judgment and intuition to mix and match. Is a particular theme or market niche readily apparent? If so, write it down.

4. In Section D, list key opportunities or constraints to developing and marketing the attraction packages you have identified.

5. Assign a member of the tourism planning team or the attractions committee responsibility for evaluating feasibility of developing each attraction package.

Prioritize

Next, use Worksheet 6.5 to identify your top development priorities for potential attractions as follows:

1. Review Worksheet 6.3. List the potential attractions that received the highest average ratings according to short- and long-term development priorities in Section A of Worksheet 6.5.

2. Complete the questions in Section B to determine how potential attraction development projects fit with existing tourism attractions and your community's overall tourism goals.

3. Review Sections A and B and identify your top attraction development priorities. List them in Section C and note potential opportunities for or constraints to developing and marketing them.

4. Appoint a committee to evaluate feasibility of developing each potential attraction.

Keep in mind that attraction development is not a completely scientific process, no matter how much information or input is collected. It is also an art. Attractions must appeal to visitors' emotions, so use creativity to juggle the attraction package until you are pleased with the results. There can be synergy between attractions, where the final product is more successful than the sum of its parts. Tourism development sometimes is the result of a "hunch" about this synergy. Have fun, and test your assumptions.

Assessing Private Sector Services

While attractions draw visitors to your town, services provide them with the things they need to have a satisfying stay. Visitor services are divided into two categories:

Primary services are services essential to the visitor's experience (e.g., lodging, restaurants, airlines, rental cars). They often are identified as being associated with tourism.

Secondary services are services that add to the visitor's experience but that are also used by local residents (e.g., gas, retail, banks, entertainment). Secondary services are not always identified as being part of the tourism industry.

Visitor services provided by the private sector are important to the community not only because they make the visitor feel welcome, but also because they generate economic activity. This is particularly true for services that are provided locally. Abundant, diverse, high-quality, community-based visitor services help communities benefit financially from tourism.

It's important to assess both existing visitor services and those needed for future tourism development. This section will help you inventory and evaluate visitor services provided by the private sector, and identify future development priorities. You will:

• Inventory and categorize private sector visitor services;

• Evaluate existing and potential private sector visitor services, identifying those that also have "attraction potential;" and

• Prioritize development of future private sector visitor services.

You may want to appoint a committee to conduct this assessment, since this process can be completed simultaneously with the attractions assessment. Consider using resident volunteers, and be sure to designate a key person to spearhead and coordinate the effort.

Inventory

Begin by completing Worksheet 6.6 as follows:

1. In the first column, check each category that represents an existing service. If multiple services are available in a category, indicate the number. If you don't know the number, use a check mark or estimate.

2. For each item, note key problems or comments in the "Description" column (e.g., local customers, location, accessibility).

3. If the category represents a potential service, check the time frame in which you think it could be developed. This is a rough estimate based on your own perspective.

Evaluate

The next step is to evaluate existing and potential private sector services.

Existing Private Sector Services

Use the following steps to complete Worksheet 6.7. Make additional copies of the worksheet if you need more room.

1. Review Worksheet 6.6. List your existing services by type (e.g., motels, resorts, campgrounds), not by specific businesses, on Worksheet 6.7 under the categories provided. Note significant weaknesses and opportunities in the right-hand column.

2. Give each entry a score in each category under "Visitor Services Assessment Criteria" using the ranking scale on the bottom of the worksheet. This is not a scientific process; rank services based upon your impressions.

3. Add the scores and divide by 4 to get an average quality and development potential rating for each visitor service category listed. Write this number in under "Average Rating."

Potential Private Sector Services

Use Worksheet 6.8 to evaluate potential private sector services as follows:

1. Review Worksheet 6.6. List any services you identified as having potential for development on Worksheet 6.8 under the

appropriate time-frame category. Note in the space provided any key weaknesses or opportunities that might influence development of the service (e.g., resources, funding, zoning).

2. Give each item a score for the project assessment criteria. Again, this is not a scientific process; just rank services based upon your impressions.

3. Once you have rated items, add the scores and divide by 4 to get an average rating for the overall development potential of each. Write this number in under "Average Rating."

4. Rank potential services in terms of priority. Give the highest ranking to the service you feel is most critical to your community's overall development of tourism. (Items with a high "Average Rating" score should be among your top-ranked priorities.) Your ranking will correlate with the number of attractions being evaluated. You may wish to rank items in each time-frame category separately.

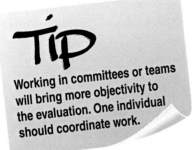

Tip

Working in committees or teams will bring more objectivity to the evaluation. One individual should coordinate work.

Prioritize

You are now ready to prioritize development of new projects or enhancements to existing private sector services. Rather than tackle too many projects at once, select a few that have the most chance for success. Usually, these will be smaller projects such as a town cleanup or a resident hospitality training campaign. Starting small and getting a few successes under your belt will improve your ability to gain community-wide support for larger projects when you need it.

Use worksheets 6.9 and 6.10 to prioritize development of services as follows:

1. Review Worksheet 6.7. List existing services that received the highest average rating for overall quality and development potential in the first column under Section A of Worksheet 6.9. Then list existing services with particularly low scores in the second column.

2. Look at the list. Consider how well your existing services support your existing attraction base. Complete Section B of Worksheet 6.9.

3. Review Worksheet 6.8. List your top-ranked potential service projects according to development time frame in Section C of Worksheet 6.9.

4. Review this list. Evaluate how well your potential service projects fit with your existing and potential attraction base. Are development priorities consistent with community tourism

goals? Complete Section D to determine if any particular opportunities or constraints emerge.

5. Review Worksheet 6.9. On Worksheet 6.10, list your top private sector service action priorities. (Make additional copies of this worksheet as needed.) Identify potential opportunities or constraints that might affect development success. Appoint a committee or individual to evaluate the feasibility of carrying out each project.

Congratulations! You are well on your way to identifying your community's tourism product potential. Take time to review your assessment of attractions and private sector services to see how well they complement one another.

Assessing Resident Attitudes

Assessment 6.1 can help you check the pulse of residents with regard to tourism. Committee members should also complete this survey to determine how closely their values and attitudes coincide with those of residents. If there is significant difference, your committee may need to better represent the community at large.

The resident survey can be mailed, handed out, or even published in the newspaper. Include a date for response. This gives all residents a chance to express their opinions and become a part of any tourism development plans.

Assessing Business Attitudes

You also need to assess the attitude of your community's businesses. Tourism-related small businesses need a positive atmosphere if they are to grow and prosper. They need support from local political officials, economic development agencies, and financial institutions. Assessment 6.2 will help you assess general attitudes of community business owners about tourism.

Photocopy the survey onto two sheets of paper, front and back. Distribute it to all local businesses, even those that seem not to be tourism related. (This will help you determine the percent of businesses that are dependent upon tourism and gauge overall support for tourism.) It is important that persons distributing the survey explain its use and assure respondents that all information gathered will be held strictly confidential by the planning committee and used only for compiling a general community profile.

Part I of the survey gathers general information about the business and how important tourism is to its operation. Part II asks for opinions about tourism. This section correlates with the community attitude survey (Assessment 6.1), so you can compare data from local residents and business operators. This is important! If the business community supports tourism but residents do not, there is potential for significant problems as development growth is pursued. Part III identifies the current level of satisfaction with community and government services.

Assessing Public Sector Facilities and Services

The public sector may provide facilities such as parking, streets, lighting, benches, rest rooms, and drinking fountains. It may provide services, such as water, trash collection, sewage treatment, public transit, roads and police, emergency medical, and information services. Services provided by the public sector are also called infrastructure. Generally used by the tourist at little or no cost, they represent a cost to the community.

Tourism development requires a careful assessment of existing public services relating to local infrastructure and the physical environment. In this section you will conduct a systematic review of your community's infrastructure, as well as key physical characteristics that impact tourism. You will:

- Inventory public services, including both infrastructure services and characteristics of the physical environment;
- Evaluate local infrastructure and physical characteristics; and
- Prioritize development of future public services.

Inventory

Begin by developing a list using Worksheet 6.11 as follows:

1. In the first column, check each category that represents an existing public service. If multiple services are available within a particular category, indicate the number. If you don't know the number, use a check mark.

2. As you check an item, note any key problems or pertinent comments (e.g., capacity limitations, environmental concerns, funding constraints) in the "Description" column. Also note the agency responsible for this service.

Use the Resident and Business Attitude surveys to "take the temperature" of your community toward tourism. Use simple descriptive statistics (e.g., Of the 150 respondents, 79% felt that...") to report the information gathered with the surveys. Share the information with the community as well as your planning group. It is an opportunity to build awareness.

3. Check categories that represent public services that are needed but not available. Indicate the time frame in which you think they could be developed. This is a rough estimate based on your own perspective.

Evaluate

Next evaluate public services using Worksheet 6.12 as follows:

1. Review the categories of services listed on Worksheet 6.11. For each, note any significant improvements needed in the space provided on Worksheet 6.12.

2. Evaluate each of the public services listed according to the categories listed under "Assessment Criteria." Assign a rating of 1 to 4 for each category, based on the scale at the bottom of the form. This is not a scientific process; just rank services based upon your impressions.

3. Add the scores and divide by 3 to get an average rating for each public service listed. Write this number in the "Average" column.

Prioritize

Assign each public service a "P" (priority) or "N" (needed but for long-term development) in the right-hand column of Worksheet 6.12.

Compare your findings with your assessments of attractions, private sector services, community attitudes, and business attitudes. Do any key themes emerge? Are existing public services adequate to support plans for tourism development, or should improvements be made before you promote increased visitation? Have any concerns been expressed in the community and business surveys that were overlooked in the public services assessment?

Discuss how all your findings relate to one another and what partners in the community or region you need to work with to accomplish identified priority public service development projects. You may want to appoint a subcommittee or planning team member to contact public agencies to determine if your priority projects are scheduled for development or improvement.

Synthesis

You have now gone through the complex process of assessing your attractions, private sector services, business attitudes, community attitudes, and public sector services and the atmosphere for tourism business growth—the cornerstones of tourism development. You should now have a fresh perspective on tourism development options and a clear view of the unique competitive advantage of your community. The information from the worksheets, along with information gathered from your situation analysis (Chapter 3), will help you as you develop your community tourism development and marketing plans. Once you have compiled this information, report back to the full planning group.

Share the information with the community at large. It will help residents see the strengths and weaknesses of their community for tourism development and more accurately determine goals and strategies for tourism development.

By now, you should be well along in your tourism development efforts. This is a good time to take stock of where your community is on the continuum, and we provide a checklist below to help. Refer back to the timeline in the Preface, as well. Always remember to ensure your tourism development planning is aligned with your community values, which ought to be identified early in the process. Check your town or region's comprehensive plan and other plans and policies, as applicable, for help in articulating values.

✔ Situation Analysis Checklist

- ❑ Tourism Planning Participants (Worksheet 3.1)
- ❑ Is Tourism Right for Us? (Worksheet 3.2)
- ❑ Task Assignments (Worksheet 3.3)
- ❑ Agenda Item Action Record (Worksheet 3.4)
- ❑ External Environment Trends (Worksheet 3.6)
- ❑ SWOT Analysis (Worksheet 3.7)
- ❑ Inventory of Attractions (Worksheets 6.1)
- ❑ Attractions (Worksheets 6.2, 6.3, and 6.5)
- ❑ Packaging Existing Attractions (Worksheet 6.4)
- ❑ Private Sector Services (Worksheets 6.6-6.10)
- ❑ Public Services and Facilities (Worksheets 6.11-6.12)
- ❑ Resident Attitude Survey (Assessment 6.1)
- ❑ Local Business Attitude Survey (Assessment 6.2)

Use the work and assessment forms on the CD-ROM included with this manual.

Once you have compiled all the information, you are ready to identify your current and target markets in Chapters 7 and 8.

Worksheet 6.1: Inventory of Attractions

A. Inventory of **Natural or Scenic** Attractions

ATTRACTION CATEGORY	Attraction Exists (✔ or #)	Potential Attractions (Time Frame to Develop)			DESCRIPTION (Notes/Problems)
		1 yr	3 yrs	5 yrs	
Beaches					
Bird-watching sites					
Botanical gardens					
Canyons and gorges					
Caves					
Cliffs					
Climate					
Deserts					
Fall foliage					
Farms, ranches, dude ranches					
Fishing streams and lakes					
Forests					
Geologic formations					
Geysers					
Headwaters					
Hiking trails					
Hot springs					
Islands					
Lakes					
Mineral springs					
Monuments (natural)					
Mountains					
Natural bridges					
Nature trails					
Oceans					
Orchards and vineyards					
Parks (national, state, local)					
Picnic areas					
Remoteness					
Rivers					
Sand dunes					
Scenic views					
Ski slopes					
Star gazing					
Swamps/wetlands					
Valleys					
Volcanoes					
Waterfalls					
Whitewater					
Wilderness					
Wildlife (natural settings, sanctuaries, zoos)					
Other:					

B. *Inventory of **Cultural or Historic** Attractions*

ATTRACTION CATEGORY	Attraction Exists (✔ or #)	Potential Attractions (Time Frame to Develop)			DESCRIPTION (Notes/Problems)
		1 yr	3 yrs	5 yrs	
Antique and craft shops					
Archaeological sites					
Art galleries					
Battlefields					
Burial grounds					
Ceremonial dances					
Churches					
Conservatories					
Costumed events					
Covered bridges					
Early settlements					
Ethnic celebrations					
Ethnic restaurants/grocers					
Exhibits					
Famous historical buildings					
Famous people					
Folk art collections					
Ghost towns					
Historic building tours					
Historic railroads					
Historical reenactments					
Indian culture					
Indian reservations					
Landmarks					
Lumber camps					
Mansions					
Memorials					
Mines					
Missions					
Monuments					
Museums					
Native folklore					
Newsworthy places					
Old forts					
Pioneer churches					
Pioneer homes					
Ruins					
Special "nationality" days					
Theaters (stage, film)					
Trains					
Unique lifestyles					
Victorian buildings					
Other:					

C. Inventory of *Recreational* Activities

ATTRACTION CATEGORY	Attraction Exists (✔ or #)	Potential Attractions (Time Frame to Develop)			DESCRIPTION (Notes/Problems)
		1 yr	3 yrs	5 yrs	
Amusement or theme parks					
Archery					
Ballooning					
Beachcombing					
Bingo					
Bird watching					
Boating					
Bowling					
Camping					
Canoeing					
Fishing					
Fossil hunting					
Gambling/casinos					
Golf					
Hang gliding					
Health and beauty spas					
Hiking					
Horseback riding					
Hot springs and mud baths					
House boating					
Hunting					
Ice skating					
Kayaking					
Kite flying					
Local food specialties					
Mountain biking					
Mountain climbing					
Pack horse or llama trips					
Picnicking					
Professional sports events					
Racing and regattas					
River tubing					
Rock hunting					
Sailing					
Scuba diving					
Shopping					
Skiing (downhill)					
Skiing (cross country)					
Spelunking					
Swimming					
Tennis					
Trap or skeet shooting					
Video arcades					
Water skiing					
White-water rafting					
Other:					

D. *Inventory of **Special Events***

ATTRACTION CATEGORY	Attraction Exists (✔ or #)	Potential Attractions (Time Frame to Develop)			DESCRIPTION (Notes/Problems)
		1 yr	3 yrs	5 yrs	
Agricultural fairs					
Air shows					
Animal shows					
Antique/collectible shows					
Art shows					
Artisan studio tours					
Auto shows					
Ball games/tournaments					
Barbecues					
Barn dances					
Card tournaments					
Comedy contests					
Craft shows					
Drama productions					
Farm tours					
Fishing derbies					
Flower shows or festivals					
Food festivals					
Harvest celebrations					
Hayrides					
Hobby shows					
Holiday celebrations (e.g., Christmas, Kwanzaa, Hanuka)					
Home tours					
July 4th celebrations					
Labor Day celebrations					
Living history festivals					
Music festivals					
Pageants					
Parades					
Photo contests					
Queen coronations					
Races (e.g., auto, motorcycle, boat, bicycle, horse)					
Rodeos					
Seasonal events					
Specialty food-tasting events					
Threshing bees					
Tractor pulls					
Triathlons/marathons					
Winery tours/tasting rooms					
Other:					

E. Inventory of **Other Attractions**

ATTRACTION CATEGORY	Attraction Exists (✔ or #)	Potential Attractions (Time Frame to Develop) 1 yr	3 yrs	5 yrs	DESCRIPTION (Notes/Problems)
Arenas					
Bakeries					
Ball parks					
Bridges					
Children's park/playgrounds					
Dams and power stations					
Ferryboats					
Fish hatcheries					
Food-processing plant tours					
Friends/Family to visit					
Government buildings					
Handcraft/craft shows					
Harbors					
Industrial plant tours					
Large city attractions					
Libraries/special collections					
Local "oddities"					
Lumber camps					
Military installations					
Most remote spot					
Most winding road					
Murals					
Nightclubs					
Observation towers					
Planetarium or telescope					
Roadside parks					
Roadside produce stands					
Settings for movies					
Shopping centers					
Showboats					
Souvenir and curio shops					
Statuary					
Swimming pools					
The biggest "something"					
The first of its kind					
The only one of its kind					
The smallest "something"					
Theaters					
Universities and colleges					
Unusual buildings					
Unusual restaurants or bars					
Windmills					
Other:					

Worksheet 6.2: *Evaluation of Existing Attractions*

ATTRACTION	Tourism Development Assessment Criteria (Rate 1-4)						Market				Months of Use												
	Product Quality	Authen-ticity	Unique-ness	Drawing Power	Activities	Average Rating	Local	Regional	US	Int'l	JAN	FEB	MAR	APR	MAY	JUN	JUL	AUG	SEP	OCT	NOV	DEC

Quality
4=Superior
3=Good
2=Average
1=Poor

Authenticity
4=Authentic
3=Somewhat Authentic
2=Minimally Authentic
1=Not Authentic At All

Uniqueness
4=National/Int'l Significance
3=Regional Attraction
2=Average
1=Lots of Similar Sites

Drawing Power
4=Multistate, national, int'l
3=Metropolitan Area
2=Regional
1=Local and Adjacent Areas Only

Activities
4=Lots of Activity Options
3=Some Activity Options
2=A Few Activity Options
1=No Additional Activities

Market(s) & Month of Use
■ =Strong
◪ =Some
□ =None

Over ⟳

Worksheet 6.2: *Evaluation of Existing Attractions (Continued)*

ATTRACTION	Tourism Development Assessment Criteria (Rate 1-4)						Market				Months of Use												
	Product Quality	Authen-ticity	Unique-ness	Drawing Power	Activities	**Average Rating**	Local	Region	US	Int'l	JAN	FEB	MAR	APR	MAY	JUN	JUL	AUG	SEP	OCT	NOV	DEC

Quality
4=Superior
3=Good
2=Average
1=Poor

Authenticity
4=Authentic
3=Somewhat Authentic
2=Minimally Authentic
1=Not Authentic At All

Uniqueness
4=National/Int'l Significance
3=Regional Attraction
2=Average
1=Lots of Similar Sites

Drawing Power
4=Multistate, national, int'l
3=Metropolitan Area
2=Regional
1=Local and Adjacent Areas Only

Activities
4=Lots of Activity Options
3=Some Activity Options
2=A Few Activity Options
1=No Additional Activities

Market(s) & Month of Use
■ =Strong
◪ =Some
□ =None

Worksheet 6.3: *Evaluation of Potential Attractions*

Potential Tourism Development Assessment Criteria (Rate 1-4)

ATTRACTION CATEGORY	Authenticity	Uniqueness	Drawing Power	Infrastructure and Support Services	Project Viability	Average Rating	Potential Target Market/ Visitor Demographics/Problems/Concerns	PRIORITY RANK
One-year Time Frame:								
Three-year Time Frame:								
Five-year Time Frame:								

Authenticity
4=Authentic
3=Somewhat Authentic
2=Minimally Authentic
1=Not Authentic

Uniqueness
4=National/Int'l Significance
3=Regional Significance
2=Average
1=Lots of Similar Sites

Drawing Power
4=Multistate, National, International
3=Metropolitan Area
2=Regional
1=Local and Adjacent Areas Only

Infrastructure and Support Services
4=Excellent Access, Services
3=Good Access, Services
2=Fair Access, Few Services
1=Poor Access, No Services

Project Viability
4=Excellent, Ample Resources/Funds
3=Good, Reasonable Resources/Funds
2=Fair, Few Resources/Funds
1=Poor, No Resources/Funds

Worksheet 6.4: Packaging Existing Attractions

Note: *This exercise may be most beneficial if a facilitator with knowledge of marketing and/or tourism in your state assists the group to work through it.*

A. Review your assessment of existing attractions and divide the top-ranked attractions into "primary" and "secondary" attractions. Primary attractions are those that are strong enough to initially draw visitors to your area, while secondary attractions are those that enhance visitor experience once they are there.

Top Primary Attractions	Top Secondary Attractions

B. What attractions are unique to your community?

How do primary attractions fit together? Do they create a strong unifying theme, or does the attraction diversity lack a central focus?

What is the primary attraction package for your town?

Does your attraction package appeal to a particular market niche?

Are there any major concerns with increasing visitors to these attractions?

C. List your top three primary attractions and, using your intuition and best judgment, group one to three secondary attractions with each to create a "package." Do any new themes or market niches become apparent?

Primary Attraction #1: _____

Secondary Attractions: _____

_____

_____

Theme/Market Niche: _____

Primary Attraction #2: _____

Secondary Attractions: _____

_____

_____

Theme/Market Niche: _____

Primary Attraction #3: _____

Secondary Attractions: _____

_____

Theme/Market Niche: _____

D. List any particular opportunities or constraints to developing and marketing the above packages. Assign a committee or team member to take responsibility for identifying, prioritizing, and implementing any required actions.

	Opportunities/Constraints	Follow-up Assigned to:
Package #1		
Package #2		
Package #3		

A. Review your assessment of potential attractions. Group attractions that received the highest average rating for development potential according to your short- and long-term development priorities.

Short-Term Priorities (1- to 3-year Development Time Frame)	Long-Term Priorities (5-year Development Time Frame or longer)

B. How do future attraction development priorities fit with existing attractions?

Are future projects consistent with community tourism goals and image?

Do potential attractions targeted for development reflect the cultural and economic heritage of the community and have local support?

Is the target market for potential attractions consistent with the type of visitors that are already coming to your area?

Are new target markets consistent with the community's goal of who it wants to attract?

Over ⊃

C. List your top potential attraction priorities and identify opportunities or constraints to developing and marketing them. Consider social, economic, and environmental impacts. Appoint a committee or team member to take responsibility for assessing total project feasibility. Make additional copies of this form as needed.

Development Priority #_____ : _____
(Potential Attraction)

Opportunities: _____

_____

_____

_____

_____

Constraints: _____

_____

_____

_____

_____

Follow-up Assigned to: _____   *Action Plan Target Date:* _____

Development Priority #_____ : _____
(Potential Attraction)

Opportunities: _____

_____

_____

_____

_____

Constraints: _____

_____

_____

_____

_____

Follow-up Assigned to: _____   *Action Plan Target Date:* _____

Worksheet 6.6: *Inventory of Private Sector Services*

SERVICE CATEGORY	Service Exists (✔ or #)	Potential Services (Time Frame to Develop)			DESCRIPTION (Notes/Problems)
		1 yr	3 yrs	5 yrs	
Accommodations					
Hotels					
Motels					
Resort properties					
Bed & breakfasts					
Campgrounds					
Condominiums					
Hostels					
Farm stays					
Inns/retreats					
R/V parks					
Other:					
Food Service					
Cafes/coffee shops					
Fast food					
Ethnic food					
Family restaurant					
Gourmet restaurant					
Convenience stores					
Taverns & bars					
Wine-tasting rooms					
Farmers markets					
Grocery stores					
Other:					
Retail/Specialty Goods					
Antique shops					
Art galleries/shop					
Bookstores					
Clothing stores/boutiques					
Drug stores/pharmacies					
Retail factory outlets					
Shopping malls					
Gift/souvenir shops					
Other:					
Miscellaneous Services					
Gas stations/auto service					
Banks/ATMs					
Auto rentals					
Taxis/private transport					
Shuttle service/tours					
Other:					

Worksheet 6.7: *Evaluation of Existing Private Sector Services*

| SERVICE CATEGORY | Visitor Services Assessment Criteria (Rate 1-4) | | | | TOTAL | Notes: Weaknesses and Opportunities |
	Quantity	Quality	Diversity	Drawing Power	Average Rating	Potential Target Market/ Visitor Demographics/Problems/Concerns
Accommodations:						
Food Service:						
Retail/Other Services:						

Quantity
4=Sufficient to Handle Tourism for Next 5 Years
3=Good for Current Needs and Growth
2=Meets Local/Regional Needs
1=Barely Meets Current Needs

Quality
4=Superior, Meets & Exceeds Guests Needs
3=Good, Meets Guest Needs
2=Fair, Meets Needs of Limited Audience
1=Poor, Limited Service

Diversity
4=Excellent Variety
3=Good Variety
2=Fair, but Need More
1=No Variety

Drawing Power
4=Multistate, National, International
3=Metropolitan Areas
2=Regional
1=Local and Adjacent Areas Only

Worksheet 6.8: *Evaluation of Potential Private Sector Services*

SERVICE	Project Assessment Criteria (Rate 1-4)				TOTAL	Notes: Weaknesses and Opportunities	PRIORITY RANK
	Need or Demand	Infrastructure and Support Services	Uniqueness	Drawing Power	Average Rating		
One-year Time Frame							
Three-year Time Frame							
Five-year Time Frame:							

Need/Demand
4=Critical/High
3=Serious/Medium
2=Average/Average
1=Minimal/Low

Infrastructure and Support Services
4=Excellent Access, Services
3=Good Access, Services
2=Fair Access, Few Services
1=Poor Access, No Services

Uniqueness
4=National/Int'l Significance
3=Regional Attraction
2=Average
1=Lots of Similar Sites

Drawing Power
4=Multistate, National, International
3=Metropolitan Areas
2=Regional
1=Local and Adjacent Areas Only

A. Review your assessment of existing private sector services. List the top-ranked visitor services that represent particular strengths in your community, and any significantly weak areas in need of development. List them in order of priority according to the significance of their strength or weakness in terms of affecting community tourism development.

Visitor Services We Have	Visitor Services We Need to Improve

B. Do any patterns or themes emerge regarding existing visitor services in your area?

Do existing visitor services support or detract from existing attractions?

Can any of these services (e.g., resorts, shopping malls) serve as attractions on their own to draw visitors?

Are physical facilities of existing services sufficient to handle increased business from tourists?

What visitor services are weak in your community?

Over ⊃

Worksheet 6.9: *Prioritizing Development of Private Sector Services (Continued)*

C. Group visitor services that received the highest average rating for development potential according to your short- and long-term development priorities. Give particular consideration to visitor service areas that were noted as particularly weak in the table in Section A.

Short-Term Priorities (1- to 3-year Development Time Frame)	Long-Term Priorities (5-year Development Time Frame or Longer)

D. How do visitor service development priorities fit with existing and potential tourism attractions?

Are potential visitor service development priorities consistent with community tourism goals and image?

Do potential visitor service projects have local industry, government, and community support?

Are visitor service development projects consistent with the type of tourists who are already coming to your area, or do they target new markets that the community wants to attract?

Worksheet 6.10: *Private Sector Service Development Action Priorities*

List your top visitor service action priorities and identify opportunities or constraints for development. Consider social, economic, and environmental impacts. Appoint a committee or team member to take responsibility for identifying, prioritizing, and implementing key actions needed to accurately assess total project feasibility. Make additional copies of this form as needed.

Development Priority #_____ : _____

(Potential Visitor Service Project)

Opportunities:

_____

_____

_____

_____

Constraints: _____

_____

_____

_____

_____

Follow-up Assigned to: _____   *Action Plan Target Date:* _____

Development Priority #_____ : _____

(Potential Visitor Service Project)

Opportunities:

_____

_____

_____

_____

Constraints: _____

_____

_____

_____

_____

Follow-up Assigned to: _____   *Action Plan Target Date:* _____

A. *Inventory of Public Services Infrastructure*

PUBLIC SERVICE	Exists [✔ or #]	Service Could Exist (Time Frame to Develop) 1 yr	3 yrs	5 yrs	DESCRIPTION (Notes/Problems)	AGENCY RESPONSIBLE
Access						
Local/county roads						
State highways/roads						
Major U.S. highways						
Commercial airport						
Train/railway services						
Public bus service						
Other mass transit						
Boat/ferry service						
Other:						
Infrastructure						
Electric power						
Gas service						
Water supply						
Sewer/waste disposal						
Storm drainage						
Telephone services						
Police protection						
Fire protection						
Ambulance service						
Medical facilities/hospital						
Other:						
Other Public Services						
Comprehensive plan						
Emergency road service						
Snow removal						
Bicycle lanes						
Public parking						
Other:						

Over ⊃

Worksheet 6.11: *Public Services Inventory (Continued)*

B. *Inventory of Public Services Physical Environment*

PUBLIC SERVICE	Exists [✔ or #]	Service Could Exist (Time Frame to Develop)			DESCRIPTION (Notes/Problems)	AGENCY RESPONSIBLE
		1 yr	3 yrs	5 yrs		
Town entrances						
Direction signage						
Downtown appearance						
Downtown lighting						
General street lighting						
Sidewalks						
Benches/rest areas						
Public rest rooms						
Drinking fountains						
Trash receptacles						
Public parks						
Multi-use trails						
Landscaping						
Handicap access						
Tourist information						
Public telephones						
Traffic flow management						
Road maintenance						
Street cleaning						
Other:						

Worksheet 6.12: *Evaluation of Public Services*

A. Infrastructure

PUBLIC SERVICE	Assessment Criteria Rate (1-4)				IMPROVEMENTS NEEDED	PRIORITY RANK
	Access/ Quantity	Quality/ Condition	Staffing/ Facilities	Average		
Local/County Roads						
State Highways/Roads						
Major U.S. Highways						
Commercial Airport						
Train/Railway Services						
Bus Service						
Other Mass Transit						
Boat/Ferry Service						
Electric Power						
Gas Service						
Water Supply						
Sewer/Waste Disposal						
Storm Drainage						
Telephone Services						
Police Protection						
Fire Protection						
Ambulance Service						
Medical Facilities/Hospital						
Emergency Road Service						
Snow Removal						
Bicycle Lanes						
Public Parking						
Other:						

Access/Quantity
4=Excellent
3=Good
2=Fair
1=Poor /None

Quality/Condition
4=Exellent
3=Good
2=Fair
1=Poor/None

Staffing/Facilities
4=Superior
3=Good
2=Fair
1=Needs Improvement

Over ⊃

Worksheet 6.12: Evaluation of Public Services (Continued)

B. Physical Environment

PUBLIC SERVICE	Assessment Criteria Rate (1-4)				IMPROVEMENTS NEEDED	PRIORITY RANK
	Access/ Quantity	Quality/ Condition	Staffing/ Facilities	Average		
Town entrances						
Direction signage						
Downtown appearance						
Downtown lighting						
General street lighting						
Sidewalks						
Benches/rest areas						
Public rest rooms						
Drinking fountains						
Trash receptacles						
Public parks						
Multi-use trails						
Landscaping						
Handicap access						
Tourist information						
Public telephones						
Traffic flow management						
Road maintenance						
Street Clearing						
Other:						

Access/Quantity
4=Excellent
3=Good
2=Fair
1=Poor /None

Quality/Condition
4=Exellent
3=Good
2=Fair
1=Poor/None

Staffing/Facilities
4=Superior
3=Good
2=Fair
1=Needs Improvement

Assessment 6.1: Resident Attitude Survey

Part I: General Opinions

Please indicate how much you agree or disagree with the following statements. Check only one response for each statement. There are no right or wrong answers. We need your honest opinions. For the purpose of this survey, "tourists" refers to visitors to the community who live outside the immediate area.

	Strongly Agree	Agree	No Opinion	Disagree	Strongly Disagree
1. Tourism has increased the quality of life in this area.					
2. Tourism provides the kinds of jobs our area needs.					
3. Tourism development unfairly increases real estate values.					
4. Tourism helps balance the economy in our area.					
5. Tourism has increased the number of crime problems in the area.					
6. Most of the businesses involved in tourism are small.					
7. Tourism contributes to local tax revenues, lowering our tax bill.					
8. Tourist attractions/facilities improve the community's appearance.					
9. Tourism only helps businesses that sell directly to tourists.					
10. Other community services receive less attention because of tourism.					
11. Tourism makes it more expensive to live here.					
12. We should encourage more tourists to come to our area.					
13. Visitors and residents have a hospitable attitude toward each other.					
14. Enough is being done to protect our environment.					
15. This community should control and restrict tourism development.					
16. Tourism increases litter in our community.					
17. Tourism provides services/activities we wouldn't otherwise have.					
18. Tourism makes the area more crowded.					
19. Tourism increases civic pride.					
20. Tourists should pay more than locals to visit area parks/attractions.					
21. We should promote our history and culture to attract more tourists.					
22. Tourism has reduced the quality of outdoor recreation opportunities due to overuse/crowding.					
23. I feel I have input in the community's plan for tourism growth.					
24. Environmental impacts resulting from tourism are relatively minor.					
25. The overall benefits of tourism outweigh the negative impacts.					
26. Tourism encourages investment in our local economy.					
27. The community should develop a plan to manage tourism growth.					
28. A good way to manage growth is through land-use zoning.					
29. My household standard of living is higher because of money tourists spend here.					
30. Tourism would help our community grow in the "right" direction.					

Over ⊃

Assessment 6.1: *Resident Attitude Survey (Continued)*

Part II. Specific Concerns About Tourism

Please list the top three major concerns (in order of priority) that you have about how tourism growth may affect you or the community. List the letters in the appropriate blank.

_____ 1st Major Concern   _____ 2nd Major Concern   _____ 3rd Major Concern

A. Traffic congestion
B. Crowded recreation areas and facilities
C. Higher prices for goods and services
D. More crime
E. Higher taxes
F. Environmental impacts

G. Social impacts
H. Overdevelopment
I. An increase in real estate/housing costs
J. Out-of-state people relocating here
K. Other:_____

_____

Part III. Specific Goals for Tourism

Please list the top three goals (in order of priority) you have for tourism growth benefiting you or the community. List the letters in the appropriate blank.

_____ 1st Major Goal   _____ 2nd Major Goal   _____ 3rd Major Goal

A. Employment opportunities
B. More or better parks and recreation facilities
C. A more vital and active local economy
D. Social or cultural interaction with people from other states/countries
E. Improvement in overall quality of life

F. Improvement in overall appearance of community
G. An increase in real estate values
H. Preservation of local culture/heritage
I. Preservation of natural/protected areas
J. Other:_____

_____

Part IV. Comments

1. Please list any concerns you may have about tourism that were not addressed in this survey.

_____

_____

_____

2. Are there aspects of the community (places, events, etc.) that you would not want promoted as tourist attractions?

_____

_____

_____

3. What is your vision of the community's future and what role should tourism have in that future?

_____

_____

_____

Please return this survey to the person who distributed it to you. Thank You!

Adapted from:

Koth, B., Kreag, G., & Sem, J. (1991). *Rural tourism development.* St. Paul, MN: University of Minnesota Extension.

Brass, J. (Ed.) (1996). *Community tourism assessment handbook.* Corvallis, OR: Western Rural Development Center, Oregon State University.

Assessment 6.2: *Local Business Attitude Survey*

Your responses to this survey will be used to assess the general attitude of local businesses toward tourism. All of your responses will be *strictly confidential* and used only to develop an overall profile. If you have questions, please contact the person who gave this survey to you. Thank you for your assistance!

Part I: General Information

1. Which category most accurately describes your type of business?

❑ Retail Sales ❑ Accommodation ❑ Manufacturer ❑ Other: (specify)
❑ Wholesale Sales ❑ Food/Restaurant/Bar ❑ Medical Services _____
❑ Service ❑ Attraction/Entertainment ❑ Professional Office

2. Are you optimistic about the future of your business?   ❑ YES   ❑ NO

3. In general, is business better than, worse than or about the same as last year?   ❑ Better ❑ Worse ❑ Same

4. How important is tourism to the success of your business?

❑ Very Important ❑ Important ❑ Somewhat Important ❑ Not Important at All

5. What percentage of your gross sales revenue is attributable to tourism? _____ %

6. Is tourism promotion in the best interest of your business?   ❑ YES   ❑ NO   ❑ Would Not Affect Me

7. Does your business distribute brochures highlighting local attractions?   ❑ YES   ❑ NO

8. Are you willing to participate financially in local or regional tourism promotion?   ❑ YES   ❑ NO

9. What type of new businesses would you like to see open in the area?

❑ Retail Sales ❑ Accommodations ❑ Manufacturer ❑ Other: (specify)
❑ Wholesale Sales ❑ Food/Restaurant/Bar ❑ Medical Services _____
❑ Service ❑ Attraction/Entertainment ❑ Professional Office

10. What type(s) of tourist attractions should be developed to attract visitors to our area? (Check all that apply.)

❑ Historic Attractions ❑ Museums ❑ Water Attractions ❑ Other: (specify)
❑ Amusement Parks ❑ Cultural Attractions ❑ Festivals _____
❑ Convention Center ❑ The Arts ❑ Recreation/Trails

11. What do you consider to be the **one most positive** factor impacting the development of your business:

❑ Market/Economy ❑ Adequate Space ❑ Modern Facilities ❑ Other: (specify)
❑ Competition ❑ Transportation ❑ Sanitary Facilities _____
❑ Regulations ❑ Labor Availability ❑ Location

12. Of the items listed in Question #11, which do you consider to be **<u>one most negative</u>** factor impacting the development of your business?

13. What type of advertising do you use to promote your business? (Check all that apply.)

❑ Tourism Guidebook ❑ State Tourism Marketing ❑ Internet ❑ Trade Shows
❑ Radio and/or TV ❑ Direct Mail ❑ Brochures ❑ Other: (specify)
❑ Newspapers ❑ Yellow Pages ❑ Co-op Advertising _____

Over ⊃

Part II: Opinions About Tourism

Please indicate how much you agree or disagree with the following statements. Check only one response for each statement. There are no right or wrong answers. We need your honest opinions. For the purpose of this survey, "tourists" refers to visitors to the community who live outside the immediate area.

	Strongly Agree	Agree	No Opinion	Disagree	Strongly Disagree
1. Tourism has increased the quality of life in this area.					
2. Tourism provides the kinds of jobs our area needs.					
3. Tourism development unfairly increases real estate values.					
4. Tourism helps balance the economy in our area.					
5. Tourism has increased the number of crime problems in the area.					
6. Most of the businesses involved in tourism are small.					
7. Tourism contributes to local tax revenues, lowering our tax bill.					
8. Tourist attractions/facilities improve the community's appearance.					
9. Tourism only helps businesses that sell directly to tourists.					
10. Other community services receive less attention because of tourism.					
11. Tourism makes it more expensive to live here.					
12. We should encourage more tourists to come to our area.					
13. Visitors and residents have a hospitable attitude toward each other.					
14. Enough is being done to protect our environment.					
15. This community should control and restrict tourism development.					
16. Tourism increases litter in our community.					
17. Tourism provides services/activities we wouldn't otherwise have.					
18. Tourism makes the area more crowded.					
19. Tourism increases civic pride.					
20. Tourists should pay more than locals to visit area parks/attractions.					
21. We should promote our history and culture to attract more tourists.					
22. Tourism has reduced the quality of outdoor recreation opportunities due to overuse/crowding.					
23. I feel I have input in the community's plan for tourism growth.					
24. Environmental impacts resulting from tourism are relatively minor.					
25. The overall benefits of tourism outweigh the negative impacts.					
26. Tourism encourages investment in our local economy.					
27. The community should develop a plan to manage tourism growth.					
28. A good way to manage growth is through land-use zoning.					
29. My household standard of living is higher because of money tourists spend here.					
30. Tourism would help our community grow in the "right" direction.					

Part III. Community/Government Services

Please indicate your level of satisfaction with the following local services as they pertain to your business. Check only **one** rating per issue.

	Excellent	Good	Fair	Poor	No Opinion
Building Inspector					
Code Enforcement					
Fire Inspector					
Fire Protection					
General Business Climate					
Government Officials					
Health Inspector					
Municipal Assessor's Office					
Municipal Engineering Office					
Planning Commission					
Police Protection					
Public Works Department					
Sewer Services and Costs					
Snow Removal					
Storm Water Drainage					
Street Cleanliness					
Street Surface Condition					
Waste Disposal					
Water Pressure and Supply					
Zoning Department					

Part IV. Demographics

1. Which category best describes your business structure:
    - ❑ Sole Proprietorship   ❑ Partnership   ❑ Franchise
    - ❑ Family Business   ❑ Corporation   ❑ Other: _____

2. Please indicate the amount closest to your business's annual gross sales revenue:
    - ❑ Less than $50,000   ❑ $100,001 - $250,000   ❑ $500,001 - $1,000,000
    - ❑ $50,000 - $100,000   ❑ $250,001 - $500,000   ❑ More than $1,000,000

3. What year was your business established in the community? _____

4. Are you a member of: The Chamber of Commerce ❑ YES ❑ NO

    A Local Tourism Bureau   ❑ YES ❑ NO

Optional Information: Name: _____

THANK YOU FOR YOUR ASSISTANCE!

Chapter 7
Assessing Your Market

Assessing your market is an integral part of tourism development. To successfully draw visitors to your community, you must know who and where they are and what they're like.

Market assessment consists of two phases. The first, *market research,* is a systematic way of acquiring and analyzing information about visitors, industry trends, local conditions, and competition. The second, *market segmentation,* involves breaking down the market you've identified through your research into subgroups so you can create and convey marketing messages tailored to the unique interests, needs, and wants of each.

In researching and segmenting your market, it's important to be alert to tourism trends. One key trend, addressed at the end of this chapter, is the growth in alternative types of tourism, including cultural heritage tourism, nature-based tourism, ecotourism, agritourism, and adventure travel.

7

WHAT'S IN THIS CHAPTER?

- **Market Research**
- **Market Segmentation**
- **Alternative Tourism**

Market Research

Market research involves four main steps:

- Determine your information needs;
- Choose a data collection method;
- Conduct your research; and
- Analyze and interpret the results.

Determine Information Needs

Before you conduct research, determine exactly what type of information you need. Define the boundaries of your tourism area so that you know who to consider visitors. The more specific you can be about your goals from the outset, the more likely it is that you will obtain accurate and appropriate information for making sound, logical decisions.

In designing your research, it is important to move beyond generalities such as "We want to know more about our visitors," to specifics such as:

- Where do our tourists come from? Where might our new visitors come from?

- What are the characteristics (age, education, occupation, income, previous visits, length of stay, party size, expenditure patterns, etc.) of our visitors?

- What do visitors think about the quality of tourist services in our community?

- What attractions, services, and features do tourists want? Have these preferences changed?

- How do tourists use their time in our town? What are their behavior patterns?

- How do visitors find out about our community? Are current advertising methods effective?

Table 7.1 details common types of information communities gather about their visitors.

Table 7.1: Types of Visitor Data

Visitor Demographics
- Age
- Sex
- Income
- Education
- Occupation
- Mode of Travel
- Point of Origin
- Party Size
- Composition of Party
- Destination

Expenditures
- Amount spent on accommodations
- Amount spent on events, attractions, other activities
- Amount spent on food, transportation, souvenirs
- Types of things purchased
- Range of expenditures

Visitor Satisfaction
- Perception of community and friendliness of resident hosts
- Preferred attractions, activities, events
- Likes and dislikes
- Overall experience (quality of service and value)
- Extent that visitor goals are met by specific attractions, services, etc.
- Interests, opinions, and values of visitors (psychographics)
- Special needs of travelers were met

Travel-Related Information
- Attractions and events visited, activities pursued
- Length of stay
- Number of times visited (repeat visits)
- Amount of planning for trip/information sources
- Reasons for visiting (motivation)
- Decision influencers (e.g., friends, family, advertisements)
- Intermediaries used (travel agents, tour operators, local chamber of commerce or convention and visitor bureau, Internet)

Choose a Data Collection Method

There are two major types of tourism market research, primary and secondary. Primary research collects data directly from the customer. Secondary research uses information compiled by someone else. Each has advantages and disadvantages.

Secondary research can be relatively inexpensive, easy, and quick. It is a good place to start gaining insight into industry and market trends, local conditions, and your competition. Existing studies can provide clues about marketing strategies that have worked or not worked in other places, or characteristics of certain market segments. Secondary research data can also keep the community current on larger travel trends and market shifts. However, the information you acquire is generally not specific to your situation, and may be outdated or unreliable. Thus, it is best used in conjunction with primary research.

Finding out where customers are from based on their hotel registration cards, counting cars on a particular road, calling your own business to assess your employees' customer service skills, and conducting interviews and satisfaction surveys with visitors are all examples of primary research. Good primary research helps you truly understand your customers. It is applicable, reliable, and up to date. However, depending on the type of information you are gathering and why you are gathering it, it can be complex, expensive (you may need to hire assistance to conduct and interpret the data), and time consuming.

Conduct Research

After you have identified what type of information you need and where you will obtain it, it's time to actually carry out the research. How you go about doing this depends on whether you are conducting primary research, secondary research, or a combination of the two.

Primary Research

Primary market research methods vary in terms of cost, quality, and practicality, depending on the situation in which they are used and the type of information being collected. In many cases a combination of methods provides the most accurate information. Table 7.2 lists pros and cons of common techniques for conducting primary research.

A community can conduct many types of research on its own if it has the time and resources. These include observation, counting cars in parking lots, tracking visitor information inquiries, collecting atten-

Research may be either quantitative or qualitative. Quantitative research provides objective, measurable data (e.g., price, number of visitors, occupancy rates, visitor expenditures). Qualitative research provides subjective information (e.g., visitor perceptions, values, attitudes, expectations). Qualitative research provides insight into what the visitor thinks and helps you see your business or community through the eyes of the visitor. When qualitative information is gathered periodically, you can compare data to detect changes over time.

Both quantitative and qualitative research are important to the tourism development process. Be sure to include both in your research efforts.

Compiling information and conducting accurate analyses can be an overwhelming task for small communities. You may want to ask experts such as county Extension educators, university faculty, or official state tourism researchers to help you obtain and interpret information.

dance figures from area attractions, monitoring local sales and lodging tax revenues, reviewing hotel registration forms, conducting interviews or written surveys, and simply talking to visitors when they make purchases, dine in local restaurants, or visit your information center. Don't forget how much can be learned about your visitors simply by being chatty at your visitor information center and other areas where you meet out-of-towners. Friendly inquiries, such as "Been here before?", "Where are you folks from?", and "How'd you find out about us?" and documentation of the responses (keep a check sheet behind the desk) are a valuable supplement to formal research findings.

If the information to be obtained is highly complex or the sample population is large, you may need to hire a professional market research firm or consultant. The validity of the research depends on many things, including the design of the survey, wording of questions, interview method, and interpretation of results. Professional assistance may be costly, but if it improves the validity of your results, it may be worth the added cost.

Table 7.2: Primary Research Methods

Direct Observation
Watching and noting how tourists behave, to get an idea of their likes or dislikes. Can be done by observers, videotape, or photograph. The key is to systematically record numbers, observations, and impressions. Examples include observing brochure selection from a rack, use of exercise room, salad bar selections.

Pros: Provides insight into visitor decision making. Works well for evaluating competitors. Is relatively inexpensive. Allows for richness of detail.

Cons: Does not explain customer behavior. Gives little insight into motivations, attitudes, and perceptions.

Counting Methods
Counting visitors to determine usage. Can use students or volunteers to do manual counts or use electronic or photographic technology. Examples include counting gate receipts, advance ticket sales, number of turnstile revolutions, traffic counts on major roads, license plate origins, and number of cars in a parking lot.

Pros: Easy to design and administer. Low cost. Provides accurate counts that can be monitored over time for trends.

Cons: May not distinguish between tourists and nontourists. Does not provide qualitative data.

Personal Interviews
Involves asking visitors a structured set of questions face-to-face. Visitors are intercepted as they register, while in transit, as they exit an area, or while at an attraction. Validity is affected by question design and whether interviewees are a representative sample of visitors.

Pros: Can provide in-depth information. High response rate, flexibility, and timeliness.

Cons: Relatively high cost. Interviewer may be biased. Respondent may be reluctant and/or inconvenienced.

Focus Groups

A variation of the personal interview in which you ask a series of set questions of a small group, then analyze the resulting discussion content. Can be used for current, repeat, or potential visitors.

Pros: Wide applicability. Can provide in-depth information that other methods miss. Allows participants to hear and react to each others' opinions.

Cons: Can be very time consuming. Usually requires professional facilitator.

Suggestion Boxes

Provides information on visitor satisfaction when positioned in highly visible and accessible areas. Boxes should be clearly identified and in good condition.

Pros: Inexpensive. Easy to design, use, and administer.

Cons: Suggestions must be followed through with action.

Written Surveys

Involves mailing or otherwise distributing questionnaires to a sample of visitors, and having them return their response by mail or to a drop box. Study design is important to minimize bias. For example, you might track changes in the market by distributing a postcard at certain times of the year asking visitors about their characteristics and activities.

Pros: Relatively inexpensive if response rate is high. No interviewer bias. Allows for large survey population, anonymity of responses, consistency in questions/responses, and convenience for respondent.

Cons: Possible low response rate. May require time and expense of follow-up to increase response rate. Impersonal.

Online Surveys

Similar to written surveys, online surveys are conducted electronically using one of several free or purchased survey programs. Individuals are contacted via email and given information on how to access and complete surveys, which they complete online.

Pros: Quick and relatively inexpensive with fast response times and no postage costs. Allows for large survey population. Most programs provide data analysis tools and ability to generate reports.

Cons: Proliferation of online surveys can reduce response. Familiarity with technology, location or age may limit access to online surveys.

Telephone Surveys

Involves calling a random sample of people and asking a series of preset questions. An increasingly popular method of gathering data. Can be used to follow up on visitors or to contact potential visitors. Can provide insights in decision making for those who requested information and did not visit.

Pros: More flexible than mail surveys. Quick and inexpensive if calling local. High potential for quality control. High response rates with trained interviewers.

Cons: More obtrusive than mail. Can be expensive if long-distance calling is needed. Usually requires professional assistance.

Experimental Method

Involves developing prototype services or marketing strategies, testing them on a limited scale, and recording consumer reaction. Minimizes risk of failure when introducing a new product.

Pros: Can provide specific information on a particular promotion or service.

Cons: Can be expensive and time consuming.

Secondary Research

Your search for secondary information might include a review of industry reports, trade journals and publications, existing data from research companies or consultants, and other library materials. In many cases, secondary data for individual communities are hard to find, so you may need to use countywide or other statistics. You can compile and analyze out-of-state or out-of-county addresses from fishing license records. Most state and national parks keep logs of visitors and conduct regular surveys.

Even if you have had no formal system for collecting visitor information, you can develop a preliminary profile of existing visitors. Be creative in thinking about the "evidence" that tourists leave behind that could help you learn more about them.

Table 7.3 lists sources of secondary tourism information you may find useful. You also can obtain U.S. tourism industry statistics and visitor profile reports from the U.S. Travel Association. Contact the association at www.ustravel.org or 202-408-8422.

Analyze and Interpret Results

Once you have collected information through primary or secondary research, your next job is to analyze and interpret it. Don't be put off by numbers and statistics. If necessary, work with a university, your local Extension service, or a small business development center expert to develop a basic working knowledge that will help you understand your research results.

It is important to:
- Organize your findings;
- Think about what they mean; and
- Talk to others to clarify the interpretation.

Table 7.3: Sources of Secondary Tourism Information

SOURCE	TYPE OF INFORMATION
International Resources U.N. World Tourism Organization World Travel and Tourism Council	International tourism statistics and trends, surveys of international travelers, demographics, travel patterns
National Resources U.S. Department of Commerce U.S. Department of Labor National Park Service U.S. Forest Service U.S. Fish and Wildlife Service Tourism industries	National tourism statistics and trends, park attendance records, other public service use records
State Resources State travel and tourism office State departments of commerce, labor, and revenue Community or economic development agencies Parks and recreation departments Natural resources, fish, and wildlife agencies Highway and transportation departments	Statewide profiles of visitors, demographic and psychographic profiles, economic impact of tourism, tourist spending patterns, traffic/public transportation counts, park attendance records, other public service use records, sales tax reports
University Extension services Economics or applied economics departments Tourism/recreation/leisure departments	Regional or local tourism statistics (note: you also may be able to make arrangements to have primary research conducted as part of a class or student project)
Existing Attractions/Services Attractions in your community Similar attractions elsewhere Visitor center	Attendance information, occupancy information, sales revenues, survey results, registration reports, existing market research
Local/Regional Resources Transportation authorities Convention and visitor bureau	Public transportation counts, existing surveys and studies, license plate counts by state
Trade and Travel Associations U.S. Travel Association National Tour Association Hotel/ Motel Associations Cruise Lines International Association International Ecotourism Society The Adventure Travel Society	Surveys and profiles of U.S. domestic travelers, specialty niche market reports, travel trends, economic impacts of domestic tourism
Research Companies and Consultants Travel Market Report Leisure Trends Group STR Global Colliers PKF Consulting	Focused studies and reports on various industry segments, consumer travel profiles, state tourism profiles, economic impact studies, niche market studies (may charge for information/subscription)
Magazines, Journals, and Newspapers *Corporate and Incentive Travel* *Successful Meetings* *Meeting Planners International* *Travel Weekly* *Travel Daily News* *Meetings and Conventions* *Business Travel News* *Hotel and Travel Index* Various consumer travel publications	Industry reports, objective analysis, business profiles, trends, industry and market segment statistics, consumer trends

Market Segmentation

Market segmentation is the process of breaking potential visitors into smaller, more uniform groups. It is valuable because it allows you to target the right message to the right group, increasing its effectiveness and maximizing your marketing dollars. The information you gather during your research phase will be invaluable to segmenting your visitor market and developing targeted strategies to encourage visitation to your community.

Communities just starting out in tourism often think that "everyone" is a potential visitor. This type of general marketing strategy is not effective in today's marketplace, where consumers are bombarded with millions of messages daily and the competition for discretionary leisure dollars is high.

No community can be all things to all visitors, nor should it try. By carefully reviewing the results of your research, you will be able to develop some profiles of key types of visitors who are already coming to your community. This information, combined with your analysis of local attractions and services, can help you identify additional market segments to target.

There are many ways to segment potential visitors—for example, by geographic, demographic, or psychographic (behavioral) characteristics; values and attitudes; trip purpose; or other common identifiers. Table 7.4 lists some of the most common.

Don't forget to look at your local market for potential visitors. Most community tourism attractions appeal to both nonresidents and residents. Also, by targeting a marketing message to local residents, you can tap into the large number of people who travel to visit friends and relatives at a significantly lower cost than marketing to these travelers in their place of origin.

For more information on traveler characteristics and market segments unique to your area, contact your state office of tourism.

Table 7.4: Tourism Market Segmentation

Segmentation Group	Description
Purpose of Trip/Descriptors Pleasure Travel Leisure, Vacation, Visiting Friends & Relatives (VFR) Business Travel Personal Business, Corporate Travel, Government Convention and Meetings Corporate, Association, Government, Incentive Educational/Special Interest Sports Travel/Tournaments	Popular and usually effective segmentation approach because the target market is actively seeking the tourism or travel product. Segments are likely to have common needs, wants, and expectations. Communities can most easily match their offerings to these types of travelers.
Geographic State, Province, Region, Country Urban, Suburban, or Rural Population Density City Size	Most common segmentation approach because these markets are readily defined and accessible. Often not the most effective approach unless used in combination with other visitor characteristics.
Socioeconomic or Demographic Age, Gender, Income, Family Size Occupation, Education Homeowners/Second Homeowners Race or Ethnic Group	This is a commonly used segmentation approach. Segments are often easy to reach and information on them is readily available. Most effective when used in combination to specifically target a group (e.g., generational marketing)
Product-Related Recreation Activity or Equipment Brand Loyalty Benefit Expectations Transportation Needs Length of Stay Special Interest	These are more difficult segments to reach, but they are well matched to specific products. Examples are frequent flyer and frequent stay programs.
Psychographic Personality Traits, Values, Lifestyles Attitudes, Interests, Opinions Motivations	An effective segmentation approach for tourism because tourism product use is extensive among certain psychographic groups. Many advertising media are segmented this way.
Use Frequency/Seasonality Heavy Users Moderate Users Infrequent Users	This can be a cost-effective method because data should be readily available on these repeat customers.
Channel of Distribution Direct Customer Sales Travel Agents Tour Operators Tour Wholesalers Internet Users Government Tourism Marketing Organizations Regional/Local Tourism Associations Airlines Cruise Lines	An effective approach for distant markets that cannot be directly reached at a reasonable cost, or where travel trade companies have a market that is closely matched to yours. Could provide cooperative advertising partners to reach mutual customers.

Adapted from Texas Agricultural Extension Service and Texas Department of Economic Development. (1999). *Developing tourism in your community.* College Station, TX: Texas Agricultural Extension Service.

Alternative Tourism

During the past two decades, several trends have emerged that are changing the face of travel. Tourists are no longer satisfied with the passive sightseeing-and-beach vacation that once dominated the industry. There is more focus on the journey itself and the magic that happens along the way. Tourists want to grow and challenge themselves, to come home changed. They want to interact with local residents, to learn about the host community's traditions and customs. They demand a more participatory experience, with hands-on educational opportunities involving local history, culture, and environment. The modern traveler seeks authenticity, personalization, personal growth, flexibility, and spontaneity.

The change has significant implications for communities interested in developing a tourism industry. It has brought growth in alternative forms of tourism, such as cultural heritage tourism, nature-based tourism, agritourism, and outdoor adventure travel.

Niche markets offer new opportunities for small and rural communities seeking to diversify their economic base. They are well suited to the rich cultural heritage, abundance of historical structures, diverse natural resources, and rich agricultural farmland of many small towns in America. For communities already involved in tourism, niche markets can help refocus tourism efforts. Specialty niches can be incorporated into your marketing efforts if your research and attraction base supports that opportunity.

The degree to which your community can provide attractions and services that cater to emerging specialty niche markets will have a major impact on your success. Niche markets depend on a sustainable tourism industry that respects its culture and natural resource assets. This places increased pressure on communities to engage in careful, long-term planning to ensure that attractions, services, and infrastructure are developed in way that sustains authenticity and resources.

Following is a brief overview of popular emerging specialty tourism markets.

Cultural Heritage Tourism

Cultural heritage tourism (sometimes called "heritage tourism" or "cultural tourism") is one of the fastest-growing sectors of the travel and tourism industry. Heritage tourism has been defined as "the practice of people traveling outside their home communities to visit his-

toric sites and areas, to participate in local festivals, to enjoy local arts and crafts, sightseeing, or recreation" (Prohaska, 1996). Cultural tourism has been defined as "travel directed toward experiencing the arts, heritage, and special character of a place" (NEA, 1995).

Every place in America, from rural areas to urban neighborhoods, can develop cultural heritage tourism. The important thing is that development is guided from within the community, and that it preserves, enhances, and promotes natural, historic, and cultural resources. Essential ingredients of successful cultural heritage tourism are authenticity, quality, education, interpretation, comprehensive planning, resource assessment, and public/private partnerships.

Many communities tend to think only in terms of historic structures when they first hear about cultural heritage tourism. It is important to think beyond structures to the rich human heritage in your area—be it a farming community, lumber or mining town, commercial fishing village, or other setting for a unique way of life. The Villages of Van Buren case study in Appendix A provides an example of cultural heritage tourism.

Cultural Heritage Travelers

In 1997, the United States Travel Association (USTA) published a profile of cultural heritage travelers. The group found that more than 25 percent of U.S. adults surveyed reported taking at least one trip in the past year that included a visit to a historical place or museum. Seventeen percent reported taking a trip in the past year that included a visit to a cultural event or festival. One-third reported taking either a historic or cultural trip, or both, in the past year.

USTA reports that as of 2003, the popularity of cultural heritage tourism has increased with more than half (56 percent) of U.S. adults including at least one cultural, arts, historic or heritage activity or event while on a trip in the previous year. This accounts for 118.1 million adult travelers. One quarter of these travelers are frequent historic/cultural travelers, taking three or more trips annually.

The 2003 study found that historic and cultural travelers are:
- Slightly older, and more likely to be retired; four in 10 trips were taken by Baby Boomers (age 35-54).
- More likely to have a college degree; and
- Less likely to involve children in the trip, although one-third of trips were generated by households with children.

Most historic/cultural travel is by auto and nearly all involves an overnight stay in paid accommodations. Overnight trips last an average of 5.2 nights and stays are most frequently in hotels, motels, or bed and breakfast establishments.

Three in 10 historic/cultural travelers indicate that their destination choice was influenced by specific historic or cultural activities, and 40 percent say they added extra time to their trip because of a specific activity.

The Internet plays a significant role in the planning of historic/cultural trips. In addition to "word-of-mouth" information, historic/cultural travelers are most likely to use the Internet for travel information and trip planning. Interestingly, frequent historic/cultural travelers are significantly more likely than those taking one or two trips annually to use the Internet for trip planning.

Nature-Based Tourism

Nature-based tourism is travel to a destination for the primary purpose of enjoying and experiencing nature. Since the early 1990s, nature-based tourism has emerged as a rapidly growing component of the travel and tourism industry worldwide, and a vital growth sector for many communities with natural resource-based economies.

Ecotourism is a form of nature-based tourism that minimizes impacts and promotes conservation of the resources upon which it depends. The International Ecotourism Society defines ecotourism as "responsible travel that conserves natural environments and sustains the well-being of local people." Ecotourism and sustainable tourism are often used interchangeably. They are similar in that both focus on minimal impact travel and preserving socio-cultural heritage of a destination. However, ecotourism is specific to nature-based tourism whereas sustainable tourism can be any type of tourism.

Ecotourism is considered the fastest growing market in the tourism industry, according to the U.N. World Tourism Organization, with an annual growth rate of 5 percent worldwide and representing 6 percent of the world gross domestic product. A similar story can be told in the United States, where LOHAS (Lifestyles of Health and Sustainability) at www.lohas.com estimates that ecotourism is among the fastest growing trends—with an estimated $77 billion market that represents 5 percent of the overall U.S. travel and tourism market.

Among the most popular forms of ecotourism being promoted in many rural areas are bird watching and wildlife viewing. A 2006 national survey by the U.S. Fish and Wildlife Service found that the number of wildlife viewers grew 8 percent from 2001 to 2006. That year, 71.1 million U.S. residents age 16 years and older spent $45.7 billion observing, feeding, or photographing wildlife. Only those participants whose principal motivation for the trip, activity, or expenditure was wildlife-related were counted, and the survey did not include trips to zoos, aquariums, museums, or circuses. The full report is available online at http://federalaid.fws.gov. A deeper discussion of wildlife tourism is found in Appendix B.

The Ecotourist

A 1996 market demand study provides insight into North American nature-based tourists. The survey was administered to general consumers, members of the travel trade, and experienced ecotourists. The general consumer survey focused on residents of Winnipeg, Toronto, Los Angeles, San Francisco, Seattle, Chicago, and Dallas/Ft. Worth in upper and middle income neighborhoods. The trade survey consisted of global companies that offered nature, adventure, or cultural experiences in a nonurban setting in North America. The experienced ecotourist survey was mailed to lists of clients generated by the trade survey respondents. Results are shown in Table 7.5.

Table 7.5: The North American Ecotourist

General Consumers Interested in Ecotourism	Experienced Ecotourism Travelers
Market Profile • Reside throughout North America • Found in all age groups, but more likely 25–54 years old • Most live in couples households, with one-third also in families with children • Generally well educated • Females and males both well represented	**Market Profile** • Reside in all major urban areas, but likelier in West Coast (California) cities • Found in all age groups, but 76% were 25–45 years old • Most live in couples households, with 25% with children and 25% alone • Very high education levels • Females and males both well represented
Trip Characteristics • Tend to be generalists* • Prefer to travel in summer, with limited interest in winter, some in spring and fall • 59% likely to travel as couples; 25% family travel • Prefer wide range of trip duration, from 4–7 days to more than two weeks. Ecotourism portion likeliest 8–14 days and over. • 38% willing to spend more than $1,500 per person	**Trip Characteristics** • Generalists and specialists* • Prefer to travel in summer • 65% travel as couples, 15% families; 13% singles • Prefer wide range of trip duration, from 4–7 days of ecotourism experience, 8–14 days for total trip • 45% willing to spend more than $1,500 per person
*Ecotourism generalists engage in nature-related recreational activity for less than 48 hours; specialists engage in activity for more than seven days. Further, general consumers provided more generalized responses regarding activity of interest, whereas experienced ecotourists were more specific (e.g., boating verses kayaking/rafting as a response).	

Source: Wight, P.A. (1996). North American ecotourists: Market profile and trip characteristics. *Journal of Travel Research, 34(4)*, 2-10.

Agritourism

Today, opportunities exist for farmers and ranchers, as well as others in the agricultural industry, to become involved and benefit from the tourism industry. Tourism can offer supplemental income for producers and provide opportunities to educate visitors about farming and agricultural production. Many tourists also seek to experience the dynamics of daily life on the farm or ranch.

Rural living has lured tourists for decades. Countries such as Austria, Italy, Australia, and New Zealand have well developed rural tourism development initiatives. Working-farm vacations, winery and vineyard tours, and farm stays draw visitors around the globe. Domestically, states such as California, Texas, Vermont, and Michigan have active agritourism programs.

Agritourism can encompass a variety of activities, including picking your own fruits, shopping at roadside produce stands, touring farms and agricultural processing plants, enjoying a working farm vacations, staying at a farm-based B&B, photographing wildlife, learning about farm life, or just observing operations. Agriculturally oriented festivals and corn mazes bring thousands of visitors into suburban and rural farm communities each year. Fee-based hunting is another form of agritourism. Many farm and ranch owners have been leasing their land to hunters for decades, but few identify this as a form of tourism.

Figure 7.1: Agritourism

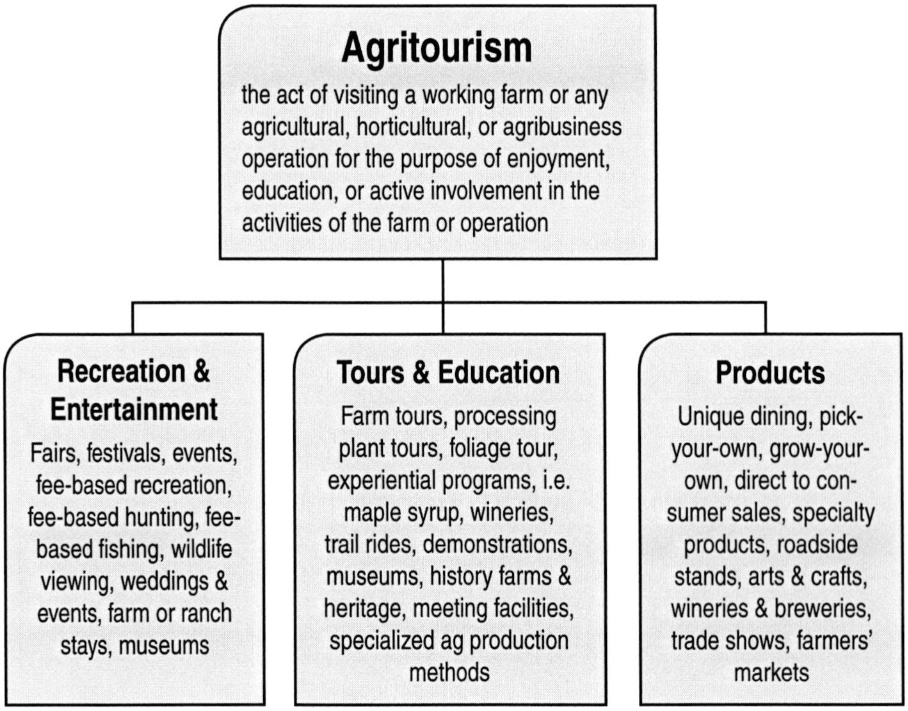

Agritourism
the act of visiting a working farm or any agricultural, horticultural, or agribusiness operation for the purpose of enjoyment, education, or active involvement in the activities of the farm or operation

Recreation & Entertainment

Fairs, festivals, events, fee-based recreation, fee-based hunting, fee-based fishing, wildlife viewing, weddings & events, farm or ranch stays, museums

Tours & Education

Farm tours, processing plant tours, foliage tour, experiential programs, i.e. maple syrup, wineries, trail rides, demonstrations, museums, history farms & heritage, meeting facilities, specialized ag production methods

Products

Unique dining, pick-your-own, grow-your-own, direct to consumer sales, specialty products, roadside stands, arts & crafts, wineries & breweries, trade shows, farmers' markets

While there may be many individual farm and ranch operations providing agritourism opportunities, there are few collaborative marketing organizations to tie the producer and consumer together. However, one example of a collaborative marketing group is the Wisconsin Agricultural Tourism Association at www.visitdairyland. com. Local destination marketing organizations, such as chambers of commerce and convention and visitor bureaus, can play important roles in organizing and marketing agritourism.

Realizing the value of America's farming culture, The National Trust for Historic Preservation launched a "Barn Again" program in 1987 that provides information on barn preservation and reuse through a hotline and various publications. Numerous farmers have restored old, dilapidated barns on their properties and turned them into retail shops, B&Bs, or "farm parks." Several state-based barn rehabilitation programs have been launched, and some states are considering tax incentives to make such projects more financially attractive. The U.S. government also offers a tax credit for rehabilitation of barns and other structures listed on the National Register of Historic Places.

As the tourism industry endeavors to become more sustainable, agricultural tourism has also begun efforts to showcase sustainable efforts. One example is "Green Routes," a Minnesota-based program to match locally based food and other products with the interests and actual travel routes of potential visitors. See www.greenroutes. org. In order to be considered a Green Routes destination, it must meet criteria such as contributing to the local economy by using local products, employing local people, conserving or enhancing the natural resource base, using sustainable products, or by actively engaging visitors in other ways. There are currently Green Route destinations in Minnesota, Wisconsin, Iowa, North Dakota, and Illinois.

Adventure Travel

Adventure travel refers to hands-on, participatory travel that is educational and challenging. It is hailed as the fastest-growing segment of the travel industry. Thousands of private travel companies and outfitters offer an array of adventure activities, ranging from hiking and camping to skydiving and survival games. In 1998, the United States Travel Association reported that half of U.S. adults took an adventure vacation during the previous five years. In 2010, the Adventure Tourism Market Report said a George Washington University study showed adventure travelers spend US $89 billion annually. The study surveyed travelers from North America, Latin America, and Europe.

Community Spotlight

Wine Trails a Growing Form of Agrotourism

Wine trails are an increasingly popular method of marketing a form of agritourism—wine tourism. Virtually every state now has grape and wine production capacity, with California, New York, Oregon, Washington, Texas, and Michigan leading the way. The introduction of cold climate grape varieties also has led to a growing grape and wine industry in such states as Minnesota, Nebraska, Iowa, Maine, and Vermont.

Wine trails typically result from a collaborative marketing strategy of vineyards and wineries in a particular geographic region. Wineries cooperate with each other to produce special events, tours, and tastings. Marketing materials such as brochures, websites, group advertising in television and newspapers, and social media exposure also help to market the cooperating businesses.

Wine trails are one way to connect the products and practices of agriculture with the tourist experience. Wineries often offer visitors an opportunity to learn first-hand how wine is made, tour the vineyard where the grapes have been grown, and sample the end product. In addition, visitors have the opportunity to purchase wine and other products, as well as patronize other businesses, such as bed and breakfast establishments or restaurants, that also contribute to the local economy.

Wine trails are usually organized by vineyard and winery owners or managers who recognize the value of "cooptition"—collaborating on some marketing programs while competing with each other on others. In the process, they learn from each other and provide additional ways to market their products and educate the public about the local wine industry in their area.

One example of "cooptation" is the Great River Road Wine Trail, which includes 10 wineries in Minnesota, Wisconsin, and Iowa. Participating wineries have developed a wine trail website, a brochure, and special events to highlight their offerings. They have utilized the geographic scope of the trail to invite other tourism related businesses, such as bed and breakfasts, to join in marketing the wine trail experience as a multi-day event. A recent special event highlighted the pairing of wines with local foods. The event exceeded expectations in both visitation and sales.

For an idea of how various wine trails are organized to market vineyards and wineries, please see:

- The Great River Road Wine Trail — Minnesota, Wisconsin, Iowa: www. greatriverroadwinetrail.org
- Uncork New York — New York: www. newyorkwines.org
- Texas Hill Country Wineries — Texas: www. texaswinetrail.org
- Idaho Wines — Idaho: www.idahowines.org
- Colorado Wines — Colorado: www. coloradowine.org

Adventure travel can be either "hard" or "soft" (Table 7.6). Hard adventure travel usually includes a higher degree of perceived danger on the part of the participant (e.g. rock climbing, river rafting, parachuting, mountain biking). Thirty-one million adults or about one-third of all adventure travelers engage in "hard" activities. "Soft" adventure offers activities with less perceived danger and often includes post-activity rewards, such as luxury camps/hotels and good food.

Table 7.6: Activities Pursued by Adventure Travelers

Soft Adventure Activities	Hard Adventure Activities
Camping	Whitewater Rafting/Kayaking
Hiking (Gradual)	Snorkeling/Scuba Diving
Biking (Road/Touring)	Off-Road/Mountain Biking
Bird/Wildlife Viewing	Backpacking (Rugged Terrain)
Horseback Riding	Rock/Mountain Climbing
Canoeing	Spelunking/Cave Exploring
Water Skiing	Skateboarding/Snowboarding
Snow Skiing	Participating in Survival Games
Wilderness Touring	Playing Paintball
Off-Road Vehicle Driving	Participating in Extreme Sports
Sailing	Roller Hockey
Taking a Photo Safari	Bungee Jumping
Visiting a Cattle/Dude Ranch	Hang Gliding
	Parasailing/Windsurfing
	Skydiving or Parachuting
	Hot Air Ballooning

References

Adams, B. (2008). *The new agritourism: Hosting community and tourists on your farm*. Auburn, CA: New World Publishing.

Jewett, J., Nelson, B., Braten, D. (2007). *Marketing local food*. St. Paul, MN: Minnesota Institute for Sustainable Agriculture.

National Endowment for the Arts. (1995). *Cultural tourism in the United States: Position paper for the White House Conference on travel and tourism* (p.1). Washington, D.C.

Prohaska, S. (1996). Planning for heritage tourism. Reprinted in *Organizational development, Heritage Tourism Planning and Management, Professional programs course manual* (p.2). Washington, D.C.: George Washington University.

George, H., Rilla, E. (2007). *Agritourism and nature tourism in California*. Davis, CA: University of California.

Reynolds, B., Stollery, S. (2007) *Expecting company? Preparing your site for agritourism*. (DVD). Alberta, Canada: Agriculture and Food Council.

Chapter 8
Marketing/Communication

When you have assessed your community's tourism potential, identified your tourism product, assessed your market, and have an organization in place to manage tourism, you are ready to develop a community tourism marketing plan.

Marketing involves communicating the availability of your tourism products and services to potential customers, and enticing them to become actual customers. It is the means by which you convince potential tourists to visit your community. Effective marketing is driven by customers' needs and your ability to meet those needs.

Tourism Marketing Basics

The tourism industry is dynamic and highly competitive on a global scale. Consequently, you must have a market orientation. Being market oriented means adopting and adhering to the philosophy that the customer's needs are the first priority, and that understanding those needs is an ongoing and long-term process. A market orientation is critical to providing a high level of customer service and a quality product, two key ingredients of the tourism experience.

Key Characteristics

Marketing is a continuous, coordinated set of activities associated with efficiently distributing products and services to high-potential markets. It is focused on providing customer benefits and satisfying needs better than the competition.

Kottler highlights several points implied in this definition:

> Marketing is a managed process. It involves carefully formulated programs, not just random activities. Marketing takes place before any selling takes place, and manifests in carefully formulated plans and programs. Marketing seeks voluntary exchange—

WHAT'S IN THIS CHAPTER?

8

- **Tourism Marketing Basics**
- **Developing a Marketing Plan**
- **Public Relations**
- **Information, Direction, Interpretation**
- **Marketing in a Digital Age**

marketers formulate a bundle of benefits for the target market. Marketing dictates the selection of target markets rather than attempting to be all things to all people. Marketing relies on designing offerings in terms of the target market's needs and desires rather than the seller's. Effective marketing is user-oriented, not seller-oriented. Marketing utilizes and blends a set of tools called the marketing mix—product, pricing, promotion and distribution.

The five key characteristics of marketing emphasized by Kottler—use of a stepwise process, identification of benefits, targeting, a market orientation, and use of multiple methods—provide a useful framework for developing a successful marketing effort.

Use of a Stepwise Process

Many communities leap into the "we need a brochure" phase as they begin promoting their area to visitors. This rarely works. Rather, successful marketing includes several steps, each consisting of a number of tasks. Some steps may occur simultaneously. All are guided by the goal of satisfying customer wants and needs.

The key steps to developing a marketing plan are:

    1. Analyze the situation;

    2. Identify your product;

    3. Select target market(s);

    4. Set marketing objectives;

    5. Create a marketing budget;

    6. Carry out promotion strategies; and

    7. Evaluate results.

These steps will be discussed below under Developing a Marketing Plan.

Identification of Benefits

Consumers who buy a vacation and those who buy the weekly groceries receive very different benefits. People usually buy travel experiences for emotional rewards rather than purely rational reasons. Therefore, you should identify both tangible and intangible benefits that your product offers. Link features to benefits that satisfy your visitors' vacation needs. For example:

- Being near shopping (a feature) offers the opportunity to purchase local arts and crafts (a benefit).

Tip

Key Characteristics of Marketing
- stepwise process
- identification of benefits
- targeting
- market orientation
- use of multiple methods

- Planned children's activities at a local attraction (a feature) frees a block of time for parents (a benefit).
- A lodging property with no television or phones (a feature) offers peace and quiet (a benefit).

Targeting

A sure way for a small community to fail in tourism is to try to be all things to all people. Primary destination areas such as major metropolitan centers, state offices of tourism, and major attractions such as Disneyland have the resources to do that; small or rural towns do not. Nor does a broad general message gain attention in the marketplace.

The trend across all retail sectors is toward market specialization:

> In a consumer landscape fragmented into dozens of niches, a marketing plan tailored to each specific group of consumers is needed. Welcome to the era of 'micro-marketing.' If marketers learned one lesson in the 1980s, it was that the mass-appeal, one-size-fits-all sell no longer sold. Instead, spurred by competition, new technology and changing tastes, products were created—and repackaged—to capture often-tiny slices of broad markets.

There are many examples of micromarketing in the travel and tourism industry. For instance, many lodging chains have different "brands" for different niches, ranging from budget to freeway stop to moderate to luxury, from suite hotels to small inns to four-star properties. Chapter 7 discussed some emerging and potential niche markets to consider. Specialize, and target, target, target!

A Market Orientation

Marketing is based on the principle that consumers will buy a product if the benefits of that product satisfy their needs. By contrast, selling focuses on the product rather than the needs of the customer. The key to gaining the attention of potential tourists is to develop a community marketing—not selling—approach:

> In fact, most of what gets passed off for marketing in tourism today is 'selling'—pushing what the community has, rather than 'marketing'—aptly described as customer satisfaction engineering. To engineer customer satisfaction, you must begin by truly understanding the customer and that is exactly where marketing begins, with market research to understand the consumer and understand the community through the eyes of … the potential

Not Just for Grownups

Winthrop, Washington (population 400), found a great way to hang out the "Welcome" sign for families with young children. The community's guidebook doubles as a coloring book, with games and entertaining information about the area.

Aim for Your Target

The Dahlonega-Lumpkin County (Georgia) Convention and Visitors Bureau uses a single website, www.dahlonega.org , to target specific markets. The home page includes tabs with targeted information for different audiences, such as festivals, weddings, wine, retirement and meeting planners. This is a low-cost way to customize information but allows website visitors to realize the variety of opportunities.

8

Estimates on the average number of ads each American sees every day ranges from 300 to thousands. Suffice it to say, it's a lot! Most of these messages are ignored. Only a few motivate a response, whether positive or negative. Only a fraction results in an actual purchase. This sheer message overload makes it essential for your convention and visitor bureau or chamber of commerce staff, local volunteer promotion committee, retail businesses, and others to be skilled in using marketing tools to increase the chances of success in the travel marketplace.

tourist. A basic tenet of marketing is this: 'people do things for their reasons, not ours.'

Tourists exchange their money for benefits provided by the community. Unless their needs are satisfied, they will not repeat the transaction.

Use of Multiple Methods

Your overall marketing strategy will be defined in your marketing plan. It is a combination of your target markets, communication methods, distribution channels, and pricing structure.

Marketing and promoting involves taking your message to the traveler through a specific delivery system using a variety of methods. Promotion is any attempt to stimulate sales by directing persuasive or informative communications to current or potential customers. Methods that are most often used in the travel and tourism industry include advertising, personal selling, sales promotions, and public relations. Used together, these methods can provide a powerful means for getting your message heard in the marketplace.

While most marketing is directed at the consumer, in fact your marketing message must be transmitted to many different publics. These include local residents, tourism business owners and suppliers, travel intermediaries, industry organizations, employees, and stockholders.

Marketing Makes the Difference

Travelers often "buy" their tourism experience sight unseen. This situation is radically different from one in which the consumer can come into the store to compare various products before making a purchase decision. It means that contact with customers before they visit—through marketing materials and activities or word of mouth by current or previous customers—is critical. Thus, well-done, attention-getting, and truthful marketing becomes an integral determinant of your community's success. Your marketing message must be honest, accurate, and consistent with your community's ability to deliver.

This is particularly critical if the marketplace is saturated, meaning there is a full range of consumer products as well as competing tourism towns. In today's global economy, your competition is not just a nearby town, but potentially towns and destinations around the world. In saturated markets, tourism destinations must produce above-average marketing in order to break through the clutter.

Marketing Must Be Responsive

Tourism marketing can be used to control crises or create opportunities. Most promotion methods have a short life span. Their immediacy enables you to respond to unforeseen changes in the marketplace. If some marketing funds have been reserved for contingencies, you will be able to mitigate the effects of negative situations (e.g., oil spills, weather disasters) or capitalize on emerging conditions (e.g., a hit movie being filmed in your area). Being proactive and developing a long-range marketing plan will help you to explore potential situations that could have a positive or negative impact on your community's tourism efforts. Know what all your marketing options are.

Reaching the Customer

Travel and tourism services and products can be sold directly to the consumer by suppliers (hotels, attractions, airlines, etc.) or through intermediaries (Figure 8.1). Most suppliers, including communities, find it effective to do both.

The most common types of travel intermediaries are tour operators, tour wholesalers, and travel agents.

Figure 8.1: The Travel and Tourism Distribution System

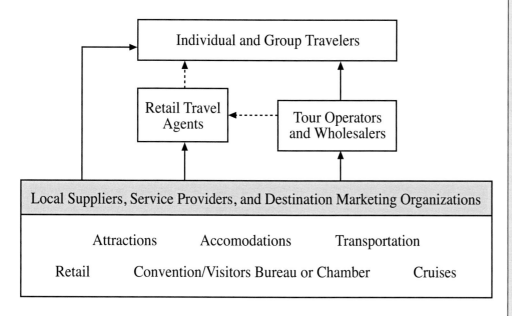

Travel Agents

According to the Airlines Reporting Corporation (ARC), there were over 16,000 accredited travel agencies in the United States at the end of 2009. The ARC is the airline industry organization that appoints

Seizing the Opportunity

A long hot spell in Texas in 1998 provided a marketing opportunity for the Northern Lights Tourism Alliance in northeastern Minnesota. The alliance's marketing committee quickly put together a campaign promoting the recreational opportunities of North Woods lakes and cool forests to the Dallas/ Ft. Worth market. A one-week TV campaign generated more than 100 inquiries. A follow-up survey was sent to all inquiries and 30 responses were received. Of these, 11 indicated a visit in 1998 because of the campaign, and the other 19 indicated plans to visit. Although the cost per inquiry was high, the campaign was deemed successful. Mary Somnis, executive director of Northern Lights Tourism Alliance, shares these thoughts about an opportunity marketing campaign:

• Be sensitive to those to whom you are appealing—don't exploit.

• Be prepared to handle the response—with TV or radio spots the response is immediate, so if it is running in the evening, you need staff to answer calls then. You may need to increase phone lines to a phone bank. These expenses can add up and need to be considered.

• Opportunity campaigns do not fit the same criteria as a strategically planned campaign within a well-formulated marketing plan.

• This type of campaign can have intangible benefits in changing perceptions and building the image of your destination.

domestic travel agents to sell airline tickets and processes airline travel sales. This number represents a majority of travel agencies, but there are also agencies that do not sell airline travel and are not included in this total count, as well as a growing number of independent agents. PhoCusWright's 2008 Travel Agency Distribution Landscape Study indicates there are approximately 31,000 independent agents in the United States.

These travel professionals sell travel services to the consumer, and counsel and help clients to:

- Make destination decisions;
- Select and book appropriate accommodations at the destination;
- Book airline, train, and/or rental car reservations; and
- Book cruise or package tours offerings.

The Internet has been an important part of the travel distribution system over the past decade. However, traditional travel agents remain a significant player in the market. U.S. travel agents sales represent approximately 40 percent of the total travel marketplace. Most agencies today focus on more complex travel arrangements, such as cruise, vacation packages or detailed independent itineraries that require greater expertise to organize and knowledge to provide consumer decision-making assistance. These agencies expect to receive commissions from suppliers, such as lodging or tour companies used in these arrangements. It is standard hotel practice to pay approximately 10 percent of the room rate to the travel agent who books the guest. Travel agents also receive commission on tour packages they sell, so any packages your community develops should include those commissions.

Tour Operators and Wholesalers

Tour operators create and sell travel arrangements for groups and individuals traveling on a tour itinerary. Tour operators normally market their packages directly to the customer, through travel agents, or in conjunction with airlines. Ground operators are tour operators who normally provide services at the destination only, and do not package transportation or market the destination.

Tour wholesalers combine existing local sightseeing tours with air transportation, hotel accommodations, and meals to create a tour product. Cruise lines, a type of tour wholesaler, offer lodging, meals, visits to multiple ports, and on-board recreation.

Group tours are one of the biggest segments in the travel industry, and are a major potential target audience for communities seeking to increase tourism. According to the National Tour Association, a single motor coach tour can bring more than $11,000 per one night's stay in a community.

One advantage of working with tour operators to market your attractions is that the operator shares the cost of promotion in print and online. These promotions can increase the visibility and customer base of lesser-known destinations.

Marketing to group tour operators should be part of an overall marketing plan and seen as a long-term marketing effort. It can take two or three years before efforts to build a working relationship with tour operators begin generating group tour visits.

Start by organizing the private sector locally, and then approach a tour operator with a history of operation in the area. Many communities work with regional groups through senior centers, community centers, and banks. Your state office of tourism and the National Tour Association can provide assistance with promoting group tourism.

A familiarization (FAM) tour can be an effective way of giving travel agents, tour operators, or group leaders a chance to see and experience your tourism product. A FAM tour is a free or reduced-cost visit to your area that includes accommodations, meals, and so on. Most FAM trips are short, no more than two or three days, and the itinerary is busy. This is not intended as a vacation. During the visit, sales managers from local lodging properties, restaurants, and sightseeing operators meet with visiting agents or tour representatives and provide inspections of their facilities. These contacts let you sell your community and make it easier for tour operators and group leaders to assemble tour offerings that include you.

A FAM tour should be included in your marketing strategy and budget and must be planned well in advance. FAM tours require careful coordination with your local tourism partners.

First and foremost, decide who you'll invite: travel agents, tour operators, or group leaders. Do not mix groups; it dilutes your ability to tailor your message to your audience. You may want to start with a small group of participants, no more than 10. The larger the group, the less one-on-one time you can spend with each participant.

8

To stay in business, travel agents must maintain a relationship of trust and confidence with their clients. Consequently, many hesitate to recommend a new destination or lodging establishment until they have personally inspected it. Many destinations and operators, therefore, make it a point to familiarize travel agents in larger markets. Consider working with the local private sector to host a familiarization (FAM) tour for a select group of retail travel agents.

The St. Paul, Minnesota, Convention and Visitors Authority, offers these tips for preparing, promoting, and hosting a FAM tour:

- Identify the purpose of the FAM tour. Promote an annual festival, community attractions, or new lodging or restaurant facilities.

- Develop an itinerary to accomplish the purpose, as well as show key elements of the area or attraction.

- Prepare a list of potential participants, with 10 more than the actual number you want to host.

- Set policies. Two people from the same company? Spouses? Transportation? Come early or stay late? Registration fees? Double or single occupancy accommodations?

Use "old-fashioned" print to make an impact – either a specially printed invitation or standard letter. Start mailings early. Follow up by phone and email. Keep in touch about the complete itinerary (including phone numbers, dress code) and descriptions of other participants.

At the local level, meet with hotel and other key hosts to discuss FAM tour responsibilities, expectations, special amenities, and so on. Careful planning and attention to detail will help ensure that things go smoothly. Consider what could go wrong and have contingencies in mind.

As a wrap-up, send thank you notes and evaluation forms to local hosts and participants. Remember the results of a successful FAM tour are long term, and will, in time, translate into business for your area.

Tip If you conduct FAM tours regularly, think about creating a yearly FAM calendar and take it to trade shows so possible participants can plan ahead.

8

Developing a Marketing Plan

A marketing plan is a written document used to guide your marketing efforts. A detailed, tactical marketing plan is generally created for a one-year period and spells out goals, objectives, and specific actions. It includes budget information, timetables, and evaluation methods for each project. In additon to this annual plan of work, a long-term marketing plan should be in place that covers goals and objectives for up to five years. This "big picture" plan is the foundation that addresses the external environments, trends, and opportunities or challenges that may affect your annual plans.

A good marketing plan is based on research and answers the questions:

Where are we now?

Where do we want to be?

How will we get there?

How do we know if we got there?

Developing a marketing plan involves seven steps:

1. Analyze the situation.
2. Identify your product.
3. Select target market(s).
4. Set marketing objectives.
5. Create a marketing budget.
6. Carry out promotion strategies.
7. Evaluate results.

The following sections elaborate on each of these steps.

Analyze the Situation

The first step in the marketing process is to conduct a situation analysis of the travel and tourism industry and its potential within your area. The goal is to answer the question, "What does our community have that travelers want?"

The situation analysis answers the question "What is?" as a basis for determining "What could be?" Your community should ask the following questions on a regular basis:

What attractions do we have that will entice people to stop and visit?

What hospitality services and facilities are available?

What experiences are visitors having in the community at present?

What promotion methods are used now, and how well do they work?

What is the community's image?

Who are our current markets?

What is the competition for our community?

How is tourism related to the community's culture, lifestyle, and goals?

What roles do community organizations play in tourism development?

What are the current trends affecting the tourism industry?

Much of the information necessary to answer these questions will have already been gathered during early phases of the tourism planning process. Review this information and transfer it into your marketing plan. For example, your attractions and services inventories (Chapter 6) will help you identify why people would want to visit your community and how prepared you are to host them.

An inventory of current markets will provide insight into the effectiveness of current promotional strategies. Complete Worksheet 8.1, using a separate copy for each market.

You must understand your competition and their strategies in order to market your competitive advantages. Neighboring communities generally are not your competitors; in fact, a number of strong travel-oriented communities working together on regional promotion can create a stronger destination image, a greater variety of attractions and facilities, wider market exposure, and a healthy degree of competition that spurs improvements. In reality, your most significant competitors will be other destinations at the national or international level.

The questions related to lifestyle and community involvement should already have been answered in Chapter 3. Understanding the roles various community organizations play in tourism development and promotion will help you see the "big picture" about your town's tourism options. Knowledge of social and economic changes that influence travel purchasing will help you develop a clear perspective of your market position and be ready to react quickly to changes when they occur—for example, the current trend toward short, get-away, "minivacations."

Identify Your Product

After the situation analysis, most communities find they are faced with multiple options for attracting tourists. The challenge is to choose one dominant one. You cannot and should not promote all of the community's attributes equally. In a tourism marketplace where consumers are faced with diverse choices, you need an "edge" to set yourself apart from the competition. You need to identify a unique product with a theme or identity that can be characterized by major promotion efforts.

First, think about the image your community already has (if any), and whether you want to enhance or shift that. Remember, one main reason people travel is to experience a new and different environment.

The situation analysis may suggest that heavy promotion of a certain attraction may create a problem. For example, if community meetings indicate residents feel area fishing lakes are overcrowded, you may wish to make lakes a secondary attraction rather than promote them heavily to tourists.

Piggybacking on Popularity

The situation analysis for Teton Valley, Idaho (pop. 3,412), indicated that the Teton Valley tourism group should try to capture a portion of the visitors already at heavily promoted and well-known Jackson Hole, Wyoming. Teton Valley residents were realistic in assessing that their town, beginning a tourism development effort, could not go head-to-head in competition with their more advanced neighbor. Like many communities with a strong but not overwhelming product and only moderate name recognition, Teton Valley first entered the tourist market by drawing visitors from existing destinations with heavy tourist traffic.

Today, the communities in Teton Valley (Wyoming) are part of the Teton Scenic Byway and are collaborating on development of a Yellowstone Grand Teton Loop Road. It includes Teton Valley, Jackson, West Yellowstone, and the National Parks to further encourage travelers to experience the entire region.

Extend Yourself with Collaboration

Stacey Reese, executive director of the Villages of Van Buren, Inc., explains how the villages in Van Buren County, Iowa, have extended their collaboration. "As you're developing tourism, regionalism and maintaining partnership is so important. We can do this on our own, but not to the extent we can do it with other counties around us." One example is a partnership with the Historic Hills Scenic Byway to bring signs to the community entrance. "There is no way we would be able to come up with $75,000 to place those three signs, but our partnership made that possible," she says.

Analysis may also bring out some advantages the community wants to promote (e.g., being a scenic alternative route to another major destination or metropolitan area), or it may indicate that the tourism product is not unique.

Work creatively with all the situation analysis information to identify a product. Sometimes the essence of the product can be captured in a positioning statement. This is a shorthand synopsis of your community's main tourism assets that serves as a guidepost to keep you on track. Your positioning statement offers the main idea or message you want to communicate, based on satisfying visitor needs. For example, the positioning statement of the city of St. Paul, Minnesota, is:

> St. Paul is a charming historic capital city with a small-town feeling and big-city access, offering a world of fun and education and a good value for the dollar.

While this is perhaps more complex and comprehensive than most small communities would prepare, it illustrates the value of having a succinct description for marketing and planning purposes.

The Vacation Package

A popular tool for attracting time- and price-conscious consumers is the vacation, weekend, or get-away package. This is simply two or more travel components (e.g., lodging, meals, transportation, entrance fees) offered together at a predetermined, inclusive price.

Packages are designed to attract individuals, families, or small parties rather than tour groups. Benefits to the customer include fixed cost, fixed amount of time, and ease of purchase (one call, one payment can buy the entire package).

To develop a package, start by having your community and local business partners prepare a packaging plan that includes preparation (e.g., market research, negotiation for services, pricing decisions), marketing, and package management (e.g., reservations, payment to suppliers, administration).

Types and functions of packages include:

Value Added: Packaging can add to the existing product during high demand periods. Visitors may be required to stay a prescribed time, or travel may be priced at a premium by adding special services.

Low Demand Periods: Packaging can add features to the product to increase sales during low demand periods. Businesses may discount services to boost volume.

Joint Marketing: Tourism businesses can reduce marketing costs by partnering to create and market a package of services.

Targeted Marketing: Packaging can tailor products to specific target markets. Examples include ski, sports, ecotourism, theater, and B&B packages.

Holiday Weekends: Packages can tie your features into a theme. New Year's Day, Valentine's Day, and Mother's Day are common holidays that generate special travel packages.

Recurring Events: You can use packages to draw people to regularly scheduled events such as sports tournaments, historical reenactments, arts festivals, or spring flower or fall color tours. Often these events develop a strong following for repeat business.

Major Events: Packages can increase attendance or encourage longer stays by linking major events with additional services or attractions.

New Products and Markets: Packaging individual services or attractions can build a stronger product that may appeal to regional, national, international, or corporate incentive markets.

Packaging success depends on good market research, an understanding of customers, knowledge of your community and tourism products, and creativity. Local lodging properties will be the key to developing a package. Lodging and transportation, usually the most expensive part of a package, are basic traveler needs. Add-ons, such as dining, tickets to attractions, and recreation, can increase salability of the package. Competitive pricing, predetermined arrangements, and access to popular activities and properties are common elements of effective travel packages.

To be successful, the package must be a good value; visitors should not be able to purchase the separate items for less than the total package price. At the same time, you probably don't want to lose money on the package. A break-even analysis can help you estimate how many packages you must sell to earn a profit.

The most frequent methods used to sell packages are:

- Direct sales to consumers through brochures, print media, Internet, and personal sales;

- Sales through travel agents (on a commission basis, usually 10 percent);

- Sales through tour operators or wholesalers, who purchase travel products in volume, add their profit, and resell them through travel agents; and

- Sales through attractions or retail outlets through joint advertising or public relations.

Community
Spotlight

Park and Ride

St. George, Utah (population 25,000), knows how to get people out to see the sights. A rent-a-car promotion with a national car rental agency there offered a reduced rate on mileage with an entrance sticker from nearby Zion National Park.

8

Select Target Market(s)

Don't try to please everyone with the same product, or to spend scarce promotional dollars appealing to people who are not prospects for purchase of your product. Rather, identify and choose target markets—groups of individuals sharing common characteristics toward whom you can direct your marketing efforts. For example, Disneyland offers more than 40 separate tickets to different target markets, ranging from senior citizens to corporate events to nearby residents.

Selecting your target markets involves three key steps:

Current visitors are a good indication of target markets attracted to your community. New prospects are likely to have many of the same characteristics unless you are planning a product shift.

1. Identify Market Segments

We discussed the process of dividing your market into target markets in the market segmentation portion of Chapter 7. If you have not already segmented out your various target markets, do so now. You may want to review Table 7.4, Tourism Market Segmentation.

2. Evaluate Target Market Potential

After identifying your target markets, evaluate each one's market potential using part A of Worksheet 8.2 (make a copy of the worksheet for each target market). As you complete the worksheet:

- Consider your product and estimate its drawing power.

- Think about your proximity to metropolitan areas and the quality of the transportation network.

- Consider size and accessibility; there must be enough members of the target market to justify the investment in reaching them.

- Consider whether you can reach the target market through a standard form of promotion.

3. Select Key Markets

Finally, select one or more of the target markets to focus on. You can concentrate on a single target market to the exclusion of all others, or you can develop campaigns for two or more markets simultaneously. Use Part B of Worksheet 8.2 to consider goals for each market, and how you will reach the market.

Set Marketing Objectives

Before implementing a promotional campaign, set clear objectives. Marketing objectives state what you want to accomplish. They keep your energy and actions focused on what's important. They help you track your successes and judge when it's time to review and shift strategies. A good objective contains four elements:

- A specific desired outcome (e.g., increased visitation, sales volume, awareness);
- A way to measure the outcome (e.g., dollars, percentages);
- A time frame within which the outcome should occur; and
- An indication of the target market you are trying to reach.

Some poorly stated or incomplete objectives are "to increase visits," "to build midweek business," and "to attract more retired couples." In contrast, an example of a well-written objective is "to increase phone and mail inquiries from fall magazine advertising by 20 percent between April 1 and June 1."

Create a Marketing Budget

A marketing budget is a critical element of a marketing plan. A good marketing budget is *comprehensive* in including all activities; *specific* in identifying not only how much money will be allocated to each activity but also the source of those funds; and *realistic*.

Many methods of budgeting are used in the tourism industry. These include "what's affordable" budgeting (spending what you think you can spend); competitive budgeting (basing your budget on comparisons to other communities); and historical budgeting (simply adding a percentage to last year's budget). These are popular because they are easy—not because they are the most effective.

One of the most effective methods of budgeting is the objective-and-task method. With this method, you can build a budget from zero each year, focusing on current objectives. The three-step process requires you to 1) set objectives, 2) determine the specific tasks and actions to accomplish your objectives, and 3) estimate the costs of each task. If several objectives and tasks have been identified, you will select the most feasible for implementation. By building your budget each year, you are forced to assess your efforts and your target markets. Although more involved, this method allows you to effectively apply your budget dollars and ensures that past marketing efforts are evaluated rather than simply continued because "it has always been done."

Investigate creative ways to supplement marketing funds. Does your state offer joint venture marketing programs that provide matching

View your marketing budget not as an expenditure but as an investment that will yield returns in increased tourism revenue.

Community Spotlight

Hometown Heroes

Related to film tourism is "celebrity tourism" in which communities develop tours and other activities around famous people who were born or raised there. Everyone knows about Memphis and Elvis Presley and Liverpool and the Beatles, but smaller communities promote celebrity tourism, too.

Examples include Duluth and Hibbing, Minnesota, birthplace and hometown (respectively) of legendary singer-songwriter Bob Dylan; Wapakoneta, Ohio, hometown of astronaut and first man on the moon Neil Armstrong; and Fairmount, Indiana, hometown of film actor and cultural icon James Dean.

With celebrity tourism, it's important to know your community's history. Do some research to find out whether any famous and/or historic people were born or raised in your town. If the answer is "yes" and you think there's enough public interest in that person to sustain tourism, you must then assess your community's willingness and ability to cultivate that interest.

Promoting your town's celebrity will require advertising and marketing, of course, but it might also require creating some new attractions. You'll have to decide what level of investment you'll want to make.

(continued)

funds for advertising campaigns on a competitive basis to local or regional nonprofit organizations formed to promote tourism? Can you exchange travel services offered by your community for advertising time or space in the media? How about considering cooperative (co-op) advertising with other communities, private attractions, or even nontourism products?

Finally, remember to hold back some contingency funds for unexpected opportunities, such as a late snowfall, a heat wave in a key target market, a "hot" trend, or a chance to benefit from a movie filmed in your community.

Carry Out Promotion Strategies

Promotion is any attempt to stimulate sales by directing persuasive or informative communications to current or potential customers, with target markets in mind. It consists of two activities: first, creating a marketing message from the product and its associated theme; and second, selecting the promotional mix that will get the message to the consumer.

Create the Marketing Message

A marketing message is the result of a creative endeavor that tries to reach a customer whose travel expectations may be complex. The personal nature and emotional appeal of travel shape the message.

It is important to make key points prominent in your message. Many things could be said about any one product, and probably an unlimited variety of things could be said about some travel destinations. However, no single message should attempt to say it all. Instead, say a few things well in each message and let the combination of your messages say it all. To set your community apart, there might even be times when it is appropriate to concentrate on only one feature. Talk to your visitors, to the experts, and even to competitors to clarify what is distinctive about your community's offerings. Then build your promotion message around this distinctiveness.

Select the Promotional Mix

A promotional mix is a combination of paid advertising, personal selling, public relations, and sales promotions. It is often described in terms of the relative amounts of effort and dollars committed to each promotional technique. Before you create a promotional mix, you need to understand the various options.

Paid advertising. Advertising is the most common promotional technique used in marketing. It is often a predominant element in the promotional mix.

There are numerous advertising media, each with advantages and disadvantages (Table 8.1). Your job is to find the combination of these media that delivers your message to the desired audience in the most cost-effective way. One way to do this is to ask the media advertising representatives for audience profiles, then choose those that most closely match the market segment you want to reach. Other factors to consider include:

- **Reach:** the number of people exposed to your message.
- **Frequency:** the number of times people are exposed to the message.
- **Impact:** the quality of the exposure in terms of consumer response.

Remember that advertising deals with cumulative effects. Visitor response usually comes from a variety of media used over a long time. A wide variety of options exist for timing your advertising campaign. You can send out your message continuously, in concentrated "bursts," or at regular intervals.

Know your target audience's media habits. Consider the type of message you want to convey. For example, a special event needs the immediacy of television, radio, or newspaper coverage, while a detailed tour package is best presented in a written format.

Cost per thousand (CPM) is a useful concept in judging the cost of alternative media strategies. It is defined as the cost to deliver one full-page black-and-white ad (or, in the case of television and radio, 30 seconds of advertising) to 1,000 households. All things being equal, lower CPM is usually better, but the quality of the media, audience type, and audience attention span must also be weighed.

Personal selling. Personal selling refers to direct or indirect consumer contact—face-to-face or by telephone. The Internet also enables creative personal selling through an interactive website, email or instant messaging. Good customer service is also a form of personal selling! Table 8.2 describes common media for personal selling.

Sales promotions. Sales promotions get potential travelers' attention by offering incentives such as vacation packages, discounts, coupons, and prizes offered through contests. Today, vacation packages and

games, minnow races, a hotdish lunch, Frostbite Frisbee, and a spaghetti dinner. In 2009, the festival also featured a "Grumpy Plunge" into the frigid river outside Slippery's Bar and Restaurant, which was featured in the movies "Grumpy Old Men" and "Grumpier Old Men." Of course, the community markets itself year-round as a scenic town on the Mississippi River with plenty of activities and attractions—including the nearby National Eagle Center.

Paris, London, Rome, Edinburgh

Movies based on Dan Brown's books "The DaVinci Code" and "Angels and Demons" have spawned a mini-tourism industry in the cities where the films were shot. Paris, London, and Rome were the biggest players in the movies, but Edinburgh, where the Rosslyn Chapel is located, also had a significant role. Various companies in these cities offer guided tours (by foot and by vehicle), with each offering a different take on the movies and books. Some companies offer package tours to all four cities, and www.fodors.com provides an online DaVinci Code do-it-yourself tour for all four locales. The effects on tourism have been particularly visible at the Rosslyn Chapel, which saw a five-fold increase in visitors following release of "The DaVinci Code" in 2006. Of course, a joint venture between Scotland's main tourist agency, VisitScotland, and Sony Pictures helped.

Evaluate your promotions with the AIDA principle—Attention, Interest, Desire, and Action. Do potential tourists see your promotions? Are they interested enough to read on or participate? Do the promotions create a desire for the product? Do they motivate a call to action?

Table 8.1: Comparison of Advertising Media

Advantages	Disadvantages	Unique Features
Newspapers (print) – see below for online advertising • Have broad reach • Are relatively permanent • Can modify with short notice • Can place ads by topic (e.g., travel section) • Use eye-catching graphics • Can use coupons to track response • Are easy to buy	• Are nonselective (difficult to reach target market) • Aren't read thoroughly • Are expensive if used frequently or with color • Don't involve reader	• Have a broad reach, are nonselective
Magazines • Target specialized audience • Have broad reach • May offer regional editions with advertising at a fraction of national rates • Have a long lifespan, several readers • Have high visual impact	• Requires major budget to be consistent • Can be expensive with color • Have a long lead time	• Have a broad reach, are selective
Direct Mail • Offers personalized approach to audience of good prospects • Is selective • Often costs less per lead • Provides rapid feedback • Recipient can save if interested	• Loses worth if list is not carefully selected • Can be expensive per unit • Costs a lot for list maintenance • Can be expensive if frequent • May be thrown away without reading	• Selective, measurable
Outdoor Advertising • Has low CPM (cost per thousand) • Offers high exposure • Is geographically selective • Can reach customer near point of purchase (depends on business)	• Doesn't provide easy way to measure audience response • Gets competition (e.g., driving, other signs) • Offers limited message • Can be expensive to cover entire market area • May irritate audience because of intrusion on landscape	• Low CPM; good at building awareness
Television • Can present product in dramatic, forceful way • Has a huge audience • Has long contact with viewer • Easily provides color and motion • Offers wide geographic coverage	• Has high production costs for smaller budget advertisers • Can be expensive to buy time • Can limit frequency because of cost • May not match your target market • Doesn't get full attention • Requires long preparation time • May not have good time slots available	• Only multi-media mass medium
Radio • Allows frequent message at low cost • Has selected audience • Offers emotional power of voice, music, and/or imagination • Is quick and easy to get on air, with short lead time if reserved in advance	• Often fails to get listener's full attention (background music) • Provides temporary message • Requires brevity and repetition • Has fragmented audience (many stations) • Offers no easy way to measure response	• Is low cost; encourages emotional involvement
Internet / Online Advertising • Has a broad reach • Can modify easily • Can target advertising • Uses eye-catching graphics • Easy to buy • Provides rapid feedback • Can track response • Can be interactive, two-way	• May be "lost" in volume of ads • Intrusive "pop-up" ads may irritate audience • Can be expensive • Limited to users of technology • May slow down websites	• Broadest reach of any ad form • Measurable • Multi-media • 24/7 access • Allows two-way communication

coupon incentives are almost expected by visitors to popular destinations both large and small.

Promotions should be used to meet short-term objectives such as increasing off-season visitation, increasing sales around major events and special occasions, or getting customers to try a new service. Target new or potential visitors and have a defined timeframe for promotions, and build in methods to track responses and gauge the value of such an effort. For example, how many packages were sold, or how many coupons distributed versus the number redeemed?

Don't forget the importance of word of mouth. Many market studies demonstrate that the primary source of tourist information is still recommendations from friends and relatives. Every interpersonal encounter between the tourist and host community has a positive or negative impact on future visitation.

Case Study

The Greater Woodfield Convention & Visitors Bureau
http://www.chicagonorthwest.com/

The Greater Woodfield CVB, representing 13 of Chicago's northwest suburbs, faced several common challenges including:

- Reduced length of overnight stays by corporate travelers
- Pressure to increase tourist visitation
- Need to better utilize and support the various attractions in the area by developing more effective marketing programs

Working with faculty at the University of Illinois, the CVB used research to inform their marketing and promotions. They conducted a study to learn about the people requesting travel information to identify important target markets and to better understand visitor experiences. They surveyed individuals requesting information over a three month period in the fall of 2002. The CVB used the findings to develop and modify their marketing efforts.

One finding was that there is a high percentage of repeat visitors with extensive knowledge and experience in the area. The CVB's strategic response was to create targeted new packages for shopping, holidays and special weekends.

Additionally, they found that their bureau can effectively use the Internet as a low cost means of communicating to existing and potential visitors. The CVB's strategic response was to upgrade their website and online communications with targeted e-mailings to special interest groups, a more effective use of sweepstakes and coupon offers, and the development of an online "graffiti wall" for visitors to share their comments with the CVB and other website visitors.

Source: Reidy, M. (2003). *Making visitor experience data come alive: Applying results to destination marketing strategies*. Presentation at censtates travel and tourism research association conference.

To get an idea of different sales promotions, attend regional tourism trade shows, read the Sunday travel sections from several metropolitan newspapers in potential market areas, or contact your state office of tourism.

Get on the digital map. A growing number of travelers are using GPS or digital maps to figure out where they want to go. Travelers access information via desktop computers and laptops, of course, but ever more so on GPS in their cars and on their mobile devices.

But do your community's most important attractions, businesses and services have a sign on this "digital superhighway?" If travelers are using GPS and digital maps to explore and make decisions, how can a community maximize the impact of this technology on tourism?

Table 8.2: Common Personal Sales Media

Medium	Description
Travel Information Centers (TICs)	Most places that draw tourists have TICs (also known by names such as visitor information centers and tourist welcome centers). Many also distribute literature at TICs in regions that draw the desired target markets. TICs distribute "take-along" advertising pieces and show promotional videos, but the primary activity that demands management attention is one-on-one personal selling. It is important that TICs are staffed with knowledgeable, enthusiastic, friendly personnel.
Telephone	Toll-free numbers are all but expected. Make it easy for an interested party to call for more information or make reservations. Be sure your telephone is answered during business hours and has voice mail for after hours. Use well-trained, knowledgeable volunteers or staff who are comfortable with low-key sales and customer contact. Use a simple form to track how callers heard about you. Respond to telephone inquiries promptly. Telemarketing has not proven effective for tourism; many people are annoyed by unsolicited phone calls.
Trade/Sports/Travel Shows	These are meetings at which the public or travel industry representatives gather information about destinations. In evaluating whether to attend, consider exhibit fees, travel and per diem expenses, literature costs, and whether the right audience will be reached. Consider teaming up with your state tourism office to reduce costs. For the general public, consider controlling costs by handing out request cards that can be returned by mail instead of brochures. (This also creates a mailing list.) With the travel trade, attend with tourism business owners in your community and schedule appointments with tour operators or travel agents to sell your community. Make sure you have a plan for following up on leads.
Public Speaking Engagements	Television and radio talk shows, presentations to clubs and organizations, and advance promotions at malls give the public a taste of what your community has to offer. Members of your community tourism organization can help spread the tourism message by participating in a speakers bureau. Prepare a simple message for speakers that "sells" your community.

For some places of interest, like the local sledding hill, you probably won't find any information when you conduct a search. Don't let that deter you. It's your job to ensure that important information does show up in the future. Record, record, record. Make a list of all the things right and wrong because this will be your work plan.

After documenting the visibility of your local points of interest, you will most likely need to make corrections and additions. Each digital mapping site has its own way of making edits and adding new information. For example, Google maintains a local (online) business center, now called Google Places, that walks you through how to update your community's digital map. This service is free. Mapquest and GPS devices get their data through a private company. You'll need to research how to update information in each digital mapping service.

Ensuring that information about your community is complete and correct is only the beginning. There are many other ways to showcase your local attractions using digital maps. Consider using picture and video-sharing websites as a way to help visitors explore. Many sites

like YouTube and Flickr allow content to be labeled with a specific location—called a geocode or geotag. Try searching YouTube for your community. You'll likely find content you didn't know was there.

Once you have updated all your local information for GPS and digital mapping sites, remember to keep it current. Continue adding to your list of assets as your community opens new businesses and creates new attractions, then submit the information.

It will take time and effort to get all your local information on GPS and digital mapping sites, but it's well worth it for your community's tourism industry. Find local resources if you need help getting started. For example, University of Minnesota Extension offers a workshop called "Roadside Advertising in a Digital World" to help communities leverage GPS technology and digital maps to increase their online presence.

Evaluate Results

Evaluation is probably the most overlooked step in marketing. It actually involves both monitoring and evaluation. Monitoring involves establishing standards for all of your marketing efforts, measuring performance against those standards, and making corrections to achieve your marketing goals. Two primary measurement tools are clear, well-defined objectives and a good budget. Monitoring is not limited to the marketing and promotional efforts of the organization. It should also be used to encourage quality products, service, and teamwork.

Businesses and communities use a variety of marketing evaluation techniques. *Sales analysis* compares actual sales (e.g., occupied room nights, number of visitors) to stated objectives. *Marketing cost and profitability analysis* evaluates the costs and profitability of elements of your marketing plan. A good analysis can be time consuming, but it's worth the investment because it can point out unproductive target markets, distribution channels, or promotional expenditures.

Probably the most common evaluation of marketing efforts is the *evaluation of advertising efforts*. These evaluations are often expressed as ratios, and may include the number of inquiries generated per ad, cost per inquiry, and cost per visitor. These form the basis of an *inquiry conversion analysis,* which evaluates the prospect's information collecting and decision-making process. In order to evaluate your advertising, you must create a method to track responses and gather the numbers you will need for your evaluation. This must be built into your advertising campaign.

As you assess your community's most important assets and investigate the visibility of key points of interest on existing digital maps, it's vital that you document everything you learn. As the related article says, "Record, record, record." It's also important to identify the most descriptive and distinctive keywords for your community's assets so they will have high visibility on search engines.

We suggest you develop a checklist to help you document information you obtain during your assessment. At minimum, you'll want to list your assets and keywords to describe them, errors to correct in existing digital maps, and additions required to existing digital maps. You also will probably want to assign roles, set due dates, and record when tasks are completed.

As noted, you will also want to continually update your list of assets as your community opens new businesses and creates new attractions. Maintaining a checklist will help you stay on track.

8

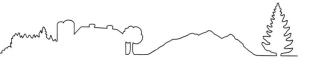

To identify which ads generate greatest response, find out where those responding heard about you. One simple way to do this is to code ads with different telephone extensions or post office box numbers. You don't have to rent multiple phone lines or post office boxes to do this. For example, you can put your phone number with "extension 2" in one newspaper ad, and "extension 3" in another. When the caller asks for "extension 2," you add a tally mark on your tracking chart to the corresponding newspaper. The same simple system works with a post office box. (e.g., P.O. Box 1234A and P.O. Box 1234B). Worksheet 8.3 can help you track response to your advertising campaign.

Cost per inquiry (CPI)—the number of advertising dollars it takes to get one person to call for information—is a simple measure of the initial impact of advertising. Most tourism destinations compare CPIs for different publications and broadcast media. But inquiries are only one step toward actual visitation.

Cost per visitor (CPV) and *return on investment (ROI)* are important measures. Conversion figures can be calculated to indicate the percentage of those exposed to your advertising who actually visit. Worksheet 8.4 shows the basic calculations. Collection of the information for these calculations can be complex, but the inquiry conversion analysis is the true "acid test" of your advertising.

In the long run, advertising is an investment that must increase profit margins to more than offset advertising expenditures. Costs must be tied to results to avoid draining budgets. Evaluating advertising results will allow you to adjust your marketing program to spend advertising dollars where they are most cost effective.

One caution: Often there is a long lag time from when travel advertising runs to an increase in consumer awareness of and interest in visiting a destination. Even if evaluation shows little consumer action, an ad program may still be building significant consumer awareness. This is particularly true for destinations just beginning to market tourism or if you are targeting markets such as tour groups that have a one- to two-year lag. In such cases it may be appropriate to maintain an advertising campaign even in the absence of evidence of payback. Watch your numbers, but use them as only one way to measure progress toward accomplishing your marketing objectives.

Table 8.3 summarizes the key steps in marketing and provides a simple format for compiling an easy-to-read, well-written marketing plan.

Table 8.3: Tips for Writing a Marketing Plan

1. Analyze the situation
Consider the rationale for your marketing efforts.
Examine the resources available for marketing.
Review the effectiveness of past marketing efforts.
Examine demographic, economic, and social trends (local, regional, national).
Analyze your competition.

2. Identify your product
Identify your community's image.
Choose one dominant activity to promote.
Find the unique product or theme.
Develop a positioning statement.

3. Select target market(s)
Identify target markets (demographics, residence, social group).
Identify what activities your target markets engage in.
Find out what your visitors are looking for.
Find out if you have repeat visitors.
Find out how far in advance your visitors plan their travel.

4. Set marketing objectives
Focus objectives on your target markets.
Make sure objectives are measurable and quantitative (number of visitors, sales, volume, etc.).
Make sure objectives are framed within a specific time period.
Make sure objectives are outcome based, focused on your end result.

5. Create a marketing budget
Be comprehensive.
Be specific about the amount for each project and sources of funding.
Be realistic.

6. Carry out promotion strategies
Identify your promotion strategies.
Define your product.
Price your product.
Consider distribution methods.
Specify your promotional mix.

7. Evaluate results
Define how you will measure success.
Decide what monitoring you will use.

Public Relations

The practice of public relations includes general functions, such as the day-to-day contact all employees have with various publics at all times. It also includes specific functions, such as the use of specific techniques by one or more individuals specially trained in the field.

Public relations techniques are used in a variety of ever-changing situations. Fazio and Gilbert identify seven guiding principles that are always present in the practice of good public relations:

1. *Every action makes an impression.* Everything we say or do has a bearing on how others perceive us; our public relations is our image.

2. *Good public relations is a prerequisite of success.* Success requires public support and support comes from a good image or perception of your organization.

3. *The public is actually many publics.* It is important to identify all those with interests in a project or those who have the power to influence its outcome.

4. *Truth and honesty are essential.* Good character and responsible performance are essential. No effort to influence public opinion can succeed on dishonesty.

5. *Offense is more effective than defense.* A proactive public relations stance is much more effective than defensive action. Prompt, honest, accurate information always prevails over the silent, "no comment" tactic.

6. *Communication is key to good public relations.* Communication is essential to establishing internal harmony, a crucial prerequisite to effective public relations. True communication is synonymous with understanding and listening is an important aspect.

7. *Planning is essential.* Planning keeps your organization on the offensive. Preplanning can calm and diffuse crisis situations. Anticipate issues, gather facts, analyze your situation, and form a plan.

The value of good public relations is usually not recognized until it is absent and needed (usually in the face of adversity). The goodwill generated by a long-term public relations effort can go a long way in helping your community achieve its tourism goals.

Media Relations

Communication with the media is the most common and prevalent form of public relations. Two factors that most strongly influence consumer decisions are word-of-mouth endorsements and editorial coverage in newspapers, magazines, and websites.

Editorial coverage of your product is often perceived as more credible and less biased than paid advertising. The negative side, however, is that the message is not totally controllable. Reporters pride themselves on their objectivity and coverage can be greatly swayed in a

positive or negative direction, based upon their experience with your product. In addition, the competition for media coverage is intense. In order to stimulate a reporter's interest, you need to stand out from the crowd. You must be a credible source of clear, consistent, creative, innovative, visual, and client-focused information.

Making and maintaining good media contacts is a priceless investment. Get to know reporters who cover travel beats and familiarize yourself with the format of their publications and stations. Know their deadlines and the format(s) in which they prefer to receive information. Ask yourself:

> What does this magazine/reporter/travel writer really need?
>
> Why is my story more important that other news topics?
>
> What is the local angle?

Keep a file of stories that are published and send thank-you letters when your town gets coverage. A media file will help you get to know which reporters produce positive coverage and which look for a negative angle. It will also help you evaluate your overall efforts in building awareness and reaching target audiences.

News Releases

News or press releases are newsworthy synopses of events or accomplishments, prepared for use by media. They are the most common tools used by public relations practitioners. Upon receiving a press release, the media will: 1) run it; 2) rewrite it or do a feature story; or 3) ignore it. To increase the chance that your news release will be used, you must find a newsworthy angle, decide who you want to reach and why, and know media deadlines.

In addition to press releases directed to travel, feature, or business reporters, submit a calendar of community events to calendar editors on a regular basis. Remember, too, that newspaper columnists may have a large following.

8

Writing Effective News Releases

One of the best ways to learn how to write an effective news release is to study how others do so. For examples, check out PRNewswire at http://www.prnewswire.com or PR Leap at http://www.prleap.com. Or visit the News or Media section of just about any business or organizational website for examples.

There are also tips and instructions on writing and formatting news releases on the Internet. Just do a search using keywords to find resources. Make sure they are credible, of course. Here are a few websites to get you started:

- The Business Insider: http://www.businessinsider.com/how-to-write-a-great-press-release-2010-7#1-learn-the-format-1
- About.com: http://marketing.about.com/od/publicrelation1/a/howtowritepr.htm
- eHow: http://www.ehow.com/how_2043935_write-press-release.html
- Ezine: http://ezinearticles.com/?Writing-a-Great-Press-Release&id=4537726
- Publicity Insider: http://www.publicityinsider.com/release.asp

News releases usually fall into three categories:

- Announcements of coming events or of personnel matters (hires, promotions, retirements, etc.);
- Information regarding a cause, a new product, or industry trends; or
- Information meant to build a company or person's image.

Media Kits

A media kit is an effective way to package information about your community. It generally includes a fact or background sheet on your town, a calendar of events, a list of area attractions, one or more press releases, a special invitation to your town, a community brochure, photographs or slides, and a press clipping or article reprint. The information should be brief and to the point.

Media kits are useful for connecting with key media. However, be selective. Costs can quickly add up, so distribute them only to outlets that are likely to provide coverage of your community.

Feature Stories

News releases and media kits often stimulate interest among reporters to visit your community and do feature stories. Most look for exclusive opportunities and unique story angles when deciding what topics warrant in-depth features.

Your community's job is to help the media tell a good story. Brainstorm about potential human interest angles and unique attractions. Spend time up front reviewing the medium's format and style. Then, when you have a strong story line in mind, contact the selected medium at least three to four months prior to publication. Write a particular person or section editor a letter describing your idea and attaching a press release and any relevant promotional literature. (Just be sure never to pitch the same story successfully to two different outlets of the same medium.) Photos can help "sell" the story, too. One to two weeks after the initial letter, telephone your contact.

Remember one or two attempts that do not result in immediate stories do not necessarily mean failure. The best strategy may be ongoing contact with media, keeping them updated about tourism in your town. Always follow through on media inquiries. The only way to gain trust and respect is by making your tourism organization a reliable source of information and assistance. Eventually they may think of your community in the context of story development.

Media Tours

A media tour, like a FAM tour, is a free or reduced cost visit to your area. The purpose of a media tour is to give media a personal look at your tourism product so they will write about your community as a destination.

For media FAMs, be selective about the media you invite and try to ensure that all attendees are "on assignment" and committed to writing a story. In the case of freelancers, keep track of who produces and who does not. With the proliferation of freelance writers in the marketplace, it is important that you not use a space on your FAM tour for someone who is just looking for free travel.

Media Relations: Proactive and Prepared

- **Be accessible.** Treat all media calls as top priority. Return calls promptly, within 10 to 15 minutes if possible.

- **Be honest.** If the news is bad, admit it and tell the reporter what your organization is doing to correct the problem.

- **Nothing is "off the record."** Stick to the facts; don't speculate. Keep information up to date and at the ready.

- **Don't babble.** Don't say more than you need to. Try to say something positive. Don't volunteer negative information.

- **Use short sound bites.** Keep your words basic. Don't use industry jargon. Keeping comments short helps reduce the possibility of being taken out of context and edited to present a totally different message.

- **Prepare a media crisis plan.** The plan should state how you would handle the news media in the first few hours of a crisis. Coordinate your plan with existing ones in effect with local government, law enforcement, and fire and rescue agencies.

- **Deal with crisis head-on.** Don't hide out. Face the media quickly. Be candid and open.

- **Involve employees.** Share your media philosophy with all employees and volunteers within your organization. Prepare a media guideline handout, including the names of those to whom they should refer media inquiries.

- **Be helpful.** Build relationships with reporters by assisting them with stories that have nothing to do with your community's tourism efforts.

Adapted from Oden, W. (1994). Tips for tackling the media. *CROA Newsletter 1(2)*. Also Patterson, B. (1993). Crisis impact on reputation management. *Public Relations Journal, 49(11)*, 16-17.

---

emails and Web visits for the Ely Chamber.

The Chamber added social media to the mix in 2009, when the April Fool's "story" was Ely's bid to host the 2016 Summer Olympics. In addition to a news release and standard public relations efforts, that story was promoted through a unique website, a blog, a Twitter account, a Facebook group, and a mock press conference on YouTube—which has drawn more than 20,000 views to date.

Once again the national media picked up the story and tens of thousands of people signed an online petition to bring the Olympics to Ely after watching the video or hearing the story elsewhere. Others bought promotional T-shirts, commented on blogs, followed Twitter postings, and joined the Facebook group, whose fans now number nearly 4,000.

In 2010, Ely officials announced that the city and the U.S. Forest Service had struck a (fictional) multiyear deal selling the naming rights of the BWCAW to Minnesota-based International Dairy Queen (IDQ)—making the wilderness area the IDQBWCAW.

Media across the country again picked up the story, and media outlets are asking "what's next." "The media, especially local media, are calling us now," Jarvis says. "We've conditioned them to expect something different."

8

TIP

Remind key hosts that in the case of the media, you are never guaranteed a "good" story; if someone has a bad experience don't be surprised if they write about it!

TIP

While it may be acceptable to offer media a complimentary visit to your community or free tickets to a special event, don't overdo it. Most national media outlets have policies against reporters accepting complimentary arrangements or gifts.

Community Relations

In addition to dealing with the media, your public relations efforts must communicate with community members (political officials, government agencies, business owners, local residents, etc.) whether or not they are directly involved in tourism. This is commonly referred to as "community relations."

Community relations is driven by the simple tenet of "be a good neighbor." Every organization and industry has an image within the community. It can be positive or negative, accurate or inaccurate. A poor image, or a group of conflicting images, can have a serious effect on the success of tourism efforts. Image also can have a significant impact on the quality of the visitor's experience. Residents' attitudes can contribute to the perception of your community as friendly or aloof, clean or dirty, safe or unsafe. Good community relations can help educate residents on the role they play in establishing a good community image and how this image affects your tourism success.

Tourism is often viewed by residents as frivolous or of little economic value. Emphasis is often on the negative perceptions of low-wage jobs, seasonal employment, traffic congestion, and increased housing costs. A well-targeted and ongoing community relations campaign can educate people about the potential positive impacts of tourism and guide community perceptions.

Common tools used in community relations by tourism organizations include sponsorship of community events, employee participation in local volunteer efforts, development of new facilities that benefit residents as well as tourists, special pricing for residents to area attractions, mentoring and job training programs for local youth, and scholarship and charitable donations for community causes. Local chambers can operate speakers' bureaus to take the tourism message to local schools, political groups, and civic organizations. Businesses, chamber of commerces and convention and visitor bureaus can donate goods, services, money, or other assistance to community programs.

Developing a positive relationship with the local community is essential to long-term tourism success. This does not mean that your community will always agree on tourism issues. Good community relations also means listening to your community with an open mind, and being willing to adjust programs to meet the community's needs.

Information, Direction, Interpretation

A third key communication function, in addition to marketing and public relations, is communicating with visitors while they are in your community. This includes providing visitor information at visitor information centers, self-serve kiosks, or directional signs, and developing interpretive programs or signs. And don't forget to update digital maps, too – see page 115. The public sector frequently takes the lead in such efforts. However, information services may also be a joint effort between local government and the tourism organization.

Information Centers

Every community needs an information center where visitors can learn about the community's attractions, its culture and heritage, things to do, and services. Staffing and management will depend on the resources available. Brochure racks in local businesses often serve as unstaffed information stations in small communities. It is important to keep these racks full, neat, and current.

Unstaffed information stations may be located at major entrance points such as airports and roadside rest stops. These can describe what the community is about, display maps, and provide literature. Direct telephone connections to the headquarters or to lodging facilities greatly increases the usefulness of unstaffed stations.

Electronic Kiosks

Computerized video display information stations or kiosks are increasingly used at points where travel converges and people congregate (freeway exits, shopping malls, etc.). Versions of these programs can also be set up to operate through televisions in lodging rooms and lobbies.

Marketing in a Digital Age

It seems only yesterday that the Internet revolutionized information distribution and marketing. A website is a necessity in almost every endeavor, and community tourism is no exception. The Internet enables travelers to get in-depth and up-to-date information about your community's attractions, lodgings and events without ever leaving home — and saves destinations the cost of handling phone or mail inquiries.

Community Spotlight

Weekly Update

The executive director of the Greater Sandpoint [Idaho] Chamber of Commerce (see case study in Appendix A) writes a column in the local newspaper addressing tourism and other business development issues. This column has helped educate the community about the financial impacts and pros and cons of tourism, how tourism dollars trickle down in the community, and the many attractions that tourism growth has developed for the benefit of residents.

8

Website Tips

There are many resources and consultants available to establish or update websites, and we suggest you research those online and in your community for more details. That said, here are some key thoughts about designing an effective website:

- Provide valuable content that answers all your audiences' questions; think like a tourist and ask yourself everything a traveler would want to know about your community;

- Make sure your site is logical and easy to navigate—as well as aesthetically pleasing;

- Craft your content so potential travelers find you via search engines; use specific key words to search-optimize your website. Remember to include your website address on all "non-browser" media, too, such as leaflets, e-mail newsletters, TV, radio, newspaper ads, and so on.

You will probably also want to create a space on your website for blogs or forums. And that brings us to social media, which is rapidly changing the way people interact with just about everything and everybody. If Web 1.0 is primarily about one-way information dissemination, Web 2.0—which includes social media—is about two-way communication.

Using Social Media

Social media allows you to make connections and build relationships with the public, who are the best boosters for your community. As Eye for Travel says, word of mouth can be a huge benefit to a brand, and social media literally is word of mouth "on steroids." Word of mouth can be negative, too, if something goes wrong, but you'll acquire valuable information to address issues and can restore confidence by participating in online conversations.

There are many forms of social media, including the aforementioned blogs and online forums. Other tools include social networking sites, such as Facebook, MySpace, and LinkedIn; photo and video-sharing sites, such as Flickr and YouTube; and microblogs—such as Twitter. All are distributed via the Internet, free of charge, and all are fundamentally user-generated.

This means blatant advertising doesn't work in social media space. Businesses and other organizations must be perceived as members of the social media community—willing to interact and listen. People use social media sites primarily to learn, not buy. That comes later.

Case Study

Adding Social Media to the Marketing Mix

Located near the Canadian border, Ely, Minnesota (population 3,700), is the gateway to the Boundary Waters Canoe Area Wilderness (BWCAW)—one of the nation's best locales for wilderness canoeing and camping. Ely also offers hiking, biking and bird-watching in the summer and cross-country skiing, snowshoeing, snowmobiling and dog-sledding in the winter— all amidst primeval forests, pristine lakes and rugged rock outcroppings.

Ely has long been a favorite destination for families and outdoor lovers alike, creating lasting memories for generations of travelers—especially those living in the Upper Midwest.

With that in mind, the Ely Chamber of Commerce launched the "Ely is Calling" campaign in 2008, featuring the theme on its website, on local and Twin Cities radio, in online ads, and (indirectly) on social media sites. The target audiences were Minnesotans and residents of neighboring states who were most likely to have visited Ely in the past.

"When you talk to people, they say they remember Ely from when they were kids—visiting as Boy Scouts or Girl Scouts or with their families," says John Jarvis, partner in Twin Cities-based Giraffe Marketing. The Ely Chamber hired him in 2008 to develop and implement an integrated marketing plan for Ely tourism. "We wanted to remind people that Ely is still out there and still like they remember, with no chain stores or shopping malls—a great place to get away and only four hours by car from the Twin Cities," Jarvis says.

Of course, sharing memories of Ely is a natural for social media, which the Chamber began to use in earnest in 2009. At the behest of the Chamber board and Administrative Director Linda Fryer, Jarvis and his team started a blog on the Chamber website, launched Facebook and Twitter sites, and posted videos on YouTube highlighting its zany April Fool's media campaign (for details, see Community Spotlight on page 122).

Online conversations about Ely soon proliferated, mostly on Facebook, where users talked about the April Fool's videos and exchanged personal stories about Ely. To date, the Ely Facebook page has drawn nearly 4,000 fans. The blog started conversations on the website, too, and local residents have since taken over the blog.

In May 2010, *Budget Travel* magazine named Ely the "Coolest Small Town in America, beating out 13 other towns in online voting. Ely captured 118,899 votes—27 percent of the total 439,411 received. The Chamber promoted online voting through its Facebook and Twitter sites.

Online voting really picked up steam in January 2010 when Ely's North American Bear Center featured real-time video on its website of the birth of a cub to Lily, a wild black bear. The center also launched a "Lily the Black Bear" Facebook page, which has drawn more than 100,000 fans to date—many of whom likely voted for Ely as the "coolest small town."

From these experiences, it's clear social media is stirring interest in Ely. How much that translates into more visitors and/or more bookings is challenging to measure at this stage. However, viewing Ely's marketing efforts in the aggregate, it's also clear that "we're doing something right," Fryer says.

As measured by lodging tax receipts and Forest Service reports on visitors to the BWCAW, tourism is holding its own in Ely, even through economic downturns.

Fryer strongly recommends that other communities integrate social media into their marketing plans. She sees many benefits to social media, including its ability to garner specifics on what interests people about Ely—thus providing valuable information (at a low cost) for future marketing efforts.

Noting that tourism is strongly influenced by word of mouth, Jarvis says that social media "allows communities to put their best foot forward" through their own blogs and by participating in others' blogs and forums. He also cites social media's role in community brand-building. "It's important for each community to establish its identity, and social media is a great way to enforce that at a fairly low cost," he says.

Both Jarvis and Fryer emphasize that substance and content still count the most, whatever the marketing tool. "You have to have a good story to tell," Fryer says. "You have to have something to promote and give people a reason to come and visit you."

8

Although relinquishing control of the message might be a problem for some organizations, the bigger issue is that monitoring social media can be quite time-consuming. However, if you're willing to make the investment, social media marketing offers real benefits. Among other things social media marketing:

- Helps reinforce community identity through story telling (yours and your customers' stories);

- Helps build brand awareness and improve how people view your brand;

- Builds relationships and strengthens connections to and among people who might not otherwise know about you;

- Helps you learn what your customers are thinking and saying about you (a virtual focus group);

- Has no setup costs or charges; your own time and labor are your only costs; and

- Helps you show up higher in search results (provided you link your social media sites with keyword content back to your main website).

Evaluate Social Media in Context

If you're thinking about adding social media to your marketing mix, evaluate it in terms of your overall goals and mission. Will it help reach your target audience(s)? Will it help you reach your objectives? Can you commit to sustaining the effort?

Once you have answered those questions to your satisfaction, you're ready to choose the social media tools that should work best for you and start using them as part of an integrated marketing campaign that features a mix of media. And remember: High-quality, meaningful content should always be your first priority whatever communications vehicle you employ.

What about measuring the results of social media? You can count the fans you attract to your Facebook page or your followers on Twitter, and you can use Web analytics to measure referrals to your website from social media sites. Assessing the most important performance indicators, including sales, profits, and customer retention and satisfaction is more challenging—not only for social media but for advertising and public relations in general.

Nevertheless, experts like Chris Lake of Econsultancy say you can measure success provided you give your social media strategy time to

evolve. Then you can look at your overall performance, as well as the performance of your social media campaigns over the duration. Lake has a number of good suggestions for assessing social media that would take up too much space here. Instead, we suggest you read his blog at http://econsultancy.com.

What's Ahead?

So what's next in online marketing? Tourism-Review.com cites two trends: mobile Internet marketing and Web 3.0. Mobile applications, which essentially put the Internet on users' phones, are a natural for tourism—enabling things like easy last-minute, in-destination bookings or plain "old" texting. Tourism also will benefit from GPS and other location-based tools combined with features like augmented reality, which—like the yellow line showing first down when you watch a football game on TV—adds a layer of virtual, computer-generated information over a physical, real-world environment. So travelers can get information about a hotel or other attraction as they're walking down the street.

Tourism-Review.com also says the next generation of the Web—Web 3.0—will make searching tasks faster, easier and more customized. Browsers will act like personal assistants, learning what travelers are interested in and tailoring responses to questions like "where should I go for my summer vacation?" to their preferences. This makes it even more important for communities and tourism organizations to create relevant and unique website content so holiday options appear high up in travelers' search results.

References

Farhi, P. (1990, January 21). Marketers bag big game in tiny niches. Article from *The Washington Post* reprinted in the Minneapolis (Minnesota) *Star Tribune*.

Fazio, J., & Gilbert, J. (1986). *Public relations and communications for natural resource managers*. Dubuque, IA: Kendall Hunt Publishing.

Kottler, P. (1982). *Marketing for nonprofit organizations*. Englewood Cliffs, NJ: Prentice Hall.

Sadowske, S. (1989). Tourism marketing for communities: Moving from hype to strategy. Sem, J. (Ed.), *Using tourism and travel as a community and rural revitalization strategy; Proceedings of the National Extension Workshop* (pp. 97-103), Minneapolis, MN.

Directions: Copy this worksheet as needed. Work with local tourism businesses and organizations to answer these questions.

Current Market: _____

    (e.g., vacationers, business travelers, convention or meeting attendees)

How many annually visit our community?

Characteristics:

    Demographic (age, gender, income, family/single/adult couple)

    Behavioral (new/repeat, length of stay, amount spent, etc.)

Where do they come from (geographic location)?

How do they make their travel plans?

How do they travel to and within our region?

When do they come?

What do they do when they are here?

Target Market: _____

Geographic location:

Demographic characteristics (age, sex, income, family/single/adult couple, etc.)

Behavioral characteristics (new/repeat, length of stay, amount spent, etc.)

A. ASSESSMENT OF MARKET POTENTIAL
Size of market (number of individuals):

Seasonal variation in this market?

Special needs of this market?

B. MARKETING EFFORT
How will market be reached? (Advertising, etc.)

Goal for this market:

Worksheet 8.3: Advertising Tracking Form

CAMPAIGN: _____

Ad Placement	Date of Ad	Tracking Code Used	Phone	Number of Inquiries Mail	Other

Directions: This worksheet will give you a quick assessment of the effectiveness of your advertising campaign. List individual advertising component costs in each column. Calculate numbers 1-7 for each component. Finally calculate totals.

ITEM	Advertising Program Components (for example: specific ads, sport show flyers)			Total Program
	#1	#2	#3	
1. Total cost = (ad production plus insertion costs)				
2. Total number of inquiries* =				
3. Total number of visitors* =				
4. Total revenue generated by travel party* =				
5. Cost per inquiry (CPI) $\frac{\text{Line 1}}{\text{Line 2}}$				
6. Cost per visitor (CPV) = $\frac{\text{Line 1}}{\text{Line 3}}$				
7. Return on ad investment (ROI) $\frac{\text{Line 4}}{\text{Line 1}}$				

*traceable to that advertising program component.

Chapter 9
Local Business Development

Tourism is important to the U.S. economy. According to the U.S. Travel Association (formerly the Travel Industry Association), almost 7.4 million people were employed in travel-related jobs in the United States in 2009. Measured another way, 1 out of every 18 people has a job resulting from travel expenditures.

At the same time, the U.S. Department of Agriculture notes that an increasing number of entrepreneurs in rural and small-town communities are identifying new ways to market previously untapped local resources and attractions to bring tourists to their area.

Many people think the tourism industry consists only of entry-level, low-wage jobs. They seldom stop to consider the impact tourism can have on building the local commercial tax base, stimulating entrepreneurship, and generating jobs at all income levels. Communities that value and encourage small business development as they build their tourism industry are most likely to reap positive, sustainable benefits.

Tourism as Economic Development

Tourism can be an important economic diversification strategy for a community. It can complement and build on existing industry. Agritourism, for example, can enhance local farm families' incomes.

Tourism can increase business and family incomes and employment. This can occur in both the businesses directly affected (e.g., hotels, attractions, restaurants) and in the businesses affected indirectly through a multiplier effect (see Chapter 2).

Worksheet 9.1 can help you begin thinking about tourism-related services and businesses that might benefit your community. Use this tool as a basis for a public forum or town meeting during the early planning stages.

9

Assessing Climate and Impact

An important step in tourism development is to assess the local business climate and the economic impact of tourism businesses on the community. The information you gather will provide a general idea of how many and when visitors are coming to your area, as well as their spending patterns. This will help you plan and market tourism and understand your community's total tourism economy. It can also help generate interest and support for tourism among community members by highlighting its economic significance and potential. Sector-specific information can be used later to compile a directory of tourist attractions and services that can be used by visitors or in marketing.

Business Surveys

Assessments 9.1–9.4 (or a modification) can help you get a handle on the business climate and economic impact of tourism in your community. You may wish to appoint a task force to distribute, collect, and tally the data.

Begin by making a list of tourism-related businesses in your area, categorized by sector. (You can use the inventory information from earlier chapters or Worksheet 9.2 to help this process.) Make a copy of the appropriate survey (lodging, food service, retail, or entertainment) for each one. Divide the surveys among survey task force members and assign a reasonable due date.

Have tourism businesses complete the survey for their particular sector. If a business doesn't fit neatly into one of four major sectors (e.g., a theme restaurant with skits could be considered both a food service and an entertainment attraction), ask the business owner which category best describes the business.

You may conduct the surveys in person or over the phone, or distribute them for business owners to complete and return. The more personalized approach may increase participation and also allows you to allay concerns business owners may have about providing this information. Explain that you are collecting general information so that the community can better understand its current tourism picture, and that you are not asking individual businesses for gross sales or profit figures.

It is important that you hold the information gathered confidential, and share only the combined data. You will probably need specialized assistance to evaluate the results and create an accurate economic

profile. You can seek assistance from your county Extension office, university tourism or business departments, or private economic consultants and research firms. Business schools or tourism departments may also be willing to help as part of a student research class project.

Existing Information

Another way to assess business climate and economic impact is to gather existing information about the tourism economy in your county or region. While this information may not be community specific, you can often identify key trends that affect your area or use it as a starting point. Table 9.1 lists some common sources of tourism-related statistics and research.

Table 9.1: Sources of Tourism Statistics and Research

State tourism office
Local or regional tourism organizations
Community and state economic development offices
Federal and state departments of commerce
Federal and state departments of labor
USDA Extension Service and local Extension offices
U.S. and state natural resource agencies (e.g., parks, forestry, fish and wildlife)
State highway or transportation departments
University departments (e.g., business, economics, recreation, tourism)

Encouraging Entrepreneurs

Small businesses are an important part of the tourism industry. Although attractions draw people to your community, services are responsible for the bulk of the jobs and income generated by tourism—and most services are provided by small businesses.

Worksheet 9.2 can help you identify which service businesses your community may need as tourism develops. Starting a business is challenging. Your community should make special efforts, both public and private, to encourage small tourism businesses. For example, you can help recruit new business owners, offer education to help residents start their own businesses, help individuals evaluate the feasibility of a business idea, and provide incentives for start-ups.

The following ideas can help individuals develop and evaluate tourism business concepts:

Help local officials understand the value of keeping investment and ownership local. The public sector is often involved in efforts to recruit and fund tourism development (hotels, restaurants, attractions, etc.). If local investment and ownership are encouraged, the profits from these developments are more likely to stay in the community, provide community benefit, and generate additional local investment.

A Boom in Brainerd Lakes

In Minnesota's Brainerd Lakes Area, tourism has stimulated community-wide economic development. The area is a popular playground for the entire state, especially the Twin Cities metro area. Crow Wing County, in which Brainerd is located, ranks fourth in the state in gross tourism revenue, and 10th in retail sales. The population of Crow Wing County has grown 41.7 percent since 1990 to over 62,700 residents, according to the U.S. Census Bureau. Businesses and jobs in the county have increased as well. In 1990, there were 1,535 firms employing about 16,000 people. In 2009, there were 2,189 firms employing more than 26,300 people. Many of the new businesses are owned by entrepreneurs who got to know the area as tourists and later chose to combine work with play. The amenities that attract thousands of tourists to the area each year are now drawing seasonal and year-round homeowners.

Tip

There are numerous resources to help you with business plans, financing options, and other aspects of creating and operating a business. Your local small business development center can assist you, as can the U.S. Small Business Administration or your state department of economic development.

- Visit other communities to observe tourism businesses.
- Obtain information from trade associations on markets and business opportunities.
- Meet with individual business owners to review the opportunities and pitfalls of a particular business opportunity.
- Discuss potential business ideas with a trusted friend.
- Take small business management classes that teach how to develop a business plan.
- Obtain information on the business you are considering from libraries, universities, and government and private organizations.
- Obtain information on managing a small business from bankers and other small business instructors.
- Survey or interview visitors to determine if a service is needed.
- Check with suppliers to see what goods sell.
- Talk with members of your family to determine their willingness to go through the rigors of managing a small business.
- Develop a business plan. Plans help you identify key components of a successful business development and communicate the idea to bankers and other investors.

Worksheet 9.3 will help individuals with a business idea assess feasibility, begin thinking in concrete terms, and develop a business plan.

Business Plans

A business plan is a document that describes a business, its product or service, the market(s) it serves, and the operations and financing. It helps an owner determine the feasibility of a new business, provides information needed to seek financing, serves as a management tool, and documents the process and information you need to manage the growth and expansion of your business. Think of a business plan as a road map to help you manage a business by clearly defining goals and outlining methods for achieving them.

Every business should have a business plan, and should review and update it periodically. To write a good business plan, you will need to carry out diligent research and to understand the marketplace.

Each section of the business plan answers questions and addresses issues. The outline on the next page, adapted from the U.S. Small Business Administration, can help you as you develop a business plan.

I. Business Description/Overview

The business plan begins with a business description and overview explaining:

What business am I in?
What are my company's products, services, and markets?
What makes my business unique?
What are the company's goals and objectives?
How will the company resolve the most threatening problems that may arise?

II. Description of Products/Services

The next section describes your products and services by answering these questions:

What does my business sell or plan to sell?
How do these products and services benefit the customer?
What makes these products and services unique?

III. Sales and Marketing Plans

In this section your business plan should answer:

Who are my customers?
What are my customers' likes, dislikes, needs, and expectations?
Who is the company competing with?
What is my competitor's pricing strategy?
What new markets will I try to enter?
What is the most effective way to promote my products and services?
How do I plan to expand my business?

IV. Operating Requirements

This section addresses the operating requirements of your business:

How is the business managed day to day?
What are the company's hiring and personnel policies?
Should the company rent or own its facilities?
What equipment is needed to produce the company's products and services?
How will I get products and services conveniently and efficiently to customers?

V. Financial Management Information

This section answers the questions:

How do I plan to finance the business' expansion?
Are the company's financial projections realistic?
Do the company's financial projections include a sales forecast, cash flow projections, a projected income statement, a break-even analysis, and a balance sheet?
How do company financials compare with those of peers?

VI. Management Profile

Next, evaluate:

Who are the owners of the company and who are its key employees?
What skills do the key employees possess?
How will I restructure the business to adapt to a changing market environment?

VII. Supporting Documents

This last section contains reports, surveys, and so on that back up your answers to the questions in the other sections.

Community Spotlight

Planning with a Heart

Terri and Larry Gray's decision to open the Riverside Bed & Breakfast and Bistro (BBB) on the shore of the Pelican River in Pelican Rapids, Minnesota (population 2,374), was essentially made "from the heart," Terri says. But the couple also backed up their choice with research and planning.

Before opening the bistro first and the bed and breakfast later, they answered all the questions required of a business plan, especially "What makes my products and services unique?" They wanted customers to enjoy a dining and lodging "experience," rather than just eat and sleep, Terri says.

Thus the Riverside BBB features varied theme menus using locally grown organic foods; cozy, cheery rooms with breathtaking waterfall and river views; and a strong European feel. The Grays also offer private parties at the bistro, and they recently started kayak rentals.

As expected, residents of nearby Fargo, North Dakota, and other surrounding areas with weekend homes on local lakes are frequent restaurant patrons, especially at dinner. However, local residents also support the bistro, as do visitors to the beautiful area, which contains more than 1,000 of Minnesota's 10,000 lakes.

The Grays advertise their business on their own website at www.riversidebbb.com, as well as through tourism websites, brochures, roadside signs, digital maps, and above all Constant Contact daily emails. Emails also capture information on customer demographics, tastes and preferences.

The Grays continue to use that information, as well as data from other sources, to update their business planning.

9

TIP

BR&E programs are used in more than 30 states and five countries. For more information, go to www.brei.org.

TIP

Before initiating a full tourism BR&E program, review the information you gathered during your tourism planning process. This can help your community identify new business opportunities and develop plans of action to help fill needs.

Business Retention and Expansion Programs

Business retention and expansion (BR&E) programs help communities improve their business climate and help businesses serve visitors. They are an important component of efforts to use tourism as a development strategy. Some 60 to 80 percent of new jobs in a community come from existing businesses that expand rather than from new businesses—yet many communities take business retention and expansion for granted when developing tourism. Failure to give priority to the survival and growth of existing tourism businesses results in missed opportunities to create local jobs and income.

BR&E programs collect information from local businesses that you can use to:

- Help solve immediate issues of local small businesses;
- Begin planning for long-term changes needed to compete in future markets;
- Begin to help businesses cooperate on implementing planning recommendations; and
- Help develop linkages to other community and state economic development programs.

Communities already involved in tourism may find a BR&E program an appropriate tool for examining opportunities to build their tourism industry. If your community has already completed a BR&E program or is implementing recommendations from such a plan, you can use the surveys in this chapter as monitoring and evaluation tools.

Support = Success

Dahlonega, Georgia (see case study in Appendix A), developed more than 40 tourism businesses. Most of these businesses were new; many were started by people who came as visitors, liked the area, and returned to go into business. Dahlonega has been successful because:

- Business development and expansion has strong support from the community. Dahlonega bank managers believe that tourism businesses are a vital part of the economy. The bank encourages the development of business plans and reviews and supports these plans.
- The University of Georgia provides support to solve business problems through a part-time small business development center in Dahlonega.
- City and county government support business development. Close cooperation between government and local institutions helps new business get started.
- Entrepreneurs committed time and personal resources. Many Dahlonega tourism businesses started small, had close ties to the community, and grew with the expansion of the tourism industry.
- Past successes have given local residents confidence to initiate development.

Key Components of a Tourism BR&E Program

- **Support**
  All development efforts must have commitment from key community groups and leaders.

- **Business development group**
  This group may consist of businesspersons, educators, economic development professionals, and community leaders. Do not give responsibility for business retention and expansion to a group with other functions.

- **Visits and survey**
  A BR&E program includes visits to, and a confidential survey of, tourism businesses. The survey should ask each business about specific problems or complaints, perceptions it has of the community as a place to do business, types of assistance it would find useful, and plans for expansion. Information gathered can help you assess the business climate. Positive data can be used to help new business start-ups or attract new businesses. Negative information is useful for formulating plans to solve problems.

- **Programs to improve the competitiveness of local firms**
  Trained employees and managers help a business compete in the tourism marketplace, keep current, and adjust to changes in the markets. Use your local school district, community college, vocational school, or land-grant university to help conduct educational programs in marketing, business development, hospitality services, management, and other business programs.

- **Cooperation among local development groups**
  Competition among community, county, regional, and state economic development groups can fragment economic development efforts. In many cases, tourism development has a much better chance of success when done on a multi-community basis, so that regional services and attractions can be packaged into a larger tourism offering.

- **Forums for addressing business problems**
  Tourism business visits, surveys, and committee meetings help create forums to begin identifying local barriers to business development. These forums can use confidential information collected from local businesses to begin solving community business problems.

- **Local economic strategic planning**
  Steps involved in planning are 1) identification of community business development goals; 2) collection of community tourism business data; 3) selection of priority actions; 4) development of action steps; 5) implementation of action steps; and 6) evaluation and plan adjustments.

- **Business development**
  Small and rural communities lacking the full range of potential businesses needed to serve visitors may need to develop new businesses. Communities can help recruit new business owners, implement educational programs to help residents start their own businesses, and provide incentives for business start-ups.

9

Encouraging Entrepreneurship

Many people underestimate the wide range of small businesses that serve the visitor. This list includes more than 120 potential businesses that could be started in rural communities. Use these ideas, along with your own, to help stimulate community leaders or local entrepreneurs. Remember, detailed analysis and business planning is needed before a community can determine if a particular business is viable.

Food service
Cafes
Restaurants
Food vendors
Caterers
Bakeries
Pie & donut shops
Farmers markets
Farm fresh produce
  shops
Fast food
  establishments
Wineries
Convenience stores
Excursion meals
Taverns & bars
Restaurant trains
Candy stores
Delis
Nightclubs

Entertainment
Amusement parks
Live theaters
Clubs
Theme parks
Festivals
Zoos
Bands
Gambling casinos
Ticket services

Accommodations
Resorts
Campgrounds
Motels
Hotels
Houseboats
B&Bs

Seasonal homes
Trailer courts
Condominiums
Spas
Retreat centers
Conference centers
Inns
Farm vacations
Hostels
RV parks

Transportation
Taxis
Limousine service
Gas stations
Shuttle services
Auto rentals
Airplane rides
Tour buses
Ferry services
Cruise ships
Hot air balloons
Helicopter rides
Carriage rides

Arts
Art galleries
Craft stores
Art villages
Specialty goods
Antique shops
Boutiques
Bookstores
Photographers
Sports shops
Clothing stores
Jewelry stores
Repair shops
Import shops

Manufacturing
  businesses
Gift shops
Flea markets
Auction houses
Bait farms
Boat dealers

General
Drug stores
Factory outlets
Grocery stores
Hardware stores
Pharmacies

Education
Arts
Tours
Sports
Specialty
  - Boats
  - Houses
Archaeology sites

Recreation
Outfitters
Guide services
Golf courses
Driving ranges
Rental services
  - Canoes
  - Snowmobiles
  - Bicycles
Hiking
Skis
Boats
Water slides
Marinas
Charter boats

Horse ranches
Ski slopes
Wave pools
Mini golf
Boat rides
Game farms
Travel agents
Trekking
Photography
Parasail rides
Fee-based hunting
Lease hunting
Fee fishing ponds
Rafting
Surf shops
Scuba diving
Spelunking
Charters
  -Fishing
  -Sailing
  -Diving
  -Snorkeling
Dude ranches
Trail rides
Naturalists
Glass bottom boats
Submarine rides
Winter tubing

Resources

Many resources exist for communities and businesses interested in economic development. Visit a library for access to databases and printed materials and check websites for online tools. A variety of private, non-profit, state, federal, and local agencies provide economic development resources. Resources also are available from academic institutions, including the following:

- Tourism Business Development Toolbox:
  www.uwex.edu/ces/cced/tourism/

  Developed by the University of Wisconsin's Center for Community Economic Development, this online toolbox provides resources to foster tourism entrepreneurship in communities. Tools on market analysis and financial planning are targeted to specific industry sectors, such as retail stores, restaurants, small resorts, nature-based tourism and agritourism businesses, and more.

- Community Retail Development Toolbox:
  www.extension.umn.edu/Retail/Downtown

  This online toolbox takes a comprehensive approach to retail market analysis for communities striving to maintain a vital economic mix. Tools combine research, analytical techniques, and the best practices of Extension educators at the University of Wisconsin, University of Minnesota and Ohio State University. Toolbox components of particular interest to tourism businesses include: 1) Trade Area Analysis to more precisely identify where customers are coming from; 2) Lifestyle and Demographic Analysis to identify types of customers in each trade area; and 3) Customer Survey Research to aid in decision-making about the direction of business districts.

Additional economic development sources include:

- U.S. Small Business Administration (SBA):
  www.sbaonline.sba.gov

  This website provides tools and describes services offered by the SBA—an independent agency of the federal government that "aids, counsels, assists and protects the interests of small business concerns."

Community Spotlight

Sustaining Vintage Village Tourism

The Mississippi Valley Partners (MVP) organization undertook a BR&E program. MVP comprises 12 vintage villages along the Mississippi River in Minnesota and Wisconsin. Trained local volunteers conducted an on-site visit and survey of 82 tourism and travel businesses.

Based on the results of the BR&E survey, strategies and related priority projects were determined by citizen volunteers and MVP members. The priority projects formed the basis of MVP's strategic plan for the next five years and have led to a number of developments including an MVP Welcome Center, increased citizen and government understanding of the impact of tourism on the economy, creation of a website and targeted marketing materials, and investment in the development of a National Eagle Center in Wabasha, Minnesota.

9

- Service Corps of Retired Executives (SCORE):
  http://www.score.org

This website outlines services provided by SCORE's volunteer mentors across the nation. Check the website for webinars and other online tools, or find the local SCORE office nearest you to make an in-person appointment with a mentor or attend a workshop.

References

Ilvento, T.W. (2001). *An overview of BR&E visitation programs.* Retrieved August 5, 2010, from University of Delaware, Department of Food and Resources website: http://www.udel.edu/FREC/ilvento/bre.htm

Small Business Administration. *Small business planner.* Retrieved August 5, 2010, from http://www.sba.gov/smallbusinessplanner/index.html

U.S. Department of Agriculture. *Promoting tourism in rural America.* Retrieved August 5, 2010, from http://www.nal.usda.gov/ric/ricpubs/tourism.html

U.S. Travel Association. (2010). *Travel powers America.* Retrieved August 5, 2010, from http://poweroftravel.org/statistics/impact.htm

Worksheet 9.1: *Identifying Business Opportunities*

Small businesses create jobs and incomes that are important to the economic vitality of smaller communities. Communities can help local businesses expand and encourage individuals to develop new tourism services. Answers to these questions can help you identify potential community business opportunities.

1. What are the potential tourism business opportunities and/or needs in our community?

2. What would businesses identified above require from our community to address needs?

3. How can we ask visitors what types of goods and services they are willing to purchase in our community?

4. Who in our community (e.g., bankers, development groups) will support local people in business start-ups or expansions? What do we need to do to get their support?

5. Can our community encourage business development and expansion through business incubators, revolving loan funds, educational programs, scholarships, and other types of development assistance? If not, what will it take to make this happen?

6. What resources are available locally/regionally for technical assistance, education, or help with data analysis?

List the types of service businesses currently found and needed in your community or region.

SERVICES WE HAVE	SERVICES WE NEED
Food Service	
1.	1.
2.	2.
3.	3.
4.	4.
Entertainment	
1.	1.
2.	2.
3.	3.
4.	4.
Accommodations	
1.	1.
2.	2.
3.	3.
4.	4.
Transportation	
1.	1.
2.	2.
3.	3.
4.	4.

Over ⊃

SERVICES WE HAVE	SERVICES WE NEED
Recreation	
1. 2. 3. 4.	1. 2. 3. 4.
Specialty Goods	
1. 2. 3. 4.	1. 2. 3. 4.
Arts	
1. 2. 3. 4.	1. 2. 3. 4.
General/Other	
1. 2. 3. 4.	1. 2. 3. 4.

Worksheet 9.3: *Evaluating a Tourism Business Idea*

This worksheet will help you develop a written evaluation of a tourism business idea.

1. What is the business opportunity?

2. Who will buy my goods and services?

3. How will I reach and communicate with my customers? (e.g., print advertising, Internet)

4. How do I take advantage of the opportunity? (e.g., open a store, work through other local businesses)

5. What resources do I need? (e.g., financing, staff, materials, training, location)

6. How or where can I obtain the resources?

7. What type of business structure is best for this opportunity?

8. What problems or obstacles will I encounter?

Assessment 9.1: Lodging Facilities Economic Survey

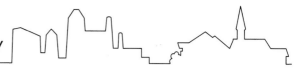

Your responses to this survey will be used to assess the current economic impact of tourism within our community. We ask for your name and address solely for the purpose of compiling a complete inventory of visitor services. All of your responses will be strictly confidential and used only to develop an overall profile of visitor services provided and associated economic impact. If you have questions, please contact the person who distributed this survey to you. Thank you for your assistance!

BUSINESS NAME: _____

CONTACT: _____ PHONE: _____

ADDRESS: _____

CITY: _____ STATE: _____ ZIP: _____

1. Which one of the following most accurately describes your lodging facility?

    ❑ Hotel   ❑ Motel w/ restaurant   ❑ Campground   ❑ Other: (specify)
    ❑ Resort   ❑ Motel w/o restaurant   ❑ RV park
    ❑ Cottages   ❑ Bed & Breakfast inn   ❑ Hostel   _____

2. What is your AAA rating, if you have one? _____

3. Total number of units: _____

4. Please indicate the number of units you have by type:

    _____Single   _____ King   _____Campsites w/hookups   _____ Kitchenette
    _____Double   _____ Queen   _____Campsites w/o hookups   _____ Other
    _____ Double/double _____ Suite   _____ Cabin

5. How many units are accessible to persons with handicaps? _____

6. What is your average daily room rate? $_____ In-Season $_____ Off-Season

7. List number of conference/meeting rooms (if any) at your establishment and capacity of the largest meeting room:

    Rooms _____   Capacity of largest _____

8. Please indicate weekday (S-Th) and weekend (F-S) seasonal occupancy rates and any months you are closed:

    Spring   Weekdays:_____ %   Weekends:_____%   Closed:_____
    Summer   Weekdays:_____ %   Weekends:_____%   Closed:_____
    Fall   Weekdays:_____ %   Weekends:_____%   Closed:_____
    Winter   Weekdays:_____ %   Weekends:_____%   Closed:_____

9. For the past year, what was the average length of stay for your guests?_____ (# nights)   Over ➔

10. Of your guests, what percent would you estimate live:

    Within the state _____ %   Out of state _____ %   In other countries _____ %

11. What percent of your guests do you estimate are traveling for: Business _____%   Leisure _____%

12. Please indicate current and projected average employment:

    Full-time employees: Current # _____   Projected # (next year) _____

    Part-time employees: Current # _____   Projected # (next year) _____

13. Do you employ more people in the summer or winter, or is your employment figure fairly constant?

    ❑ More in Summer   ❑ More in Winter   ❑ Fairly Constant

14. Can your staff give accurate information, including directions, regarding community attractions?

    ❑ YES (Go to Question 17)   ❑ NO (Go to Question 15)

15. Would you be willing to have your employees attend a hospitality/tourism training class?

    ❑ YES (Go to Question 16)   ❑ NO (Go to Question 17)

16. Would you be willing to pay a fee to cover the costs for your employees to attend a hospitality/tourism session?   ❑ YES   ❑ NO

17. Are you willing to participate in community organizations to promote tourism? ❑ YES   ❑ NO

18. Are you planning any additions or renovations within the next 12 months?   ❑ YES   ❑ NO

19. If YES, what do you plan to do and how will it increase or change your ability to cater to tourists?

    _____

    _____

    _____

20. Who is your primary target market?

    ❑ 25–50 years   ❑ Families w/children   ❑ Specialty travelers

    ❑ 50 + years without children   ❑ Business/convention   ❑ Other _____

21. Which of the following most accurately describes the location of your primary competitors?

    (Check all that apply.)

    ❑ Local community   ❑ Local county   ❑ Surrounding counties   ❑ Your state

    ❑ Adjacent states   ❑ Other states _____   ❑ Other

22. Please provide any additional comments about how tourism impacts your business:

    _____

Assessment 9.2: *Food Service Economic Survey*

Your responses to this survey will be used to assess the current economic impact of tourism within our community. We ask for your name and address solely for the purpose of compiling a complete inventory of visitor services. All of your responses will be strictly confidential and used only to develop an overall profile of visitor services provided and associated economic impact. If you have questions, please contact the person who distributed this survey to you. Thank you for your assistance!

BUSINESS NAME: _____

CONTACT: _____ *PHONE:* _____

ADDRESS: _____

CITY: _____ *STATE:* _____ *ZIP:* _____

1. Which one of the following most accurately describes your dining establishment?
    ❑ Family restaurant   ❑ Ethnic/gourmet   ❑ Fast food   ❑ Supper club
    ❑ Restaurant/bar   ❑ Ice cream shop   ❑ Coffee shop   ❑ Other:_____

2. What is the total seating capacity of your restaurant? _____ Persons

3. Do you serve alcoholic beverages?   ❑ YES   ❑ NO (Go to Question 5)

4. What percentage of your business' gross volume is generated through beer/wine/liquor sales?_____

5. Do you accept reservations?   ❑ YES   ❑ NO

6. Is your establishment accessible to persons with handicaps?   ❑ YES   ❑ NO

7. What is the average check per customer? (excluding alcoholic beverages, tax, and tip)

    Breakfast $ _____   Lunch $ _____   Dinner $ _____

8. List number of banquet rooms (if any) at your establishment and total banquet capacity:

    # Rooms _____   Capacity _____

9. Please list your operating hours for each day of the week you are open. (Indicate days closed with an X.)
    Monday _____ to ____   Wednesday _____ to _____   Friday _____ to ____   Sunday _____
    Tuesday _____ to ____   Thursday _____ to _____   Saturday ____ to ____   to _____

10. Approximately how many customers do you serve each month? (Indicate closed months with an X)
    _____ January   _____   _____   _____   April
    _____ February   _____   _____   _____   May
    _____ March   _____ June   _____ September   _____   Over ➜

11. What percentage of your business is conducted on: Weekdays _____% Weekends _____%

12. What percentage of your guests are residents of your county? _____%

13. Are brochures highlighting community attractions available at your establishment? ❏ YES ❏ NO

14. Which of the following most accurately describes the location of your primary competitors?
    (Check all that apply)

    ❏ Local community ❏ Local county ❏ Surrounding counties
    ❏ Your state ❏ Adjacent states ❏ Other

15. Please indicate current and projected average employment:

    Full-time employees: Current #_____ Projected # (next year) _____
    Part-time employees: Current #_____ Projected # (next year) _____

16. Do you employ more people in the summer or winter, or is your employment figure fairly constant?

    ❏ More in summer ❏ More in winter ❏ Fairly constant

17. Can your staff give accurate information, including directions, regarding community attractions?

    ❏ YES (Go to Question 20) ❏ NO (Go to Question 18)

18. Would you be willing to have your employees attend a hospitality/tourism training class?

    ❏ YES (Go to Question 19) ❏ NO (Go to Question 20)

19. Would you be willing to pay a fee to cover the costs for your employees to attend a hospitality/tourism
    training session? ❏ YES ❏ NO

20. Do you currently participate in community organizations to promote tourism? ❏ YES ❏ NO

21. Are you willing to participate in community organizations to promote tourism? ❏ YES ❏ NO

22. Are you planning any additions or renovations within the next 12 months? ❏ YES ❏ NO

23. If YES, what do you plan to do?

    _____

    _____

24. Who is your primary target market?

    ❏ 25–50 years ❏ Families w/ children ❏ Local residents
    ❏ 50 + without children ❏ Business/convention ❏ Other _____

25. How do you currently market your business? _____

26. Please provide comments about how tourism impacts your business:

    _____

Assessment 9.3: Retail/Services Economic Survey

Your responses to this survey will be used to assess the current economic impact of tourism within our community. We ask for your name and address solely for the purpose of compiling a complete inventory of visitor services. All of your responses will be strictly confidential and used only to develop an overall profile of visitor services provided and associated economic impact. If you have questions, please contact the person who distributed this survey to you. Thank you for your assistance!

BUSINESS NAME: _____

CONTACT: _____ *PHONE:* _____

ADDRESS: _____

CITY: _____ *STATE:* _____ *ZIP:* _____

1. Which one of the following most accurately describes your business?

    ❑ Gift/souvenir shop   ❑ Factory outlet   ❑ Auto/gas station   ❑ Other retail sales
    ❑ Craft/antique shop   ❑ Food/gourmet shop   ❑ Services (misc.)   ❑ Other: (specify)
    ❑ Clothing store   ❑ Sporting goods   ❑ Professional services   _____

2. What do you consider to be the most important factor(s) leading to the success of your business?

    ❑ Quality product   ❑ Diversity of selection   ❑ Rare/unique items   ❑ Other: (specify)
    ❑ Customer service   ❑ Price of goods   ❑ Location   _____

3. Please list your operating hours for each day of the week you are open. (Indicate days closed with an X.)

    Monday _____ to _____   Wednesday _____ to _____   Friday _____ to _____   Sunday _____
    _____

    Tuesday _____ to _____   Thursday _____ to _____   Saturday _____ to _____   to _____

4. Are your operating hours consistent year-round or do they fluctuate according to seasonal demand?

    ❑ Consistent year round   ❑ Seasonal (explain)_____

5. What is the average purchase per customer? $ _____

6. Is your establishment accessible to persons with handicaps ?   ❑ YES   ❑ NO

7. Do you have public rest rooms?   ❑ YES   ❑ NO

8. Approximately how many customers do you serve each month? (Indicate closed months with an X)

    _____ January   _____ April   _____ July   _____ October

    _____ February   _____ May   _____ August   _____ November

    _____ March   _____ June   _____ September   _____ December

9. What percentage of your business is conducted on: Weekdays_____% Weekends_____%

    Over ➔

10. What percentage of your customers come from:

Local community _____%   Local county _____%   Outside the county _____%

11. Is information highlighting community attractions available at your establishment? ❑ YES   ❑ NO

12. Which of the following most accurately describes the location of your primary competitors? (Check all that apply)
     ❑ Local community   ❑ Local county   ❑ Surrounding counties
     ❑ Your state   ❑ Adjacent states   ❑ Other _____

13. Please indicate current and projected average employment figures:

Full-time employees   Current #_____   Projected # (next year)_____

Part-time employees   Current #_____   Projected # (next year)_____

14. Do you employ more people in the summer or winter, or is your employment figure fairly constant?
     ❑ More in summer   ❑ More in winter   ❑ Fairly constant

15. Can your staff give accurate information, including directions, regarding community attractions?
     ❑ YES (Go to Question 18)   ❑ NO (Go to Question 16)

16. Would you be willing to have your employees attend a hospitality/tourism training class?
     ❑ YES (Go to Question 17)   ❑ NO (Go to Question 18)

17. Would you be willing to pay a fee to cover the costs for your employees to attend a hospitality/tourism training session?   ❑ YES   ❑ NO

18. Are you willing to participate in community organizations to promote tourism? ❑ YES   ❑ NO

19. Are you planning any additions or renovations within the next 12 months?   ❑ YES   ❑ NO

20. If YES, what do you plan to do?

_____

_____

21. How do you currently market your business?

_____

22. Would you support community-wide retail and/or tourism promotional events? ❑ YES   ❑ NO

23. Please provide any additional comments about how tourism impacts your business:

_____

_____

Your responses to this survey will be used to assess the current economic impact of tourism within our community. We ask for your name and address solely for the purpose of compiling a complete inventory of visitor services. All of your responses will be strictly confidential and used only to develop an overall profile of visitor services provided and associated economic impact. If you have questions, please contact the person who distributed this survey to you. Thank you for your assistance!

BUSINESS NAME: _____

CONTACT: _____ *PHONE:* _____

ADDRESS: _____

CITY: _____ *STATE:* _____ *ZIP:* _____

1. Which one of the following most accurately describes your business?
   - ❑ Amusement park
   - ❑ Museum/gallery
   - ❑ Event/festival
   - ❑ Historical attraction
   - ❑ Arts/cultural attraction
   - ❑ Outdoor recreation/park
   - ❑ Entertainment (list)_____
   - ❑ Sports attraction (list)_____
   - ❑ Other (list) _____

2. What do you consider to be the most important factor(s) leading to the success of your business?
   - ❑ Quality product
   - ❑ Customer service
   - ❑ Authenticity
   - ❑ Price
   - ❑ Uniqueness
   - ❑ Location
   - ❑ Other (specify)
   _____

3. Please list your operating hours for each day of the week you are open. (Indicate days closed with an X.)

   Monday _____to _____   Wednesday _____to_____   Friday _____ to _____   Sunday _____
   _____

   Tuesday _____to _____   Thursday _____ to_____   Saturday _____ to _____   to _____

4. Are your operating hours consistent year-round or do they fluctuate according to seasonal demand?
   - ❑ Consistent year round
   - ❑ Seasonal (explain)_____

5. What is your basic admission fee per person?

   $_____Adult $_____Children $_____Seniors   _____No admission fee

6. Are brochures available at your establishment for other community attractions?   ❑ YES   ❑ NO

7. Is your establishment accessible to persons with handicaps?   ❑ YES   ❑ NO

8. Do you have public rest rooms?   ❑ YES   ❑ NO

9. What is your estimated monthly attendance? (Indicate closed months with an X)

   _____ January   _____April   _____July   _____October

   _____ February   _____May   _____August   _____November

   _____ March   _____June   _____September   _____December   Over ➜

10. What percentage of your business is conducted on: Weekdays _____ %   Weekends _____ %

11. Please estimate the percentage of your customers who come from OUTSIDE the county: _____ %

12. Of your visitors from outside the county, what percent would you estimate are from:

    Within the state _____ %   Out of state _____ %   Other countries _____ %

13. Which of the following most accurately describes the location of your primary competitors?
    (Check all that apply)

    ❑ Local community   ❑ Local county   ❑ Surrounding counties
    ❑ Your state   ❑ Adjacent states   ❑ Other _____

14. Please indicate current and projected average employment:

    Full-time employees: Current # _____   Projected # (next year) _____

    Part-time employees: Current # _____   Projected # (next year) _____

15. Do you employ more people in the summer or winter, or is your employment figure fairly constant?

    ❑ More in summer   ❑ More in winter   ❑ Fairly constant

16. Can your personnel give accurate information, including directions, regarding community attractions?
    ❑ YES (Go to Question 19)   ❑ NO (Go to Question 17)

17. Would you be willing to have your employees attend a hospitality/tourism training class?
    ❑ YES (Go to Question 18)   ❑ NO (Go to Question 19)

18. Would you be willing to pay a fee to cover the costs for your employees to attend a hospitality/tourism
    training session?   ❑ YES   ❑ NO

19. Are you willing to participate in community organizations to promote tourism? ❑ YES   ❑ NO

20. Are you planning any additions or renovations within the next 12 months?   ❑ YES   ❑ NO

21. If YES, what do you plan to do and how will it increase or change your ability to cater to tourists?

    _____

    _____

22. Who is your primary target market?

    ❑ 25–50 years   ❑ Families w/ children   ❑ Specialty travelers

    ❑ 50+ without children   ❑ Group tours   ❑ Other _____

23. How do you currently market your business?

    _____

24. Please provide any additional comments about how tourism impacts your business:

    _____

Chapter 10
Infrastructure/Appearance

The appearance and infrastructure of a community are important factors for both residents and visitors. They impact the quality of life for residents and the quality of the visit and/or perceptions of the tourist about the community. Assessing and upgrading the elements of your community's infrastructure and attractiveness for tourism not only establishes a solid foundation for tourism development, but benefits your citizens.

Infrastructure

One of the first areas of dissatisfaction for both residents and tourists as tourism develops is insufficient infrastructure. Communities need to anticipate how tourism will impact public services and take steps to reduce negative impacts before they occur. The inventory and the assessments in Chapter 6 will help the community accomplish this.

WHAT'S IN THIS CHAPTER?

• Infrastructure
• Appearance

10

Accommodating increased traffic is often one of the first challenges. Streets become jammed with traffic; parking areas can't handle the demand from RVs, buses, and cars with trailers and boats; intersections are snarled. If traffic trouble isn't resolved, residents can easily become disenchanted with the growing tourism industry.

Communities should begin addressing potential impacts of tourism on roads and traffic patterns long before problems arise—as long as 20 years in advance. There are many possible ways to prevent or alleviate problems. Shuttle buses and temporary parking may help meet intermittent needs created by attractions. Downtown parking pressure may be eased by using areas behind Main Street buildings for parking and adding back-door entries to shops. Highway engineers and consultants can help find ways to improve traffic flow.

If your community is pursuing international tourists, you also need to consider factors such as transportation linkages, safety and security issues, and communication needs. You may need to provide visitor information or signage in a foreign language.

Appearance

Community appearance is important in forming positive visitor opinions. It is also a source of pride for local residents. Appearance sets a community apart from other destinations and projects an image of what the community thinks of itself.

Visitors are influenced by the community's appearance at several points during their visit. A first impression is often made at the gateway to your community or along the road as the visitor approaches your community. First impressions are hard to overcome, so it is important that you make a positive one! Travelers are also greatly influenced as they move through the community, particularly in areas of high visitor use such as attractions, hotels, restaurants, retail areas, and public rest rooms.

Every community has its own individual character. The goal is to develop the community's visual appeal in a way that enhances its existing character and maintains a strong community identity. Attention to detail and compatibility are fundamentals in guiding improvements to community appearance. Concentrate on improving areas used by both residents and visitors first to get the most impact.

Two strategies to implement community appearance goals are:
- Review or inventory opportunities to improve community appearance. Focus on areas of the community where visitors travel or stop.
- Take a gradual approach to community improvement, beginning with simpler, smaller, less costly activities, and adding more difficult projects later. Small, immediate improvements will build pride and encourage further improvements.

Appearance as Attraction

The physical appearance of your community can serve as the main attraction. This is especially apparent in many small communities where unique Main Street programs have captured national attention. Towns like Telluride and Grand Junction, Colorado; Sedona, Arizona; and Viroqua, Wisconsin, are just a few examples. Visitors travel to these communities from all over the world to experience their uniqueness. In many cases the natural physical environment of the community—mountains or scenic roads—adds to the appeal. There are many assistance opportunities for communities, including the National Main Street Center, which offers technical assistance, research, and information to communities seeking preservation-based commercial district revitalization. More information can be found at the group's Web site, www.mainstreet.org.

Another popular example is the development of tourist towns along scenic highways and byways all across the United States. Such travel routes are designated for their unique natural physical appeal, and small towns along the route are well positioned to capitalize on the resulting tourist traffic, if they retain their unique character and authenticity over time. Popular scenic byways that have stimulated tourism communities include the Blue Ridge Parkway through North Carolina and Virginia.

Is your community on an already-designated scenic highway or byway, or on a road that could be so designated? Such designation—formal or informal—can boost visits to your community.

Through communications with successful scenic highway program administrators and members of the conservation community, Scenic America has produced six recommendations for developing local scenic highway programs or designating a new scenic highway corridor. These steps should be taken to protect the scenic, historic, and cultural characteristics of scenic highways. Table 10.1 summarizes these recommendations.

Contact the National Scenic Byways Program:
1200 New Jersey Ave., SE
HEPH-30
Washington, D.C. 20590
1-800-4BYWAYS (1-800-429-9297)
1-202-366-1586

Blue Ridge Benefits

Scenic byways can be beneficial in many ways—helping to protect the natural resources and the cultural authenticity, and bringing economic benefits to nearby communities. Visitors spent $1.8 billion in counties adjacent to the Blue Ridge Parkway, according to a study by researchers at North Carolina State University. These expenditures resulted in more than $147 million in tax revenue and supported more than 74,614 jobs in the region. (Brothers, Gene, and Rachel Chen. 1996. *1995–96 Economic Impact of Travel to the Blue Ridge Parkway, Virginia and North Carolina*. Raleigh: North Carolina State University. As cited on the Scenic America Web site, www.scenic.org.)

10

Table 10.1: Recommendations for Developing a Scenic Highway Program

- Develop a corridor management plan. The plan should identify natural resource protection zones and future development zones. It should also include a visual inventory and viewshed map identifying important scenic, historic, and cultural resources to be protected; commercial and residential site development requirements and design guidelines; and guidelines for roadway reconstruction and roadway safety improvement.

- Establish a tree protection policy. The policy should prohibit clear-cutting of trees immediately adjacent to the roadside but allow clearing of vegetation to create or restore obscured scenic views if identified in the corridor management plan.

- Establish visual pollution controls. Prohibit new off-premise outdoor advertising structures other than approved, uniform motorist information. Set limits on size, height, and number of new on-premise signs. Prohibit or buffer junkyards, gravel pits, mines, etc., within the scenic corridor viewshed.

- Establish a system of uniform motorist information and directional signage such as those currently in use in Maine and Vermont.

- Identify sources of funds for acquisition of scenic easements in key resource protection zones. In order to protect certain critical parcels within the scenic viewshed, you may need to acquire scenic easements or purchase critical "gateway" parcels along the corridor.

- Purchase development rights or scenic easements when expanding or constructing new roads.

Beautification and Community Image

A good starting place for improving community appearance is with facility and landscape maintenance. Clean up the grounds. Control litter. Repair or replace parts of buildings, fences, roads, sidewalks, and other structures that have become old or worn out. Paint structures and spruce up lawns, gardens, trees, and shrubs.

Focus on creating compatibility and attention to detail.

Begin by identifying appearance needs. This may seem simple, but residents often take their community's appearance for granted. Some ways to get a new look at your surroundings:

- Have residents tour your community, looking at it as though they were visitors arriving for the first time.
- Ask visitors about your community's appearance — what they like, what bothers them, and how appearance could be improved.
- Get opinions from professionals — architects, historical experts, landscapers, artists, students of design.
- Photograph or videotape your community and have groups analyze the views you capture.

A clean, attractive community:

- Promotes pride in a neat, beautiful hometown
- Reflects the kind of people who live there
- Provides a pleasant and desirable place to live and raise a family
- Is attractive as a place for retirement
- Invites tourists to visit and stay
- Attracts people who want to relocate their business to the community
- Exists in harmony with the natural beauty that surrounds the community
- Increases property values
- Conveys an asset instead of a liability to future generations

Getting Started

Improving community appearance doesn't have to be complicated or expensive. It can begin with simple projects that can be accomplished by a small group working on its own. Civic, business, youth, and church groups, as well as garden clubs, often volunteer to help with community appearance projects. State or local historical societies can help with historical restorations. Tourism groups may be a source of assistance. Many states have programs to get professionals or students into the community as volunteers to help prepare a community beautification plan.

Prioritize your needs. Focus first on main areas, especially those used by both residents and visitors, in order to get the most impact. Table 10.2 suggests areas on which you may want to concentrate.

Table 10.2: Beautification Priorities for Tourism

High Priority Areas	Low Priority Areas
• highway and freeway service areas • community entrances • attraction and travel corridors • attraction settings • unique features • waterfront areas	• parks and natural areas • public restrooms • downtown and retail shopping areas • motel, restaurant, and entertainment areas • residential areas • industrial, wholesale, and warehouse areas • rail and trucking yards • schools
(Note: low priority areas may need to be addressed if located within major travel corridors or historic/cultural areas.)	

10

18 Ways to Improve Community Appearance

✔ Eliminate trash and accumulated junk, eyesores, old signs, and graffiti.

✔ Mow or control weeds on streets and ditch banks early in the season and during the summer before weeds become large.

✔ Grade unpaved streets and ditch banks.

✔ Repair or replace nonfunctional, bent, or dilapidated traffic signs, street signs, trash receptacles, benches, and fences.

✔ Periodically paint homes, porches, fences, benches, storefronts, parks, and public facilities.

✔ Remove debris from streets and develop a street-sweeping plan.

✔ Screen objectionable sights, such as junkyards and gravel pits, with landscaping, fences, and trees—or relocate them to a less prominent area.

✔ Formulate a community street tree-planting policy and initiate a planting program.

✔ Develop creative designs for community entrances, public trails, public waterfront, scenic highways, or streets.

✔ Control storage of boats, recreational vehicles, trucks, or other large equipment in street and yards.

✔ Create a lighting plan for special features (e.g., statues, fountains, monuments, trails).

✔ Protect special features, create historic zones, and buffer areas around key attractions, such as waterfronts.

✔ Obtain public access for waterfront areas.

✔ Develop hiking and biking rights of way and trails.

✔ Control sign and billboard proliferation. Adopt a community signage plan. Consider instigating a uniform logo sign program and eliminating billboards.

✔ Develop a plan to eliminate overhead wires in downtown and other areas.

✔ Develop a scenic easement plan and purchase or obtain scenic easements.

✔ Develop a scenic highway program.

Chapter 11
Human Resources

Tourism can provide good jobs for all skill levels. It also can provide many volunteer opportunities. To make the most of tourism, a community must make a special effort to develop its human resources.

Workforce Development

Tourism does not just bring minimum wage jobs. It offers a variety of employment opportunities, from front-line service in hotels, retail shops, and attractions, to professional management. According to the U.S. Bureau of Labor Statistics, median annual wages of lodging managers were $45,800 in 2008, with the highest 10 percent earning more than $84,270.

Tourism benefits the community when jobs are filled by local citizens. When planning tourism, be sure to assess employment needs and opportunities, match the skills required to the local potential labor pool, and identify training resources.

Tourism businesses and communities need to look to the broader community for employees and offer a workplace that accepts diversity and provides opportunities for education and training. By partnering with schools and colleges, local businesses can provide internships and hands-on training for youth. School-to-work programs can help businesses by helping prepare a pool of new workers who understand the needs and expectations of business. For youth, understanding the diversity of opportunities in tourism can build enthusiasm and career interests while they learn transferable work skills.

Retirees are another potential source of workers. These individuals have years of work experience and skills to share, and part-time or seasonal jobs often meet their needs and lifestyles. Check with your community senior programs. In many communities, the Service Corps of Retired Executives (SCORE) program offers small business counseling.

WHAT'S IN THIS CHAPTER?

- **Workforce Development**
- **Hospitality and Customer Service**
- **Working With Volunteers**
- **Volunteering in America**

11

Local colleges and Extension offices and state offices of education, trade, and economic development can provide assistance with workforce issues and trends.

One of the primary issues in tourism employment is seasonality. Most tourism areas experience fluctuations in demand. During peak travel seasons, employment opportunities in tourism can double or triple—far exceeding the capacity of the local labor market. Table 11.1 offers ideas on how to find and retain workers that can help you meet seasonal demand.

Table 11.1: Ideas for Recruiting and Retaining Employees

- Reorganize jobs to allow more part-time work.

- Recruit minorities, retired people, international students.

- Find ways to use less labor (e.g., switch restaurant to buffet, cafeteria, or family-style service).

- Recruit more extensively (e.g., arrange internships with universities, colleges, high schools).

- Advertise jobs more widely or start earlier in the season.

- Recruit over the Internet.

- Provide more training to prepare employees for the position and for advancement.

- Offer job sharing.

- Learn and use motivational and team-building skills.

- Develop incentives for length of service (e.g., end-of-season bonus).

- Develop motivational programs with nonmonetary rewards.

- Raise wages.

- Offer wage incentives for completing training programs (these could be offered within the community, and sponsored by business groups).

Community Spotlight

Filling Seasonal Needs

Valleyfair! amusement park in Shakopee, Minnesota, is only open during the summer. The park fills its needs for hundreds of seasonal workers by working with local schools and colleges to recruit staff. It also uses the Internet to recruit employees regionally and from around the globe. For more information, see www.valleyfair.com.

Hospitality and Customer Service

Service is not as much about good actions, as it is about good feelings—creating them in others, and experiencing them within. It is not so much about 'doing,' as it is about 'being'; being one's best, being one's higher self.   —Anonymous

Creating a welcoming atmosphere for visitors is an integral part of the tourism industry. For communities willing to make a serious commitment to customer service and hospitality, rewards can be enormous.

Keep hospitality and customer service in mind at all times. Managers and workers need to be taught and regularly reminded about the

importance of hospitality and customer service skills—especially if worker turnover is high. Consistent, high-quality service doesn't just happen; it must be planned, taught, and implemented.

Hospitality skills are centered around:
- Maintaining a service attitude, even in trying situations;
- Understanding how people communicate, not only with words, but also with body language and tone of voice;
- Recognizing key moments when your response will have an important impact on the visitor's impressions; and
- Practicing good hospitality habits:
    - Make a good first impression;
    - Communicate clearly;
    - Know what your job is as it relates to visitors;
    - Know your community;
    - Handle problems effectively; and
    - Make a good last impression.

Quality Service

Quality service is good business. Good service benefits both residents and visitors!

Good customer service starts with management. In businesses, management must ensure that the systems, marketing, and operational elements of the business are geared to meeting and exceeding customer expectations. Quality service is not just a few staff practicing hospitality skills; it should be infused throughout the business or community.

Quality service is defined by the customer. Business and public leaders need to ask customers to help identify the components of quality service that matter to them, identify the key contact points within each business and the community that can affect customers' perceptions, then act upon customers' suggestions.

Policies should provide guidance and support for staff to handle problems, respond to emergencies, and satisfy customer requests. Service standards not only provide guidelines for employees, but also provide a tool for evaluating how well you are meeting customer needs. Training, motivation, reward, and a teamwork orientation all support quality.

Every resident, not just tourism employees, can affect a visitor's perception of your community. Everyone needs to use good hospitality skills, to show pride, to keep the community clean, to know about community, to be willing to help visitors. Building pride and community spirit will benefit your tourism development. Think about hosting citizen FAM tours or having competitions to "spruce up" the community. Brainstorm other ideas.

11

Customer service and hospitality training programs are available from both public and private sources. Restaurant, hotel, and retail trade associations and many chain businesses have training programs. Private consultants offer a variety of programs. University Extension and vocational training programs and state tourism offices often have training or educational materials that teach basic skills in customer service, hospitality, and understanding visitor needs.

Look for programs that your local groups can conduct themselves and integrate into the community. Be sure to include training about the local community—attractions, activities, and services—as well as a bit of history and culture of the area. Trainees can pass the information along to visitors.

Working with Volunteers

Because volunteerism is so important to tourism, volunteer management is critical to keeping a tourism program competitive. The individual in charge of volunteer management is responsible for everything from identifying volunteer needs to recruiting, training, supervising, and recognizing volunteers. The following pages examine volunteer management practices that will assist your community develop an effective volunteer program.

Why Volunteer?

Effective volunteer management begins with understanding who volunteers, why they volunteer, and how they volunteer. There are many reasons why people volunteer to share their time and effort. The different motivations require different management techniques. It is important to recognize the different reasons motivating volunteers and make volunteer assignments accordingly.

> People tend to support that which they help to create. —Unknown

> A volunteer is a person who believes that people can make a difference—and is willing to prove it. —Anonymous

Table 11.2 provides some ideas on volunteer motivations. Use these ideas to help you place volunteers in a way that creates win-win experiences for volunteers and organizations.

Table 11.2: Motives for Volunteering

Achievement Motive

— needs opportunities for success, excellent performance, innovation
— looks for unique accomplishments and can be competitive

Select tasks that:

- Allow latitude in setting work pace and methods
- Challenge the volunteer's abilities and skills
- Provide the opportunity to learn new materials and skills
- Require a high degree of performance
- Provide clear and unambiguous feedback on performance

Affiliation Motive

— works with others for personal interaction and friendship
— wants to be liked and respected

Select tasks that:

- Let the volunteer interact with others
- Require cooperation from other volunteers
- Allow time for social interaction
- Provide for stable working relationships

Altruism Motive

— pursues the general good or public interest
— strong sense of values and justice

Select tasks that:

- Involve developing goals and generating commitment from residents and organizations
- Address identifiable community goals and needs
- Involve other groups with similar goals and values

Recognition Motive

— wants recognition for work
— may prefer short-term tasks with clear beginning and end

Select tasks that:

- Can be completed in a short time
- Are visible to others in the group or to the community at large
- Are newsworthy
- Offer tangible rewards (e.g., plaques, citations, announcements)

Power Motive

— likes to influence programs and policies
— may have strong need and ability to supervise or lead

Select tasks that:

- Allow opportunity to direct co-workers and make changes
- Allow time for personal interaction while working
- Require dealing directly with tourism committee or manager
- Allow personal control over work pace and methods
- Require managerial skills

Adapted from Greger, G., & Yandle, E. (1983). *Volunteer program training guide and volunteer for Minnesota: Trainer's manual*. St. Paul: Minnesota Office of Volunteer Services.

Recruitment

A good volunteer recruitment program is important to the maintenance of a volunteer program. Recruiting takes time and effort up front, but will help you find new volunteers and improve volunteer commitment and quality programming.

Key items include:

- A well-planned recruitment effort, targeted at recruiting people with skills your community needs. Use several different recruitment methods to solicit volunteers.

- Up-to-date volunteer applications providing information that will enable you to match volunteer interests with program needs.

- Development of a recruitment package to make available to potential volunteers. This package should include potential volunteer jobs, the functions of the organization and other important volunteer information.

- Job descriptions that reflect the needs of your tourism program. Today's volunteers are interested in shorter assignments.

- Assignment of committee members to solicit volunteers for assignments from community residents (80 percent of the people who don't volunteer list as the primary reason that they were not asked!).

- Solicitation of special groups (e.g., youth, the elderly, students, unemployed seeking re-entry into the job market) and organizations for volunteers.

- Use of local media to help advertise your community's need for volunteer service.

- Recruitment efforts renewed every year. It helps your community recruit new volunteers and prevents burning out your existing volunteers.

- Follow-through. The long-term success of a volunteer program depends on follow-through in all aspects, including job descriptions, appropriate placement, orientation and training, supervision, recognition, and continual evaluation.

Volunteer Job Description

A written job description is an important part of a volunteer program because it helps committees organize and plan for the role of volunteers in your tourism program. It also helps the volunteers understand their duties and responsibilities and can be used as an agreement between the volunteer and community organization.

A job description is valuable because it:

- Defines the job and tasks a volunteer is asked to perform
- Clarifies the duties and responsibilities of the volunteer in relation to the tourism committee, its chair, and hired personnel
- Helps the volunteers understand their time commitments and duties
- Enables the tourism manager or committee to plan, organize, and distribute the work load among volunteers
- Helps the tourism manager or committee set the standards and expectations for volunteer work
- Assists recruiting and screening of volunteers
- Identifies volunteer training needs
- Helps to avoid misunderstandings between the volunteer and tourism committee or manager
- Aids in supervision because duties, expectations, and timeliness can be outlined in a job description
- Correcting volunteer job performance is easier because standards are in writing
- Makes it easier to identify management problems and make adjustments, if necessary

Volunteer job descriptions should be short, one-page descriptions to help your community organization and volunteer understand what is expected of the position. The job description should include:

1. Job title

2. Purpose of the job

   - Need for the job
   - Nature of the job

3. Responsibilities and duties

   - Each duty and job responsibility (be specific)
   - Tasks in terms of quantity, quality, and timing (this becomes the performance standard)

4. Requirements and qualifications

   - Background and qualifications needed for the job
   - Skills, knowledge, and abilities needed to perform this job
   - Specific training or qualities needed for the job
   - Training that will be provided (includes the nature, specific content, and approximate hours for orientation and training)

11

5. Time commitment

- Hours per week the job will take
- Time of day
- Days of the week
- Length of the job commitment

6. Reporting responsibilities

- Name, location, and telephone number of the person in charge of the activity
- Person to whom the volunteer reports progress
- Relationship of the volunteer to other committee members or volunteers
- Schedule of feedback on performance

7. Benefits to the volunteer

- Skill development
- Letters of recommendation
- Compensation—expenses, awards, etc.

The job description can become a valuable management tool for your community organization. It can be used in the following ways:

- *Recruitment.* Use the job description when recruiting volunteers.
- *Contractual.* Have the volunteer and committee chair or manager sign the job description to act as an agreement between your organization and the volunteer.
- *Self-evaluation.* Ask the volunteers to use the job description to report their progress on the job duties.
- *Checkpoint.* Check with the volunteer on a regular basis to review job duties completed.

How can the job description help the tourism committee or manager?

- It helps organize work and is useful for recruiting volunteers.
- It helps the supervisor manage problems of work performance. You can focus on the job description, rather than personalities.

Orientation and Training

Community volunteers are usually the individuals making front-line contacts with the public. If volunteers are not well trained and supervised, and do not feel involved with the community or organization, the quality of volunteer services and the organization's products will suffer greatly. Time spent on training and orienting volunteers and on planning for ongoing communication will pay off in quality of volunteer product and production. It will also pay off in volunteer retention.

Key items to consider in an orientation are:

- Organizational history;
- Purpose of the organization, its role in tourism development, the project to which the volunteers are assigned, and the individual role of the volunteer;
- Staff and volunteer lists and the administrative structure of the governing body, including responsibilities to the public, clients, and governing body;
- Fund-raising policies, funding sources for the project, and procedures for asking for funding decisions;
- Volunteer policies as they relate to safety, insurance, etc.;
- Volunteer policies as they relate to volunteer rights, duties, and chain of command;
- Tour of the job sites of the volunteer;
- Review of the volunteer job descriptions;
- What to do in case of an emergency; and
- How the volunteer will be informed about organizational activities and policy changes.

Supervision

Supervision provides volunteers with guidance and helps them coordinate their activities with other volunteers. Supervision also helps with feedback, so the volunteers know that the job is being performed properly and that they are contributing to the overall goal of the organization. Following are the rights and responsibilities of both volunteers and organizational managers.

11

The volunteer has a right to:

- Be treated as a co-worker, not just as free help
- Have a suitable and worthwhile assignment
- Be kept informed about the organization's programs, policies, and activities
- Participate in the activities of committees and organizations
- Be asked to be part of the organization's planning efforts
- Have safe working conditions
- Receive guidance, direction, and training
- Be recognized and rewarded for volunteer efforts

The volunteer has a responsibility to:

- Accept only realistic assignments
- Follow through on job assignments and deadlines
- Respect confidences
- Follow the rules and guidelines of the organization
- Keep the organization informed about his/her volunteer activities
- Respect professional attitudes and methods used by the organization

Management has the right to:

- Decline the help of unacceptable volunteers
- Expect that volunteers will communicate with committees and managers
- Expect volunteers to keep their commitments and meet deadlines

Management has the responsibility to:

- Provide an accurate job description
- Know the limitations of volunteer assignments
- Treat volunteers as co-workers with acceptance and trust
- Prepare volunteers for their assignments and provide training if necessary
- Give the volunteer significant tasks
- Keep volunteers informed about the activities and policies of the organization
- Give volunteers feedback on their performance
- Recognize and reward volunteer efforts
- Manage the volunteer program in an efficient, effective, and professional manner

Evaluation

Evaluation is a valuable tool for improving the product and avoiding future problems. Evaluation is frequently ignored by communities because people feel they may not have the skills or that it takes a special effort to complete this activity. Evaluation, planned as a part of the volunteer management program, does not have to be difficult, but is critical to the creation, maintenance, and retention of a good volunteer program.

> Questions to ask before conducting an evaluation:
>
> - Who needs the information?
> - Why do they need it?
> - How will the results be used?
> - What information is needed and what questions should be asked to get this information?
> - Who will gather the information?
> - How many resources will be needed to complete an evaluation?
> - When is the evaluation needed?

Ideas to help collect information and feedback from volunteers:

- Make a folder for each volunteer job. Ask the volunteers to write comments about their work and place them in the folder for future reference by other volunteers.

- Hold exit interviews with a select group of volunteers. These personal interviews can gather data that are difficult to obtain from surveys.

- Ask an individual from another community to evaluate your community's volunteer program.

- Have a member of the tourism committee visit volunteers while on the job. It will help identify needs in training, supervision, communications, or other problems that can detract from the tourism program.

Local tourism programs cannot be maintained without volunteers, which are a community's most valuable resource. Failure to draw up and implement a comprehensive volunteer management program will detract from developing an effective tourism development program. The enthusiasm, energy, and commitment levels of your volunteers can be maintained if they are consulted and treated with respect.

Recognition

Simple recognition may be the difference between keeping and losing volunteers. Recognition is often forgotten because it occurs after the activity is completed and everyone is tired. In a small community, organization managers may be very familiar with the volunteers and are in contact with them all the time. It is easy to forget a "thank you" under these conditions.

Planning for recognizing volunteers must be an integral part of volunteer management.

A good recognition program can:
- Reduce turnover rate among volunteers.
- Provide information to others in the community on a volunteer's commitment to the community.
- Encourage others to volunteer.

A good recognition program should be:
- Honest. Do not recognize false achievement.
- Sincere. Avoid overproduced recognition.
- Consistent. Do not recognize some and not others.

Ways to Provide Recognition

- Give personal praise in public and in presence of peers
- Send notes of thanks and certificates of appreciation
- Ask volunteers' advice (only if you are willing to follow good advice)
- Include volunteers in important meetings
- Recognize volunteers in the media
- Ask schools, businesses, or churches to recognize members' efforts
- Conduct special award programs
- Invite volunteers to special events or training sessions
- Provide letters of recommendation
- Provide buttons, T-shirts, or identification pins

Reference

U.S. Bureau of Labor Statistics. (2010). Lodging managers. *Occupational outlook handbook, 2010-2011 edition*. Retrieved August 5, 2010, from http://www.bls.gov/oco/ocos015.htm#earnings

Volunteering in America

- A total of **63.4 million volunteers**, or 26.8 percent of the adult population, contributed 8.1 billion hours of service in 2009.

- The hours of service provided by volunteers were **valued at $169 billion**, or $20.85 per hour.

- The **volunteer rate increased in 2009** to 26.8 percent, up from 26.4 percent in 2008.

- The increase was primarily driven by **higher volunteer rates among women**, especially women ages 45-54. The volunteer rate of women increased from 29.4 percent in 2008 to 30.1 percent in 2009, while the volunteer rate for men, at 23.3 percent, was essentially unchanged.

- **By age**, 35-to-44-year olds and 45-to-54-year-olds were the most likely to volunteer in 2009. Their volunteer rates were 31.5 percent and 30.8 percent, respectively. Volunteer rates were lowest among people in their early 20s (18.8 percent) and those age 65 and over (23.9 percent).

- Volunteer rates were higher among **married persons** (32.3 percent) than those who had never married (20.6 percent) and those with other marital statuses (21.5 percent). **Parents** with children under 18 were substantially more likely to volunteer than were persons without children under 18 years of age—34.4 percent compared with 23.9 percent.

- Americans report that being **asked to volunteer** makes a difference in their willingness to give their time. About 44 percent of volunteers report becoming involved after being asked to volunteer, most often by someone in the organization to which they are contributing their time. A slightly smaller proportion, 40.9 percent, became involved on their own initiative.

Source: Corporation for National and Community Service. (2010). *Volunteering in America 2010.* Retrieved July 29, 2010, from http://www.volunteeringinamerica.gov/

Note: The Corporation for National and Community Service and the Bureau of Labor Statistics (BLS) are federal agencies that partner to collect Volunteering in America data through the Current Population Survey's (CPS) annual Supplement on Volunteering, which is conducted every September. The CPS, in turn, is a monthly survey of about 60,000 households (approximately 100,000 adults), conducted by the U.S. Census Bureau for the BLS.

11

Chapter 12
Funding

Effective and competitive tourism programs need local funding. Tourism planning and marketing organizations, government, and nonprofit organizations need money to develop public services and attractions for visitors. Small businesses need financing to create tourism jobs and provide incomes for community residents. This chapter will help you develop fuel for the engine—financial resources needed to implement a community tourism program.

Tourism Funding Areas

Successful community tourism programs require strategic funding in four key areas:

WHAT'S IN THIS CHAPTER?

- Tourism Funding Areas
- Funding Strategies

Tourism Organization Support

Tourism organizations develop and implement tourism projects and activities, and often handle marketing as well. Funding provides the resources they need to do their job. Stable and adequate funding is needed to maintain a tourism program over time.

Small Business Development

Small businesses provide jobs and income from the tourism industry. Commitment of local businesses and bankers to developing new businesses and expanding existing businesses is important. Communities will need to commit time and effort to assist the business sector as a part of a successful tourism program.

Infrastructure/Attraction Improvement

Local governments must provide public facilities and investments to meet visitors' needs. Communities often lack the infrastructure or attraction improvements needed for a strong tourism program.

12

(continued)

Plan such improvements carefully to avoid costly mistakes. A tourism improvement program allows you to plan improvements in an effective sequence, initiate funding and development plans, and plan for long-term maintenance of improvements.

Festivals and Events

Festivals and other public events develop community solidarity and help strengthen the community attraction base. Developing means to recover costs of events will reduce the need for annual funding requests to local organizations, improve the event's financial base, and make managers more sensitive to the marketplace.

Funding Strategies

Over the years tourism planners have developed a variety of strategies for funding each of these four areas of tourism development. Following are some common strategies that others have found successful:

Tourism Organization Support

Most communities have an organization, such as a convention and visitor bureau, chamber of commerce, economic development committee, or nonprofit tourism committee, that hires professionals to help organize, develop, and market a tourism program. Following are a few of the key methods used to finance these organizations.

- Organization dues

  Membership dues are a common method of financing tourism organizations. Some charge flat fees to all membership. Many have a sliding fee scale based on number of employees or gross revenue. Sliding fees can usually generate more funds and are considered more equitable, since larger businesses can afford higher fees.

- Local government

  City or county governments are often asked to contribute to the operation of tourism organizations. The ability of government to tax constituents provides more accessible resources, especially for small communities. However, governmental bodies may not wish to provide support over a long period.

- Selling advertising

  Some tourism organizations sell ads in their brochures, magazines, flyers, and other marketing materials. This method ensures that those who benefit pay.

Developing a Funding Base

Developing and maintaining a reliable funding base is one of the more difficult tasks faced by a community tourism organization, small business, or festival. Most entities that fail do so because they did not go through a planning process to define realistic financial goals and objectives and develop an implementation plan. Use these ideas to improve funding success:

• Develop an action plan

As part of your development and marketing plans, you have identified funding needs and resources. These plans will be helpful in approaching funding sources. It is difficult to solicit funds without a well-defined plan of action. Before groups or individuals contribute, they need to know the details of the proposed program, the overall goals and objectives of the organization, and how the project will help meet those goals. Planning can also help you focus your efforts and achieve results in a timely manner.

• Start small

Many organizations attempt to start a tourism program with large and complex projects that take considerable time to develop. Communities and businesses that start with simple projects that can be completed within six months begin developing a track record of successes. Funding support is easier to obtain once successful projects are completed.

• Diversify funding sources

Successful organizations rely on several sources for funds. Select funding sources that can generate adequate funds and begin efforts to develop special funding sources. (e.g., a lodging tax to fund a tourism organization). One common mistake is to spend major effort on a funding program that simply cannot produce the funding needed.

• Use grants or gifts for start-up

Grants and gifts often provide the resources to begin projects. Generally, smaller projects with a definitive timeline, clear outcomes, and clear benefits to the community are viewed more favorably than larger, less specific projects. Maintain clear records of grant and gift usage so you can report to the granting agency.

• Cultivate relationships with potential funders

Don't wait until you have a proposed project and are looking for funds to approach funding sources. Identify potential funding sources, meet their managers, and learn about their programs and funding policies ahead of time.

• Move toward self-sufficiency and stability in funding

Grants and voluntary contribution funding strategies are not reliable long-range funding methods. Develop funding sources that can be counted on year after year to generate the needed funds. In the long run, the community and tourism businesses must provide most of the funding.

Ingalls family, "Little House on the Prairie." Today, almost 30 years after the show ended, thousands of travelers visit Walnut Grove annually. Most of them come in the summer when the community stages the Wilder Pageant, a family-oriented drama based on Laura's life in Walnut Grove, over three weekends in July.

In addition to the pageant, the community created a small museum in response to the TV show and continues to build its collection of period items and Laura memorabilia. Walnut Grove's website at www.walnutgrove.org provides information on the community, the pageant, the museum and other attractions, including a Family Festival, lodging, campsites, and historically accurate sod houses at Sanborn, Minnesota.

Everything a visitor needs to arrange a visit to Walnut Grove is housed on the website, including the ability to order pageant tickets and information about the Wilder Museum, the Ingalls dugout site, the Family Festival, unique shopping, lodging, camping, a Walnut Grove map and much more. And if you want to learn even more about Laura and her family, the website includes links to Ingalls and Wilder historical locations around the country. It's all a festival for Laura lovers.

- Lodging taxes

  Charging room or bed taxes to help finance marketing efforts is common. A tax of 1 to 5 percent is levied against room sales for hotels, motels, and B&Bs. Often there are both lodging and sales taxes charged on lodging. Lodging taxes are not always dedicated for tourism uses, and the laws governing them vary greatly from state to state. Check your state laws for details.

- Donations and gifts

  Communities often ask state organizations, larger businesses and organizations, and foundations for grants to help them start or expand a tourism program. Such gifts are usually of a limited duration and should be used only for special start-up program costs. Funding sources may be found both inside and outside the community.

- Earned income

  Organizations can generate income from a variety of sources, such as space rental at buildings or festivals, administrative services of the organization, advertising sales, ticket sales, vendor fees, or sale of retail goods such as books, T-shirts, and pins at events or visitor centers.

- Food and beverage taxes

  Organizations or governments levy special taxes or find unique funding sources to help finance tourism marketing projects.

- Free publicity

  Third-party endorsement and recommendation from travel writers, travel agencies, meeting planners, and news feature stories don't actually raise money, but they can highlight an area without cost to communities.

- Voluntary contributions

  Tourism businesses volunteer to pay a set fee or a percentage of gross sales to help finance marketing. This can be classified as a "fair share" method of voluntary assessments.

- Matching funds

  State tourism departments, foundations, and corporations sometimes provide matching grants to help communities finance innovative marketing or develop new industries. Many allow matched funds—those the organization must come up with—to be in the form of "in-kind" services (e.g., staff time, mailings, printing) rather than cash. Applications detailing the proposed use of the funds are required, and often funds are granted at

certain times of the year. Check with your state tourism office and regional development groups for information.

- For-profit business operations

  Communities own or operate businesses that create profits (e.g., by selling shirts, caps, and other retail goods).

- Special district levies

  Communities create special taxing or development districts that levy taxes.

Use Worksheet 12.1 to identify potential funding sources that may be viable for your organization. Consider multiple funding sources to provide stability and sustainability.

Small Business Development

Small communities often have difficulty attracting, developing, or expanding tourism-related businesses. Business development requires entrepreneurs (people willing to risk their money to start up or expand into a new area), community support, financial assistance, and help from professionals acquainted with problems of small businesses. Small businesses are financed mainly through five sources of funding:

- Personal savings

  Most banks or individuals will not lend the total amount needed to purchase a business and provide operating expenses. Entrepreneurs generally need to use savings and assistance from friends and relatives to provide initial financing to start a business.

- Debt financing

  Most individuals approach a bank, credit union, or savings and loan first for funds for business start-ups and expansions. Other frequently used forms of financing are contracts for deed and personal notes from friends and relatives. Debt financing is most frequently based on the ability to pay the interest and repay principal from the profits of the business, and often depends on the development of a good business plan.

- Equity financing

  Equity financing refers to the resources offered by individuals or institutions to help start or expand a business. Equity financiers offer to take the same risks as the business owner and expect to receive some reward from the profits of the company. Most small business equity financing comes from personal savings or from money provided by family or friends.

12

- Government or nonprofit programs

  Some small businesses qualify for financing programs managed by federal, state, and local governments. Examples are federal loans from the Small Business Administration and U.S. Department of Commerce, state loan or grant programs, or local revolving funds designed to help business start-ups and expansions.

- Business profits and retained earnings

  Most existing businesses finance at least part of their expansion from profits. Expansion through this method may be slower, but it places all control in the hands of the business owner.

Other financing options include loans from suppliers on attractive repayment schedules, loans from life insurance policies, deposits from customers, and loans from small business development companies.

For More Information

U.S. Small Business Administration, 409 3rd St., S.W., Washington, DC 20416; 800-U-ASK-SBA; www.sba.gov; or local offices in your state.

Seminars on economic development financing, The National Development Council, 51 East 42nd St., New York, NY 10017; 212-682-1106; www.ndc-online.org.

Infrastructure/Attraction Improvement

Public services cost money. Funding needs may be minimal (e.g., for cleanup projects) or major (e.g., for new highway projects).

Who should pay for public services needed for tourism development? There is no simple answer to this question. Many public services benefit residents and tourists alike. In addition, funding affects control. If funding comes exclusively from tourism-related sources, tourism industry leaders will wish to have a great influence over public tourist service decisions. If funding comes from both tourism and nontourism sources, other sectors of the community will likely want to share control.

Table 12.1 lists some key steps you can take to build support for funding public services and to identify funding roles.

Table 12.1: Strategies for Building Funding Support for Public Services

1. Set up meetings of tourism leaders and local officials (mayors, councils, planning commissions, county leaders, area planning boards and organizations, etc.) Establish ongoing communications to keep public officials informed about tourism activity and to listen to the concerns and interests of the public.

2. Delineate public, private, and joint public/private tourism roles. Obtain community input as needed. Determine how leadership will be provided for joint roles: Will the public or private component be the overall leader? Will leadership be split for individual functions?

3. Coordinate with local officials to identify and prioritize public tourism projects and activities. Assist as needed in developing and implementing selected projects.

4. Discuss general funding issues with local political and industry leaders:
   - Funding strategies for ongoing tourism operations and facility maintenance
   - Funding for specific tourism development projects
   - Supervision, control, and reporting procedures for public funds used in joint operations
   - Incentive and development strategies to encourage local investment

12

The issue of how to finance large, complex projects (e.g., development of a tourism information system, trails, or a public art display; downtown improvements; a major land purchase) is encountered at some point by most communities. Projects may range from a few thousand dollars to millions. They are usually one-of-a-kind physical improvements not easily financed by annual budgets. Communities use a variety of funding methods to finance such projects. Most-used methods are:

- General revenue bonds

  The local government sells municipal revenue bonds and pays principal and interest from project revenue.

- Private investment

  Private investors finance the project. However, they may ask for public help with financing, zoning, or public utilities and services.

- Grants or loans

  State, federal, or private foundation grants or loans are provided for a specific program or project. Costs funded are usually major acquisition, building, or development costs that occur once in the project's lifetime.

- Government financing

  City and county governments use their financing and taxing powers to provide funds for projects. Recreation areas and parks are usually funded by government.

- Local fund-raising

  Local organizations ask citizens and civic and social organizations to help fund projects.

- Development of a nonprofit corporation

  A nonprofit corporation is formed to finance projects. The corporation may sell shares or memberships and take out loans.

- Venture capital funds

  Venture capital funds finance large projects. Commercial venture capital funds expect sizable returns if the project is successful. Local venture capital funds are formed to help develop small businesses and community projects.

- Debt or equity financing

  Lending institutions provide debt financing, or individuals invest their own monies to become part owners of the project.

- Revolving loan funds

  Local governments or nonprofit economic development groups create revolving loan programs that provide low-interest loans for projects. When funds are repaid, additional loans are made. Funds may come from a variety of sources, including foundations, state government, banks, or local groups.

- Special funding methods, tax incentives, and tax increment financing

  Economic development professionals help communities organize several funding strategies into a package.

- Grants and gifts

  Monies are made available by state and federal agencies, foundations, and corporations for one-time costs.

- Sales tax

  Communities enact sales taxes to help fund projects.

- Local foundations

  Communities create local foundations, solicit funds to create an endowment, and fund projects through the interest from the endowment. This is an excellent way to develop long-term funding.

12

Tips for Project Financing

- **Learn from other communities' successes and failures.**

  Has another community completed a similar project? Learn about how it handled financing and management. This may give you valuable ideas for your project.

- **Have an outsider evaluate the feasibility of the project.**

  Projects often fail due to poor planning and evaluation of the basic project idea. A critical review of your project by an outside evaluator can help identify major problems.

- **Determine if the project will improve your attraction base or increase jobs and income for your community.**

  Projects that fail to fit into your overall community tourism development plan and do not add to the economic base of your community will be difficult to maintain.

- **Select an organizational structure appropriate to the project.**

  Every organization has strengths and weaknesses. Evaluate your project to determine which local organization has the skill to complete it.

- **Don't underestimate the funds needed to complete the project.**

  Lack of adequate funding can doom a project. Ask tourism or finance professionals to help your community develop realistic financing plans.

- **Select the appropriate financing tools.**

  Choose tools that will provide adequate monies and can be repaid with revenue generated by the project.

- **Develop a financing plan.**

  The plan should outline which funding tools you will use and how you will fund the maintenance of the project, and detail how your community will repay the debt.

- **Use multiple sources of funding involve community, government, and business.**

  Most projects require more than one source of financing. Multiple sources of financing will provide a more stable funding base. Projects that include the broadest set of potential partners and gain strong community support have the best chance for funding and success.

- **Leverage community resources with other sources of funding.**

  Many funding sources do not wish to take the total risk for a project. Cost sharing is frequently used to distribute the risk among funding sources.

- **Separate operating and project development expenses.**

  Project development expenses are usually one-time expenditures needed to complete a project. Operating expenses (costs needed to keep the project functioning) are often financed through funds generated by the project. Over the lifetime of a project, the operation and maintenance cost will be much larger than the development costs.

- **Evaluate the risks.**

  All projects have some risk of failure. Careful review of risks can help you design a better project, plan for risks, and reduce the chance of failure.

- **Consider a public-private partnership for your project.**

  Public sector and private business cooperation is an excellent strategy for reducing the risk of project failure and ensuring long-term viability. Private businesses are flexible and can keep up with market conditions if the project relies on project revenues to fund the debt.

Adapted from: Kinsley, M. (1997). *Economic renewal guide* (3rd ed.). Snowmass, CO: Rocky Mountain Institute.

For More Information

Kinsley, M. (1997). *Economic renewal guide* (3rd ed.). Snowmass, CO: Rocky Mountain Institute. Institute website: www.rmi.org

North Central Regional Center for Rural Development. (1990). *Take charge: Economic development in small communities.* Ames, IA: Iowa State University. NCRCRD website: http://ncrcrd.org/

Festivals and Events

Festivals and events are excellent tools for developing and expanding a tourism industry. Funding usually comes from local government, chambers of commerce, or businesses. As a community festival develops and expands, organizers should think about ways to charge for events so the festival becomes self-supporting.

Definitions

Event - a temporary occurrence, planned or unplanned.

Special Event - a one-time or infrequent event outside the normal program or activities of the sponsoring or organizing body.

Festival - a public, themed celebration.

Source: Getz, D. (1997). *Event management and event tourism.* New York, NY: Cognizant Communication Corporation.

A variety of techniques have been used to raise money for festivals, events, and other community activities. Among them:

- Fees

  Many festivals charge fees (e.g., vendor fees, parking fees, admission fees, contest entry fees) to help cover basic costs. While fees may generate substantial revenue, they may also limit participation for those unable to pay them.

- Sponsorship

  Event sponsors—public or private sector organizations willing to provide cash or in-kind support in exchange for product placement, publicity, or other considerations—are a major and growing source of festival revenue. Sponsors must be chosen carefully, however, to ensure compatibility with the goals of the event. The larger the sponsor's contribution, the greater its potential influence on the festival or event.

- Sales

  Items such as buttons, T-shirts, and mugs can be sold as part of a festival. One disadvantage is that the festival assumes the loss for unsold items. Also, the needed sales force and sales outlets increase administrative costs.

- Miscellaneous

  Funding strategies for festivals and events are limited only by the creativity of the event organizers. Special fund raisers, raffles, and assessments can also produce revenue. However, they

lack long-term sustainability, may be hard to organize, and they may cost more in terms of time and effort than the value of the cash they bring in.

Many people think of financial resources only in terms of cash. Other types of resources to consider are:

- In-kind contributions such as printing and donated goods or services
- Volunteer time of employees or managers
- Free or reduced-price equipment
- Free public-sector services
- Earned income from festival sales

Five Tips for Event Fund-Raising

1. Know the purpose of the event and how fund-raising ideas fit into it.

2. Develop a plan for the event, including funding.

3. Refresh your fund-raising skill. Raising funds for events is different than raising funds with events. Remember the three rules for fund raising:
   - People give to people
   - Friends give to friends
   - Peers give to peers.

4. Research funding sources early.

5. Evaluate the event regularly.

Funding and other basics of organizing, managing, and operating festivals and events are covered in the Festival and Event Management program offered by the University of Minnesota Tourism Center. For more information, see www.tourism.umn.edu.

Worksheet 12.1: *Thinking about Funding*

Answering the following questions will help you identify and tap funding sources.

1. What are potential local sources of funding? (e.g., organization dues, local government, selling advertising, lodging tax, donations and gifts, earned income, food and beverage tax, voluntary contributions, matching funds, special district levies, retail sales)

2. Will the funding source generate adequate income for our tourism efforts?

3. What problems will we encounter in "selling" the funding idea?

4. Which groups need to support the idea?

5. What administrative procedures or legal actions are required?

6. How will our organization develop plans to justify the need for these funds?

7. How will we keep community groups and citizens informed about our programs?

8. What is our long-range funding plan?

Chapter 13
Maintaining Tourism Vitality

As tourism grows in your community, it will bring both benefits and costs that need to be addressed. Your tourism organization, industry, and government will want to build monitoring and management into your tourism development plans to ensure that tourism maximizes the economic, social, and environmental benefits while minimizing negative impacts for both the community and the visitor.

The processes, tools, and assessments discussed throughout this manual establish a foundation for monitoring and management. Fostering community-wide participation in the tourism development process and building a solid development plan that incorporates local values and creates short-term and long-term strategies are fundamental to successful tourism management. So too are using research, creating effective marketing, and building local human and business resources. Reviewing your tourism plan and periodically updating the information will allow you to assess changes, make adjustments, and anticipate the effects these changes may have on your community.

WHAT'S IN THIS CHAPTER?

- **Tourism Management**
- **Crisis Management**
- **Conclusion**

Tourism Management

Tourism management is not about limiting growth, but ensuring that it is aligned with the community's values and interests, protective of natural and cultural resources, and economically viable. Effective tourism management builds profitability while protecting the resources upon which it depends.

There is no single formula for managing tourism, nor is any single person or organization solely responsible. Your tourism management strategy should address community goals, reflect the character of your community, and respond to local conditions. It may include setting standards, establishing regulations, and integrating principles of sustainability into public and private aspects of tourism. Open com-

13

munication and collaboration in managing the various aspects of tourism gives residents, government, and businesses an active voice in your collective future.

Monitoring

Effective monitoring establishes systems for gathering, storing, and comparing information. It is an important function of tourism management. It helps your community and local tourism industry know if it is achieving the benefits expected from tourism, or if undesirable effects are developing. It allows you to gauge progress, identify issues, and adjust management strategies to accommodate change, unexpected occurrences, and developing trends. Systematic monitoring of quantity and quality changes provides important information you can use to make decisions that will help you maintain tourism vitality.

Monitoring is carried out in many ways and for many purposes. You may find you have many monitoring mechanisms already in place. For example, businesses and tourism organizations generally count inquiries and visitors to gauge the effectiveness of advertising campaigns. They track occupancy rates as a basis for staffing and other management decisions. Tourism organizations monitor residents' attitudes through local forums and town meetings to get a sense of concerns before they become major issues. They also use other monitoring and evaluation methods to guide marketing decisions.

Visitor satisfaction is essential to maintaining tourism vitality. As visitor numbers grow, it is valuable to carefully monitor the quality of the visitor experience. Many tourism businesses use guest surveys. You might conduct annual visitor satisfaction surveys (e.g., during events or peak travel season) and share the results with residents. Contact local or regional resources such as your Extension service, local colleges, or your state office of tourism for assistance in developing and conducting surveys.

Other monitoring ensures compliance with zoning ordinances, building codes, laws, tax regulations, and environmental standards. Such monitoring generally is the responsibility of government.

Tools for monitoring tourist volume (e.g., traffic counts, state park usage) may already be in place. You can work with local, county, or state transportation departments to access this information. Comparing these over time can provide a quantitative picture of growth.

To establish a monitoring system for your tourism development efforts, begin by identifying aspects of your community that may be particularly vulnerable to changes from increased tourist visits. These may be economic, social, or environmental. Next consider your community's values. How are these factors currently monitored? Who currently collects the information? Does it measure changes sufficiently? Can current monitoring methods attribute changes to specific sources (e.g., tourism versus other industry)? Use Worksheet 13.1 to help you identify current monitoring efforts.

As you develop tourism, you have the opportunity to develop new monitoring and evaluation systems. Build in mechanisms for determining whether tourism is generating the intended benefits, and whether or what adjustments need to be made in your development plan.

Table 13.1 suggests some specific areas you may want to monitor as part of your community's tourism development effort.

Indicators

Indicators are tools for measuring information that can be used to guide tourism management decisions. Most indicators are quantitative (e.g., counts, sizes, rates of change). They measure economic, social, or environmental conditions (e.g., GNP, population, ozone levels). Indicators can identify key types of information tourism managers need to monitor in order to measure changes over time.

In 1993, the United Nations World Tourism Organization (UNWTO) began developing indicators for sustainable tourism. Since then, a subset of core indicators has been developed for use by tourism decision makers at the local, regional, and national levels. These core indicators constitute the base level of information recommended to manage sustainable tourism in any destination. Supplementary or destination-specific indicators also have been developed so individual communities can monitor impacts unique to specific sites. Table 13.2 lists the core indicators for sustainable tourism adopted by UNWTO. Take some time to consider how you can adapt these indicators for your community.

For help in developing local indicators:

United Nations World Tourism Organization. (1996). *What tourism managers need to know: A practical guide to the development and use of indicators and use of indicators of sustainable tourism.* Madrid, Spain: UNWTO. Website: http://www.ustravel.org/

Hart, M. (1999). *Guide to sustainable community indicators* (2nd ed.) North Andover, MA: Hart Envrionmental Data. Website: http://www.sustainablemeasures.com/

13

Table 13.1: Possible Targets for Systematic Monitoring

Economic
Accommodation occupancy rates
Number and types of tourist facilities and attractions
Attendance records at attractions
Number of visitors
Tourist expenditures
Amount of benefits accruing to locals
Level of tourism employment
Business development and expansion

Social
Effect on lifestyles and community activity
Tourism role in conserving or revitalizing cultural traditions and customs (e.g., arts, crafts, belief systems, ceremonies)
Attitudes and perceptions of residents toward tourism

Physical
Congestion
Cleanliness
Water quality
Air quality
Noise
Ecological systems
Land use
Vegetation and wildlife
Monument conservation (historic and cultural)

Infrastructure
Transportation facilities and services
Utilities (water, electric, gas)
Waste management collection, treatment, and disposal
Telecommunications
Community health and safety facilities and services
Housing and community services for tourism employees

Tourism Image
Acceptable standards of quality
Perception of quality of product and services
Customer service quality
Level of tourist satisfaction
Repeat visitation levels

Marketing
Current markets
Visitor characteristics
Effectiveness of marketing campaigns
Match of market and product
Niche market opportunities

Table 13.2: Core Indicators of Sustainable Tourism

Indicator	Specific Measure
• Site protection	Category of site protection according to the World Conservation Union
• Stress	Tourist numbers visiting site (per annum/peak month)
• Use Intensity	Intensity of use in peak period (persons/hectare)
• Social Impact	Ratio of tourists to locals (peak period and over time)
• Development Control	Existence of environmental review procedure or formal controls over development of site and use densities
• Waste Management	Percentage of sewage from site receiving treatment (additional indicators may include structural limits of other infrastructure capacity on site, such as water supply)
• Planning Process	Existence of organized regional plan for tourist destination region (including tourism component)
• Critical Ecosystems	Number of rare/endangered species
• Consumer Satisfaction	Level of satisfaction by visitors (questionnaire-based)
• Local Satisfaction	Level of satisfaction by locals (questionnaire-based)
• Tourism Contribution to Local Economy	Proportion of total economic activity generated by tourism only
• Carrying Capacity	Composite early warning measure of key factors affecting the ability of the site to support various levels of tourism
• Site Stress	Composite measure of levels of impact on the site (its natural and cultural attributes) due to tourism and other stresses
• Attractiveness	Qualitative indicator of attributes that make a site attractive to tourism

Source: United Nations World Tourism Organization. (1996). *What tourism managers need to know: A practical guide to the development and use of indicators of sustainable tourism* (p. 9). Madrid, Spain: UNWTO.

What to Manage

Aspects of tourism that require monitoring and management are:

Progress

Managing completion and regular evaluation will help keep you on track with specific development projects. As part of your planning efforts, you should have established methods for monitoring and managing progress toward your community's overall development plan. Several of the forms in this manual are designed to help you monitor and evaluate progress of specific projects or actions.

Quality

Tourism management's goal is to balance the needs of your community and visitors in a way that provides long-term benefits for the community, and a quality experience for the visitor. Tourism businesses and communities can use performance standards—service levels, health and safety, environmental, architectural, and so on—to ensure a high-quality tourism experience. Government will set standards for health safety and comfort. Businesses set their own stan-

Community Spotlight

Travel Green

Travel Green Wisconsin is a voluntary program that reviews, certifies and recognizes tourism businesses and organizations that have made a commitment to reducing their environmental impact. Specifically, the program encourages participants to evaluate their operations, set goals and take specific actions toward environmental, social, and economic sustainability.

Travel Green Wisconsin was launched in 2007. Today over 280 businesses have completed the voluntary program.

13

dards for service, operation, and productivity. Tourism and community organizations can provide a forum for communication and collaboration to ensure a shared vision of quality.

Quantity

Your goal in developing tourism is to increase visitors and benefit from their spending. However, if the growth is too fast for the community, or inadequately planned, the effects can be negative. Quantity control helps you avoid exceeding your carrying capacity—the degree of development that provides the volume of tourism needed and expected without exceeding the real and perceived capacity of your community and the natural systems that sustain it to absorb change and growth. Decide what intensity of tourism is desirable for your community and consider possible quantity control mechanisms before you reach that level. For example, you might limit numbers of visitors to a sensitive recreation area or number of guests at an attraction, or set a seating capacity in a restaurant. Remember that capacities may change over time. Incorporate mechanisms to monitor and modify limits into your tourism management strategy to help ensure that tourism remains beneficial.

Location

Is your strategy to confine tourism to a specific area (e.g., a resort area around a lake or remote beach), integrate it into the heart of the town, or simply "let it happen"? Some location elements such as natural attractions or historic sites will help dictate some development patterns. Considering where tourism activities exist or will develop within the community will help to preserve the character and authenticity of the community as well as protect natural resources. Each community is different, and no single strategy is appropriate for all communities. Determine your community's strategy for tourism location early in your development planning. The questions about community values and vision in Chapter 1 can help you.

Financing

Careful management of financing efforts is critical to effective tourism development. Funding sources establish strict criteria and time lines that need to be managed with knowledge and care. Do projects have sufficient and appropriate financing? Review Chapter 12 for ideas. Communicate with local finance and government resources regarding specific project and development issues.

Management Methods

Tourism management can take many forms. Some management efforts are obvious—for example, restrictions on the number of visitors who can use an attraction at one time. Others are more subtle—for example, good planning that ensures that adequate transportation infrastructure is in place to handle increased volume generated by increased tourism.

Prevention

Obviously, the best way to deal with problems or negative impacts is to prevent them. Poor planning, inadequate design, and lax administration are often responsible for many of the unacceptable impacts attributed to tourists. Identifying and building in management strategies at all phases of tourism design and development is an effective means of prevention. Forethought rather than hindsight should guide tourism development.

Education

Education of both the visitor and the community is one of the most important methods of tourism management. Tourism awareness education provides visitors and residents with knowledge they can use to make the tourist experience in your community the best for residents, business, and visitors alike.

Most people want to be responsible tourists. Because tourism is an interactive experience, visitors who behave responsibly actually enhance their own experience.

Education can be built into the experience. For example, you can offer a nature hike at a resort, or offer simple tools designed to share information with tourists and generate responsible tourism. Many hotels offer guests the option of reusing towels and bedding rather than changing it daily to reduce the use of detergents and water.

For residents, education communicates that tourism has more than simply economic value. It engages them in the design and maintenance of your community's tourism product. Education also ensures a knowledgeable and trained work force to support tourism.

Communication

Establishing and maintaining communication among community residents, tourism managers, and government is an effective technique for fostering tourism vitality. Regular sharing of information through private and public channels will keep interested parties informed and up-to-date.

- Boundary Waters Canoe Area Wilderness total use permits
- Effective property tax rates by market value of property
- Age distribution of population
- Noise levels at various locations
- Public and private land holdings
- Land use permits issued by type of use
- Land use variances
- Average daily traffic volume at various locations
- Rare and endangered plant and animal species
- Five-year highway improvement plans
- Housing values
- Auto crash facts
- Arrests
- Earnings by industry
- Business starts and closures and related jobs for selected counties
- Labor force characteristics for selected areas in Minnesota
- Selected hourly mean rates
- Household income by interval
- Estimated economic impact of domestic travel in Cook County and Minnesota
- Visitor Center walk-up inquiries
- Comparison of median income for region and state
- Tax levy by district
- Source of county taxes

Source: University of Minnesota Extension Service and Humphrey Institute of Public Affairs. (1998). *Land use guide planning indicators for Cook County, Minnesota*. Minneapolis: University of Minnesota.

13

Limits and Regulation

Limits are frequently used to manage capacity and patterns of use. They can be set by businesses or government and be either voluntary or regulatory. Some limits are accepted more readily than others.

There are many examples of beneficial limits and regulations. Traffic signals help alleviate traffic congestion; campsite reservations prevent overcrowding. Public and private facilities may voluntarily restrict hours of use, behaviors (e.g., alcohol consumption), age of users, and so on for safety and visitor satisfaction.

A common example of limits is the maximum occupancy level established for facilities such as restaurants, sports centers, and amusement parks. Maximum levels are established by government regulation, but facility managers frequently monitor attendance, and may set lower maximums if they feel the users' satisfaction is being negatively affected.

Pricing strategies are a method of self-limit often used by tourism businesses. Pricing strategies include setting higher room rates or admission fees during peak seasons, and lower rates during less busy periods.

Fees can also be used to limit access and control usage to both protect the environment and enhance the tourist experience. Fees can be adjusted seasonally or by type of use (e.g., guided vs. self-guided tour). Both private attractions and public parks and facilities use fees to manage crowding and prevent overuse.

Some communities have used zoning and design regulations to guide the development of tourism areas and retain authenticity and cultural character. Your community should determine appropriate zoning and building regulations for both current and future needs.

Crisis Management

An important management function is being able to respond rapidly and effectively to the unexpected. A crisis can come in many different forms. It may be a drought, forest fire, lack of snow, pollution, or some other natural disaster. Some crises have a direct effect on tourists; sometimes there is little or no impact. Even if the crisis has no impact on the tourist experience, broad coverage of it can discourage visitors from coming to your area.

Before crisis strikes:

- Form a crisis team of a few individuals who can come together on short notice to handle a crisis if one occurs. This committee should coordinate its plan with your community's crisis planning committee.

- Brainstorm possible events and their potential negative impacts on the tourism industry. Develop a list of strategies for managing the impacts.

- Develop a backup communication plan. Have remote radios or cellular phones on hand and charged at all times at attractions and other places where tourists gather so you can communicate with emergency personnel and disseminate information to media, residents, and tourists in case of a crisis.

- Decide in advance where your crisis team will convene if a crisis occurs. Distribute a phone list to all team members with current numbers for emergency personnel, city officials, local media, and team members.

- Develop a media information plan to get your story out to the public. Target specific news media you think can have the greatest impact. Make sure your media list is always up to date.

When facing a crisis:

- Agree upon key points that affect tourism businesses. Statements to media and customers should present a similar message.

- Prepare fact sheets on the situation and what is being done to manage it. Distribute to tourism businesses and public information people. Do not make statements until facts can be verified!

- If the crisis could affect future tourism, ask local tourism businesses to help communicate your message to potential visitors. For example, if an amusement park is damaged by fire, local hotels could use their advertising to assure potential visitors that it is still in operation.

- Prepare information packets that tourism businesses can share with their customers. Keeping visitors informed in advance and while they are in your area will decrease anxiety.

- Keep your community well informed through newsletters, meetings, phone calls, and news articles. If residents handle the crisis well, it can help reduce visitors' concerns.

Crisis Management

The United States Virgin Islands Department of Tourism's national marketing firm, Martin Public Relations, successfully implemented an aggressive crisis communications plan before, during and after Hurricane Georges passed through the USVI in September 1998. With only a few days to implement a complete crisis communications plan, the firm worked to prevent long-term damage to the reputation of the territory's tourism industry which could have been caused by inaccurate and negative news reports. Martin PR communicated with dozens of contacts to ensure accurate information about the islands' condition was readily available to hundreds of news outlets, as well as the USVI's major travel partners. The USVI team consistently disseminated accurate information to spread the positive news about the territory's readiness to receive visitors.

(Adapted from U.S. Virgin Islands press release, July 2, 1999.)

Limiting Access to Wilderness

More than 1 million acres in size, the Boundary Waters Canoe Area Wilderness (BWCAW) in northern Minnesota contains hundreds of lakes and rivers, has 1,200 miles of canoe routes, is home to threatened and endangered species, and is visited by more than 200,000 people a year. It is the most heavily used wilderness area in the country. Entry permits are used to regulate entry to and use of the BWCAW in order to protect the resource and maintain a quality wilderness experience for tourists. For details on the entry permit program, visit www.bwcaonline.com.

13

Conclusion

Tourism is a growth industry and will continue to be a major influence globally. Tourism has the potential to be a valuable economic diversification strategy for communities. Throughout this manual we have presented strategies, tools, and worksheets to help your community develop tourism in a manner that is sustainable and beneficial. Tourism will bring change to your community because—unlike other industries—it brings people to the product (local attractions and services). Tourism's impacts will be more obvious in smaller communities because the visitors are obvious. As tourism increases, changes will occur.

Is there a saturation level for tourism development? Views on this question vary from person to person. Most will agree that rather than a question of saturation, tourism development should be based on individual resources, the inherent limitations of geography and environment, and, most importantly, the interests of the community. The more effort that is taken to make tourism grow in harmony with the interests of the community, the more satisfaction the community will have with tourism.

Directions: Use this worksheet to help identify current monitoring efforts in your community.

What	Measure used/method	Frequency	Responsible Agency

Appendix A
Case Studies

These communities are featured in a case study film available from the University of Minnesota Tourism Center.

A

Dahlonega, Georgia

Population: 4,950
Economy: Tourism, education, government, retail trade, and manufacturing
Employment: Tourism, education, service, government, retail, manufacturing
County: Lumpkin, population 27,000
Website: www.dahlonega.org

Quaint shops in Dahlonega's beautifully preserved downtown historic district are filled with regional art, antiques, and collectibles. Photo by Cynthia Messer.

Authentic Regional Experience

The city of Dahlonega is located in the foothills of the Blue Ridge Mountains in North Georgia, approximately 70 miles northeast of Atlanta. The county seat of Lumpkin County, Dahlonega has a permanent population of approximately 4,950. The name Dahlonega is derived from a Cherokee word for "yellow money" or gold and the city was named in 1883. The city of Dahlonega was the site of the first major gold rush in the United States in 1828–20 years before the California gold rush. A U.S. Branch Mint was located here from 1838 to 1861. North Georgia College and State University, founded in 1873 in the abandoned Mint Building, is one of six senior military colleges in the United States, with an enrollment of 6,000 undergraduate and graduate students.

Much of Dahlonega's downtown commercial district, including the public square and historic Gold Museum located in the former Court House, is listed on the National Register of Historic Places. The Gold Museum is the oldest public building in North Georgia and one of the most visited historic sites in Georgia. Dahlonega's Better Hometown Program was also accredited as a 2008 National Main Street Program for meeting the commercial district revitalization performance standards set by the National Trust Main Street Center.

Background

Dahlonega was first profiled in the 1991 National Rural Tourism Development Project because the community's tourism leaders had successfully positioned Dahlonega's unique historical, cultural and geographic assets to cater to the growing number of visitors looking for an authentic regional experience. That successful strategy is still in place.

"Thinking back to 20 years ago, tourism was doing well but probably somewhat in its infancy. It has evolved to have greater diversification," said Jimmy Faulkner, retired banker and long-time community leader. "The wineries that are now in Lumpkin County didn't exist 20 years ago. When you look around the town square, you don't see vacant buildings. Tourism has helped us keep those buildings occupied, helped us to keep people coming here."

In 1991, Dahlonega's tourism strategy focused on visitors from the state of Georgia and northern Florida. At that time, most visitors were using Dahlonega as the base for one- to two-week vacations, or were coming for long weekends. Initially, visitors traveled to Dahlonega for the gold history; the authentic, well preserved town square; and outdoor recreation and events.

Today, Dahlonega's focus is still primarily on visitors from Georgia and neighboring states, but the community has expanded its attraction base to appeal to new travelers. This includes wine tourism and the performing arts. Five locally owned and operated wineries have been established in the rich, fertile hillsides of Lumpkin County, creating a growing wine industry for the state and increasing visitor traffic in the region. Several venues in Dahlonega draw visitors seeking authentic blue grass music, and the historic Holly Theatre Community Center offers live theater productions, movies and concerts.

The history, arts and culture of Dahlonega are key elements of the community's tourism product. The historic downtown forms the centerpiece of Dahlonega's tourism. Dozens of retail shops and restaurants housed in buildings from the 19th century face the historic square with its beautifully preserved courthouse, which now houses the Gold Museum. These shops and restaurants cater to visitors with quality products and services – many produced by local artists.

The centerpiece of Dahlonega's square, the Courthouse Gold Museum offers visitors a look at the mining history of Georgia. Dahlonega's gold strike was the largest east of the Mississippi River. Most of the gold that could be mined economically has been mined, but the rich mining history remains. The courthouse was built with locally made brick that includes traces of gold, and it served as the seat of Lumpkin County

government from 1836 to 1965. It is the oldest existing courthouse in Georgia and was restored and adapted to its current use by the state of Georgia. Visitors can tour the museum, and the Chamber has created a "Gold Fever" package that includes admission to the museum and two gold mines and a chance to pan for gold.

Dahlonega's former courthouse, which holds the Gold Museum, is listed on the National Register of Historic Places. Photo by Cynthia Messer.

The outdoor recreational opportunities in the Dahlonega-Lumpkin County area also draw many tourists. Nearly one third of Lumpkin County is covered by the Chattahoochee National Forest. Visitors can go kayaking, tubing or fishing along the Chestatee River, and hunting, fishing, rock climbing, horseback riding, biking or hiking in a number of areas—such as

Amicalola Falls State Park. This popular state park is located approximately 20 miles from Dahlonega. The 729-foot Amicalola Falls is one of more than 30 waterfalls in the area. An eight-mile approach trail leads from the park to Springer Mountain, the southern end of the 2,135-mile Appalachian Trail.

One of Dahlonega's strengths over the years has been its proximity to major population markets. Chamber Director Amy Booker said, "We have great markets to draw from if you look at the three hour timeframe." Cities within that radius include Charlotte, North Carolina; Chattanooga, Tennessee; and Atlanta, which is accessible via Highway 400, designated Hospitality Highway. "Those are some great markets that we can draw from and continue bringing people," Booker noted.

Successes and Challenges

Dahlonega has successfully used its historical and natural assets to attract visitors from a well-defined geographic market. By offering a variety of events and retaining the authentic downtown character, the community has generated a strong repeat visitor industry. However, recognizing the advantage of bringing in new visitors, Dahlonega has enhanced existing attractions and encouraged new opportunities with wine tourism, the arts, and a growing interest in outdoor recreation.

Stephen Smith, Tourism Director for the Dahlonega-Lumpkin County Chamber of Commerce and Convention & Visitors Bureau (CVB), identifies four key targets for the community's marketing efforts: 1) cultural-heritage, 2) young families traveling for short distances or for weekends, 3) outdoor enthusiasts, and 4) wine aficionados.

The Chamber and CVB market Dahlonega to these target audiences through a variety of

means, including print media such as the visitor's guide, as well as electronically with a comprehensive website, Twitter and Facebook. Positive word-of-mouth and repeat visitors have been important as well. The CVB marketing efforts are funded by a 5 percent lodging tax. Said former CVB director Hal Williams, "The state of Georgia enacted the lodging tax in the mid-1990s. Dahlonega was one of the first communities to engage the tax and that was with the agreement of all of our lodging owners and all of our business owners. The Chamber of Commerce acts as the marketing agent for the lodging tax. The law says that 40 percent of the revenues from the state lodging tax must be used in conjunction with a marketing agency to promote tourism. Recognizing that tourism is the second largest business in Dahlonega, the county and city both have devoted 100 percent of that revenue to tourism which has made a big difference for us."

The Dahlonega General Store takes visitors back to an earlier, simpler time. Photo by Cynthia Messer.

Over the years, Dahlonega has evolved into a center for the performing and visual arts. Festivals are popular with tourists and help build communities. In 1991, Dahlonega hosted at least six large and successful events, including the Gold Rush, the Mountain Top Rodeo, the Mountain Flower Fine Art Festival and "An Old Fashioned Christmas Celebration." Several of

Lumpkin County is home to five vineyards that produce wine and cater to tourists. Photos by Cynthia Messer.

these were listed among the Top 20 Events in the Southeast and most were run by volunteers or civic organizations.

Festivals and events continue to be an important part of Dahlonega's tourism strategy, and the community hosts some type of event almost every month. Gold Rush Days remains a major event each October, bringing over 300 arts and crafts exhibitors and an estimated crowd of more than 200,000. New festivals and events are periodically added to this solid base. Targeting wine tourists, the Georgia Wine Country Festival was started in 2001 by the owners of Three Sisters Winery. A second wine event, the Georgia Fine Wine Festival on the grounds of Black-Stock Vineyards & Winery, is held on the same weekend. In 2010, a new festival, Georgia BluesFest, will be added.

"Being recognized as Georgia's festival community was a deliberate strategy," Williams said. "We do 16 festivals and major events every year and having volunteers step forward is really not a problem for us."

In 1991, Dahlonega's future plans for tourism development included the development of one of the still active gold mine areas into an attraction, building a golf course, and attracting upscale lodging and dining options. Today, Dahlonega has achieved those plans. The recently built Achasta Golf Course is a semi-private course offering limited public hours. Two gold mining facilities are now open as attractions, including Consolidated Gold Mines and the historic Crisson Gold Mine, a family-owned and operated business offering a gold panning experience and a gift store.

A full variety of dining and lodging options are available in Dahlonega from casual to upscale. More than three dozen dining establishments offer everything from fast food to fine dining experiences. Visitors can enjoy local fare, or choose from an eclectic variety of ethnic dining choices. Lodging options in Dahlonega-Lumpkin County include historic hotels, country inns, B&Bs, resorts, cabin rentals, camping and motels. The four limited-service chain motels and B&Bs in Dahlonega account for more than 300 rooms. The Chamber offers a searchable lodging database on its website.

One of Dahlonega's strengths is the retention of the authentic feel of its downtown. Visionary community leaders early on recognized the benefit of maintaining their unique historic buildings, and the entire downtown business district was placed on the National Historic Register in 1983. The downtown historic district reaches beyond the square, too, incorporating 22 blocks of businesses and residential property. This move has protected the downtown by limiting development and helped retain the cultural heritage that is attractive to visitors and residents.

Dahlonega's Gold Museum gives visitors a chance to pan for gold. Photo by Cynthia Messer.

"We use planning and zoning with our historic commission," said Mayor Gary McCullough. "They have control of our historic square and all of the historic sites in Dahlonega. So we have certain guidelines, color schemes, what you can do and what you can't do. Anyone who wants to do something on the square has to go before them and then the city council also, so you have two levels to go through before you can do anything on the square."

Shopping is a mainstay of the square, and wide brick sidewalks, baskets of flowers, historic lighting and benches invite visitors to spend time around the square. The Chamber operates a Welcome Center with a friendly staff and information on the community and tourism opportunities in the area. Numerous shops are filled with regional arts and crafts, décor and gifts. The Dahlonega General Store retains the traditional atmosphere of the original general stores created to serve the needs of the miners. Visitors are invited to "step through the door and step back in time" as they browse home-made fruit butters and preserves, old-fashioned candy, marbles by the pound, and wooden toys.

According to the city's 2008 downtown master plan, "While the community members treasure their historic heritage and want future plans to help preserve and protect it, they are also aware of the need to adapt to the demands of a growing population and the importance of providing a mix of uses toward the core. The city needs to link itself with its surroundings like the vineyards, trails, mines and mountains."

Dahlonega has tapped into the growing wine industry to expand tourism opportunities around the county. No wineries existed in Lumpkin County in 1991, but today the county has five vineyards that produce wine and cater to tourists. Located within a few minutes' drive of Dahlone-

A

ga, each of the wineries is unique and locally owned and operated. All five host wine-tasting opportunities, and several offer other tourism experiences—including summer music concerts, festivals, and wedding and meeting facilities. Several tasting rooms have also opened on the square in Dahlonega. These wineries are bringing a new group of visitors to the region and complement the traditional cultural heritage and outdoor recreation tourist markets.

"You have to be aware of what's going on around you—you can't get stuck," said business owner Dana LaChance. "In 1980 it was the Gold Rush town; it has been known for that since the mid-1800s. Then we embarked on 'discover Dahlonega, cool little town up in the mountains; step back in time.' We rode on that for five or six years, then the wineries started popping up. The wine, the arts and recreation have now become the new magnet for Dahlonega. You have to look for new ways to go, and be able and flexible enough to go there."

Growth Issues

"Tourism benefits the locals by keeping taxes low, [creating] a stable base here of employment and more importantly, property ownership and improvement," Faulkner said. These benefits help create a positive attitude and continued support for tourism on the part of residents. However, with the success of tourism over the last two decades, traffic and parking issues continue to be an issue, despite significant improvements. As noted, the historic main square is built around the courthouse, which is convenient for pedestrians but has required rerouting of traffic.

"Traffic was very much considered an issue 20 years ago. Every vehicle traveling north, south, east, or west had to come around [the courthouse]," Faulkner said. "Some 15 years ago, the

community started planning an east-west connector and there was a lot of outcry from merchants on the square. That connector became a reality 10 years ago, and the square has done nothing but boom. The Downtown Historic District continues to be the focal point for tourism."

The development of this connector by the State Transportation Department has enabled the community to direct development of other service industries away from the historic downtown.

The city also has taken other measures to address traffic and parking issues downtown. Non-commercial traffic now moves one way through and around the square, and public parking on the square is metered. The North Georgia College and State University built a 450-car parking deck for students adjacent to downtown

and allows visitors to use it after 5 p.m. and on weekends. This conveniently helps the city meet the needs of visitors during peak travel times.

Despite these steps, downtown infrastructure—including parking—remains a concern for the community, according to City Manager Bill Lewis. "Unfortunately, the way the community has grown has not been conducive to providing additional parking downtown," he said. "Growth we are experiencing in terms of tourism is creating some additional parking problems that we are going to have to address in the near future. Some of the ideas on the table for addressing parking was one of the issues addressed in our recent downtown master plan; there were recommendations made in there. I think it is going to require some cooperation and partnerships with the private and public sectors working together to accomplish that."

Lessons Learned

The city of Dahlonega has embraced tourism as a critical part of its economy, even citing it in the community comprehensive plan. The city, Chamber and community organizations actively work to maintain and attract tourism-related business. Dahlonega's tourism leaders also understand that providing a quality experience is critical to generating positive word-of-mouth and repeat visitors. The Chamber provides customer service training to businesses, and it continues to work with residents and businesses to maintain a positive attitude toward visitors.

Said Karl Boegner, owner of the Wolf Mountain Winery, "It is the experience and how you are treated when you get there, and the desire to want to come back, and the desire to want to speak favorably about where you have been. So our main marketing push is hospitality and that word-of-mouth marketing that comes from a good experience."

Dahlonega, like many other towns, has seen great benefits from tourism, but it has also experienced challenges. Tourism also means that there is added strain on the local infrastructure, especially downtown.

"We are well prepared for water/sewer services in the future," Lewis said. "However, tourism puts a pretty heavy stress on those services because [visitors] don't pay for those, so our people pay a little bit higher sewer and water rates because of the tourism activity downtown. On the other hand, tourism generates a lot of sales taxes, too, and helps keep everyone's taxes down. In our earlier years as we began to grow there wasn't a whole lot of emphasis put on future needs like parking, solid waste removal and those kind of things. We really have a problem with where to locate dumpsters for our downtown businesses. A lot of times we are asking people to walk several blocks to dispose of their trash. We need to address those kinds of things in the future."

Future Vision

Tourism is a significant part of the Dahlonega-Lumpkin County economy. Citing research in the 2005-2025 Comprehensive Plan and state figures for 2008, the Chamber of Commerce says tourism accounts for 300 jobs and approximately $37 million dollars in visitor spending. Dahlonega-Lumpkin County is well positioned to continue enjoying the benefits of tourism because of supportive and involved leaders and residents who have a strong appreciation for their community's assets. This has helped the community retain authenticity and local control and has enabled development of targeted marketing efforts matched to assets.

"Tourism will continue to be a major part of the Dahlonega-Lumpkin County economy so long as the leadership and the local people support it. I cannot envision that changing," said Jimmy Faulkner.

A

Persons Interviewed

Jimmy Faulkner
Retired banker and long-time community leader

Stephen Smith
Tourism Director,
Dahlonega-Lumpkin County
Chamber of Commerce & CVB

Amy Booker
Director
Dahlonega-Lumpkin County
Chamber of Commerce & CVB

Hal and Carol Williams
Former CVB Director & downtown business owner

Bill Lewis
City Manager
City of Dahlonega

Ben and Dana LaChance
Business owners
Appalachian Outfitters &
Crimson Moon Café

Doug Paul
Owner
Three Sisters Winery

Karl Boegner
Owner
Wolf Mountain Winery

David Harris
Owner
BlackStock Vineyards & Winery

Gary McCullough
Mayor
City of Dahlonega

Source ("Growth Issues"): Dahlonega Downtown Master Plan. (2008). Dahlonega, GA: Prepared for the City of Dahlonega and the Downtown Development Authority by Urban Collage, Inc., in association with PBS&J and Bleakly Advisory Group. Retrieved August 9, 2010, at http://www.cityofdahlonega.com/index.php?option=com_content&view=article&id=227:downtown-master-plan&catid=142:downtown-master-plan&Itemid=128

Sandpoint, Idaho

Population: 8,337
Economy: Tourism, timber, agriculture, retail trade, government, and manufacturing
Employment: Construction, retail, forest-related activities, agriculture, light manufacturing, finance, service jobs
County: Bonner, population 41,400
Website: www.sandpointchamber.org

Full-page color ad from the Idaho Official State Travel Guide.

Diverse and Distinctive Attractions

Sandpoint, the county seat of Bonner County, was established in the late 1800s in North Idaho on the northern shore of Lake Pend Oreille and at the foot of the Selkirk Mountains. The community has a strong history tied to the railways and timber industry. By 1910, Sandpoint was a thriving city with a population of 5,000.

Over the next 60 years, its timber-based economy experienced many ups and downs. By 1970, the population had dropped to 4,355. Then skiers, retirees, and young people looking for a rural, outdoor-recreation lifestyle began discovering North Idaho. The population increased 55 percent into the early 1980s, when a national recession dramatically slowed economic growth and the timber industry fell on hard times.

Newcomers and established residents alike realized that the economy had to be diversified; tourism was viewed as the quickest and most cost-effective way to do so. Blessed with a moderate four-season climate, Sandpoint has long been known as a hunting and fishing mecca and outdoor playground. Many people who visit later relocate to the area. Sandpoint's population increased from 5,203 in 1990 to 7,598 in 1998 and to more than 8,300 in 2009, according to U.S. Census data. During that same period, the Bonner County population increased 34 percent, from 26,622 to 35,226, and in 2009 climbed to over 41,000.

The attraction base in Sandpoint is diverse and distinctive. The most significant asset is Lake Pend Oreille, stretching 43 miles between the Selkirk and Cabinet Mountain ranges with 111 miles of shoreline. Known as one of the premier freshwater lakes in the United States, Lake Pend Oreille has a depth of 1,150 feet and beckons boaters, skiers, and anglers.

A

The lake and mountains are home to an abundance of wildlife, ranging from moose and goats to woodpeckers and bald eagles. Just 11 miles north of Sandpoint lies Schweitzer Mountain Ski Resort, ranked by *Snow Country* magazine as one of the top 50 ski resorts in North America. A four-season resort, Schweitzer boasts a 2,400-foot vertical drop spread over 2,900 skiable acres and serves as gateway to North Idaho's wilderness.

Downtown Sandpoint is the center stage for an eclectic mix of shops, galleries, and events that draw tourists year round. A major tourist attraction is Coldwater Creek, a national women's apparel retailer and mail-order giant. Across the street from the anchor store is the Cedar Creek Bridge, the nation's first passive solar shopping plaza.

Coldwater Creek store and mall interior.
Photo by Duane D. Davis © 1994.

Sandpoint has more artists per capita than any other town in Idaho and is nationally recognized as one of the 100 finest small arts towns in America. The Panida Theater, a historic community-owned vaudeville-era theater, hosts a wide variety of performing arts and fine art films, including national-caliber presentations. Music lovers flock to Sandpoint each year for the Festival at Sandpoint, a 10-day series of outdoor concerts. Hundreds of antique cars and thousands of rock-n-roll enthusiasts converge on downtown for the "Lost in the 50s" event. Other activities include the Idaho State Draft Horse Show International, and Timberfest.

Idaho State Draft Horse Show. Photo by Duane D. Davis © 1994.

Visitor services are abundant and varied. Lodging establishments include local and chain hotels, B&Bs, and guest ranches, as well as private vacation and condo rentals. Commercial lodging establishments in the immediate area provide almost 700 rooms. Vacation rentals and condos provide another 300+ units. More than 50 dining establishments serve fare to please any palate, including local seafood, fine dining, ethnic cuisine, and fast food. The area also has RV parks, campgrounds, and marinas. The Greater Sandpoint Chamber of Commerce estimates Sandpoint hosts 45,000 to 55,000 visitors per year.

While the community does not keep exact visitor counts, our 1991 profile estimated that 45,550 visitors stopped at the visitor center in 1990. That same year, skier days at Schweitzer Mountain were estimated at 150,000. That number increased to 160,000 in 1998 and to 217,000 skier visits in the first half of 2010. The Chamber reports that there are several weekends each year during which all lodging establishments are full and rooms are scarce.

Background

Sandpoint was profiled in the 1991 National Rural Tourism Development Project for its successful creation of an effective tourism organization and its year-round festival and events strategy. The Chamber of Commerce is the primary coordinating agency for tourism in the area. A board of directors oversees the work of several standing committees.

Sandpoint is accessed from the south by Long Bridge on Interstate 95, which crosses the west arm of the lake, or by Interstate 2 from Spokane, Washington. Interstate 90 runs east and west just 44 miles south of Sandpoint, while Interstate 95 is a major trade route to Canada. The city is also served by a private airport, bus services via North Idaho Community Express, and freight and passenger rail service, including Burlington Northern/Santa Fe, Union Pacific, and Amtrak.

Sandpoint is a popular stopover and drive-through tourist market capturing visitors on their way to Glacier National Park or the Canadian Rockies. A 1991 study found that Spokane is the area's primary year-round drive market, while most ski visitors are day-trippers from Seattle. "One advantage we have is a large population base in Spokane and Coeur d'Alene that view us as their backyard playground," said Amy Little, Executive Director of the Greater Sandpoint Chamber of Commerce. The area is also popular with Canadian visitors.

In 1991, tourism marketing was handled by the Chamber and the Resort Association, a loosely knit organization consisting of property owners, restaurants, attractions, arts groups, and other tourism-related businesses. Sandpoint's marketing and promotion strategy, begun in the early 1980s, focused primarily on creating a variety of events to draw tourists and on developing a cooperative marketing program. The community lacked one dominant player that could carry the local industry, and it had become clear that only by pooling resources could the community hope to achieve its tourism marketing goals. Under the umbrella of the Chamber of Commerce, the Resort Association began with a budget in 1984 of $12,000 to market Sandpoint in the winter. Its budget grew to almost $100,000 by 1991, including attendance at international trade shows to capture the Canadian tour bus market.

Welcome signage along I-95 North/Long Bridge into Sandpoint.
Photo by Duane D. Davis © 1994.

In the early 1990s, the Resort Association evolved into Destination Sandpoint!, a tightly knit organization with an executive committee and a tourism marketing manager. This entity became known throughout Idaho as a model tourism marketing organization. Destination Sandpoint! operated with a marketing budget of $125,000 generated solely from grant dollars from the Idaho Travel Council (ITC). In 1999, Destination

Sandpoint! received $80,000 in grant money from the ITC; the remaining $45,000 was a cash match from the county, generated by the return of 45 percent of the revenues from the state of Idaho's 2 percent lodging tax on the various travel regions.

The Chamber increased its emphasis on marketing existing attractions to visitors outside the state in the intervening years and used other community resources to support festivals and events. The name Destination Sandpoint! was later dropped and the organization has been restructured as a committee within the Chamber. Today, the Recreation and Tourism Council has 13 appointed positions representing various sectors of tourism. These positions are renewed or filled annually.

According to the Chamber website, the council's charge is "to promote tourism in the Greater Sandpoint area, particularly for the benefit of our Visit Sandpoint members, through effective membership communication and networking and maximization of Idaho Travel Council grant funds in public relations, Web presence and cooperative advertising opportunities." Visit Sandpoint is a state-sponsored website, linked from the Chamber's website, which promotes attractions and activities in the area. The Chamber also operates and funds the Greater Sandpoint Visitor Center.

Coldwater Creek store, tourist Information, and kiosk.
Photo by Wendy L. Oden.

In 1991, Sandpoint reported that its tourism strategy was focused on developing events and festivals that would attract tourists year-round. The premise was that the quickest and least expensive way to bring visitors to Sandpoint would be to create a variety of events to entertain them. Key events highlighted in 1991 included the Festival at Sandpoint, Winter Carnival, Waterfest, Octoberfest, the Idaho State Draft Horse Show International, and the Great Northern Bluegrass Festival.

Sandpoint also reported it hosted a major event drawing at least 2,000 visitors in each of 10 months out of the year. Emphasis was also on promoting expansion of other tourist attractions, including Schweitzer Mountain Ski Resort, Hidden Lakes Golf Course, and Silverwood Theme Park. The community assumed that if it could draw people to Sandpoint and improve the tourism economy, increased capital investment in physical attractions would result. It was also hoped that by exposing more people to Sandpoint, the community would attract light industry.

City beach and marina. Photo by Duane D. Davis © 1994.

Much of Sandpoint's success with tourism in 1991 was attributed to the high degree of community involvement in various events and in the creation of successful partnerships. Numerous individuals, arts groups and nonprofit organizations were involved in tourism activities that were loosely coordinated with the Chamber.

Volunteers were the key to the success of many events sponsored by nonprofit organizations, including the Festival at Sandpoint, the Pend Oreille Arts Council, the North Idaho Draft Horse Association, and the Lake Pend Oreille Idaho Club. Local artists hosted the festival and the annual Arts and Crafts Show; the agricultural community hosted the draft horse show; and the timber industry promoted its heritage with Timberfest.

The historic Panida Theater hosts a variety of performing arts and fine arts films. Photo by Cynthia Messer.

Successes and Challenges

Today Sandpoint enjoys a booming tourism industry that is well balanced with other key economic sectors (timber, agriculture, retail trade, government, and manufacturing). Tourism accounts for 15 percent of the local economy. Direct tourist spending in Bonner County, of which Sandpoint is

the principal city, was $92 million in 1997. Tourism-related jobs increased from 1,033 in 1988 to 1,609 in 1998. Approximately 2,000 jobs were generated in the 2004 peak summer season.

The Sandpoint Chamber focuses on educating the community about the importance of tourism. "I have done speeches to different organizations about the numbers—how much money is contributed to our economy and how many people are employed in the industry—to get people to really understand how important tourism is," said Amy Little. "We also write articles in the newspaper every month [to help] people understand where the tourists are coming from and how they are supporting the community."

A locally owned business offers popular cruises on Lake Pend Oreille. Photo by Cynthia Messer.

Since 1991, the attraction base has expanded considerably, building upon the outdoor recreation and arts focus. A number of new businesses have sprung up on Lake Pend Oreille, including resorts, marinas and water recreation services, such as parasailing, watercraft rentals, fishing charters, and guided canoe and kayak adventures. A locally owned business now offers popular cruises on Lake Pend Oreille. Many existing events have become stronger and some formerly significant ones have been replaced by others that have proven to be of greater appeal.

For example, Octoberfest and the Winter Carnival have declined in popularity and participation. The Great Northern Blue Grass Show and Waterfest are no longer scheduled. Major new events include the Idaho State Chili Cook-off and the Pend Oreille International Fiddle Competition. Long-time favorites, such as the Festival at Sandpoint, Lost in the 50s, Idaho State Draft Horse Show International, Timberfest, Long Bridge Swim, and two fishing derbies, still draw record crowds. The Pend Oreille Arts Council sponsors numerous cultural events throughout the year, including an annual Arts and Crafts Fair, Artwalk and Concerts on the Lawn. The community-owned Panida Theater is home to art shows and more than 100 performances annually, including first run movies, musical events, plays, and vaudeville shows.

Schweitzer Mountain Resort and Lake Pend Orielle continue to be Sandpoint's major attractions. The community is host to a variety of sports tournaments and events, and North Idaho Bikeways has created an 11-mile paved bike path from Sagle to Sandpoint. Other new tourism businesses and activities since 1991 include disc golf, mountain biking, climbing wall, bungee jump trampoline, and other outdoor pursuits.

Much of the success of tourism in Sandpoint can be attributed to the willingness of the community and various sponsoring organizations to monitor, evaluate and adapt its tourist product to the demands of a changing market. Flexibility and a keen sense of balancing community needs with tourism goals are apparent.

Festival at Sandpoint Turnaround

The Festival at Sandpoint was created in 1982 to bring symphonic music to the area. As the festival grew, it expanded its vision to include jazz, blues, folk, world, and popular music. The Festi-

val at Sandpoint struggled financially during the mid-1990s and almost ceased to exist in 1996. The festival had started staging large commercial concerts that did not draw enough attendance to be profitable, yet drew large-enough crowds to spark neighbors' complaints about noise. In conjunction with the Schweitzer Institute of Music, the festival also ran a young musicians' educational program that proved to be a financial drain. Festival staffing also had become management-heavy, and it became apparent things needed to change if the event was to be salvaged. As a result, the summer music institute was discontinued in 1996, and the festival was refocused.

Festival at Sandpoint. Photo by Duane D. Davis © 1994.

"Between 1991 and 1996 the festival got away from listening to what the community wanted us to be," explained Dyno Wahl, Executive Director of the Festival at Sandpoint. "We really had to redefine what we are. Maybe we aren't a festival that puts on the Beach Boys and draws crowds of 8,000. We cut staff and decided to voluntarily limit the attendance to 2,500 people per event.

"In the last few years, we have gotten back to really listening to the community, knowing what our limitations are, and knowing what is appropriate for the community both financially and physically," Wahl continued. "You have to calibrate your tourism to what your community can bear or wants to bear. This is now the community's festival."

Now back on track, the festival celebrated its 28th year in 2010, has a $500,000+ budget and draws upwards of 20,000 people over the nine-day program. Wahl attributed much of the turnaround to a new board (consisting of a diverse group of individuals with specific skills), transition to a committee structure, a highly successful transferable season pass, "audience-friendly" policies, varied sources of funding (ticket sales, corporate sponsorships, grants), and a highly motivated, 200-strong volunteer base. The festival also launched a 5th grade music outreach program in 1999 and has expanded the organization's educational mission.

Ski Resort Turnaround

Schweitzer Mountain Ski Resort has a similar tale of transition and growth. After undergoing a major expansion in 1990–91, the resort suffered financial losses when anticipated skier numbers and condo sales did not materialize. In 1997, the owners went into bankruptcy, and the business struggled to stay afloat. In 1999, Seattle-based Harbor Properties purchased the resort, and in 2005, ownership was transferred to the McCaw Investment Group (MIG) of Seattle.

"A big concern with a large outside company buying the resort was whether they would take business out of the area. We have made a conscious effort to use local suppliers whenever we can," said Deanna Harris, former director of base area services. "The success of the mountain is dependent upon the success of the town. We are working on a lot of ways to tie in the lake and community. We will work more closely to make sure the whole product is successful."

A

year-round jobs. According to Schweitzer news releases on its website, the year-round strategy has steadily increased annual visitor numbers. The resort saw more than 217,000 skier visits in the first half of 2010, an increase of 7.5 percent over the previous ski season.

As noted, MIG took ownership of the resort in 2005, and it has focused on developing sustainable practices through participation in the National Ski Area Association's Sustainable Slopes Initiative. In 2009, a new housing project added LEED-certified (Leadership in Energy and Environmental Design) lodging to the mountain village.

Lost in the 50s Expands

Other events have been so successful that they have reached a critical point in their life cycle. Lost in the 50s began in 1986 as the brainchild of two local residents who wanted to create a fun and exciting way to celebrate the music and cars of the 50s and 60s, while also raising funds for the festival. The event centers on a "show and shine" car show downtown and a dance at the fairgrounds with music of the 50s and 60s performed by original artists. Since its inception, eight volunteer organizers and an additional 100-150 on-site volunteers have run the event. What began as a two-day event with 26 cars and three key activities has evolved into a multi-day affair drawing hundreds of cars from around the country, a parade, a free public street dance, a rock-n-roll ticket dance at the fairgrounds, and a Sunday fun run.

"Success has its price. The more people you have come, the more problems you have to deal with," said Carolyn Gleason, founder of Lost in the 50s. "It started out as a party for us; now it's like a job. From a volunteer standpoint, it's not as much fun. We are bursting at

Selkirk Lodge at Schweitzer Mountain Resort.
Photo by Duane D. Davis © 1994.

Schweitzer has undergone several expansions in the past decade to improve infrastructure and recreational facilities, and expand lodging options. The Selkirk Lodge offers 77 rooms and suites, and the resort also includes the condo-style White Pine Lodge and private condo homes. Further improvements included replacement and expansion of the ski lifts. In 2008, a new snowmaking system was installed, and today the resort features 10 lifts providing access to the 2,900-acre terrain.

The resort also has transitioned from a winter resort to a year-round playground, offering mountain biking, hiking, horseback riding and other outdoor activities—thus creating more

the seams. There are more costs. We are not bringing in as much profit as we used to. It becomes passé to the locals after awhile. They see it as a way to make money for themselves, but they don't think about giving back to share in the work load."

Canoe on Sand Creek. Photo by Duane D. Davis © 1994.

Despite these challenges, Gleason said most businesses see the value in Lost in the 50s. She credited much of the event's success to keeping the core of activities downtown, which generates significant revenue for local merchants. Lost in the 50s no longer serves as a fund raiser for the festival, which is now self-sustaining. After 25 years, the event is a well-regarded part of the tourism offerings in Sandpoint.

Growth Issues

While Sandpoint has witnessed much success with its tourism efforts, it continues to face significant challenges in coping with a rapid influx of visitors and a population growth rate well above the national average. In 1991, traffic congestion, downtown parking, and the cost of housing were the primary concerns. Nearly 20 years later, these concerns remain, but several key actions are in place to help alleviate problems.

One key issue identified in 1991 was traffic congestion generated by Interstate 95, a major trade route to Canada. This highway carries all leisure and truck traffic through the middle of downtown Sandpoint, and traffic has increased more than ten-fold in the last two decades. Combined with more tourism and rapid population growth, this causes major backups stretching south of town in summer months. Many residents say they feel they give up their town in summer.

"My sense is that the traffic issues grew so quickly that they were not planning clearly up front. Now it's like trying to play catch-up and wondering whether [we] will even solve the problem," said Christie Robinson of the Downtown Sandpoint Business Association. "It's important to have good cooperation with the people in charge of transportation issues."

Truck traffic on Main Street. Photos by Wendy L. Oden.

Plans to construct a bypass to downtown have been discussed for nearly 60 years, and work has finally begun. As of mid-2010, the Idaho Transportation Department was constructing a new 2.1-mile bypass east of downtown. The $98 million project, which includes six bridges, 65 retaining walls, and a pedestrian/bike pathway, is expected to be complete by 2012.

Availability of affordable housing is another key issue for the community. Many people have chosen Sandpoint as a place for a summer home, while others have built expensive year-round homes in the region. This has driven up housing prices to the point where some local residents find it difficult to obtain housing. Infrastructure problems have also multiplied as a result of tourism's rapid expansion.

All these issues have not reduced Sandpoint's commitment to tourism. However, they have forced the community to search for solutions more frequently than communities that do not face multiple impacts from tourism.

Lessons Learned

Most city officials agree that proper planning is the key to dealing with the effects of growth on Sandpoint. The community updated its comprehensive plan in 2009 to address the growth that has occurred since the plan was first drafted in 1977. The comprehensive plan cites tourism in a number of sections—acknowledging its role in the local economy and its influence on planning for public facilities.

Recognizing tourism's significant role, the city also took a unique approach in its comprehensive planning process. According to City Planner Jeremy Grimm, visitors were invited to participate in some planning sessions. "There was some debate about whether tourists should be shaping the future of Sandpoint," he said. "But it was decid-

ed that these folks represent a significant portion of our local economy, and therefore we certainly want to be sure that whatever we are designing and planning takes their concerns into account."

Tourism leaders also noted that while the city and businesses value tourists, some local residents do not favor continued growth in tourism out of fears that the community will change too much.

"If you are successful [in] marketing and showing the world your best amenities, people are going to naturally be attracted to that," said one leader. "As a result, communities are going to have to deal with [short-] and long-range planning to make sure that success doesn't destroy what initially attracted people to the area."

Hikers overlooking Long Bridge. Photo by Duane D. Davis © 1994.

Regional cooperation and cross-sector collaboration are key themes expressed by many in the Sandpoint area. The Greater Sandpoint Chamber of Commerce also represents communities bordering the city and works cooperatively with other chambers throughout Bonner County. The Chamber has several working committees, including agriculture and forestry, business development, recreation and tourism, and leadership. The forestry, or timber, group has established a bridge between the tourism industry and public land agencies. The agricultural sector also collaborates on various tourism events.

Cooperation and trust between the public and private sector are also cited as vital keys to success. "I want to stress how important it is for every community to step back and try to establish trust within organizations—public and private—that have the ability to make change happen," said Kevin Clegg, former city planning director. "[There should be] a basic trust between business associations and the city agencies that have control over what happens in your community. It's all about partnerships. I didn't have a full appreciation of that until I came to Sandpoint. But it really is critical, because if not everybody feels that they are on board, you're more likely to run into stumbling blocks."

Public-private cooperation is found in several regional efforts. One example is the Downtown Sandpoint Business Association (DSBA). The DSBA is a 501c6 non-profit corporation created by downtown merchants. According to its website, the DSBA mission is "to work in a cooperative effort with the community to enhance the economic vitality and the aesthetic and cultural character of Sandpoint for this and future generations."

The DSBA receives funds from the city via assessments on businesses within a business improvement district (BID) created in 2000. Key strategies include making physical improvements, collaborating on economic development efforts, conducting focused marketing for downtown, and determining tourism's role in the vitality of downtown. The BID has been controversial since its inception, but it has withstood several petition attempts to disband it.

Future Vision

Many local officials told us that tourism has turned around Sandpoint's economy and made it a viable community. Tourism has lived up to initial expectations, playing an increasingly important role in the local economy. "Using tourism to boost

Sandpoint's economy has worked, but I don't think that it was as quick as people necessarily thought it would be," said Amy Little. "Just advertising something doesn't guarantee [visitor] traffic, so it has been an evolving process of branding the community and really figuring out where people are coming from, how to target them, and how we can get them to keep coming back."

Osprey on Pend Oreille River. Photo by Duane D. Davis © 1994.

Tourism is solely responsible for the development of resorts that grace the shores of Lake Pend Oreille, and for the current extensive remodeling and expansion at Schweitzer Mountain Resort. Other lodging properties also have undergone remodeling and expansion; several new B&Bs have been developed; and a variety of new events and activities have been created in response to the growing visitor presence.

Sandpoint aerial view. Photo by Duane D. Davis © 1994.

It has been estimated that the Festival at Sandpoint brings in at least $3 million in revenue for the region during its two-week annual season. Lost in the 50s and the draft horse show are both said to generate more than $1 million during the single weekend they are held each year. Because tourism has stimulated community and county-wide growth, it is also said to be indirectly responsible for expansion of other community services and facilities, such as a recent addition to Bonner General Hospital. Light industry has also come to

Sandpoint, but it is being attributed to local community recruitment efforts rather than tourism.

While Sandpoint views tourism as important, many are aware that it is only one segment of a successful, balanced economy. Timber and agriculture continue to play key roles in the area, and there is recognition that support for these sectors must be sustained. The Greater Sandpoint Chamber of Commerce works collaboratively with the Bonner County Economic Development Association and the Downtown Business Association to promote economic development.

"Tourism will continue to be important and a significant part of our economy as long as the vision is compatible with traditional industries," said Idaho State Senator Shawn Keogh. "We are very cognizant of what the area can bear. We can continue to grow, but we need to manage that growth in a planned fashion. [We must] look at the limits of land capacity and have a plan in place that allows for a light touch on the land for future generations. Planning ahead is key."

Persons Interviewed

Amy Little
Executive Director
Greater Sandpoint Chamber of
Commerce

Lisa Derr
Past President
Greater Sandpoint Chamber of
Commerce

Kevin Clegg
Former Planning Director
City of Sandpoint

Jeremy Grimm
Planning Director
City of Sandpoint

Deanna Harris
Services Director
Schweitzer Mountain Ski Resort

Marilyn Sabella
Board Member
Pend Oreille Arts Council

Carolyn Gleason
Founder
Lost in the 50s

Dyno Wahl
Executive Director
Festival at Sandpoint

Shawn Keough
Idaho State Senator
Timber Information Program
Manager, Greater Sandpoint
Chamber of Commerce

Karl Dye
Executive Director
Bonner County Economic
Development Corporation

Linda Mitchell
Owner
Lake Pend Oreille Cruises

Deanna Harris
Former Director of Base Area
Services
Schweitzer Mountain

Christie Robinson
Downtown Sandpoint Business
Association

A

San Luis, Colorado

Population: 739
Economy: 90 percent agriculture
Employment: Mostly farming, education, local government
County: Costilla, population 3,232

Rich History, Culture

The town of San Luis is the oldest in Colorado, established in 1851. The county seat of Costilla County in the beautiful San Luis Valley, it is known for its rich history and culture. The predominately Hispanic population has close ties to religious, cultural, and artistic traditions of Spain. Today, the county remains primarily a rural area with an agriculture-based economy. It is also one of the poorest counties in Colorado, with a high population of elderly citizens and children living on assistance. People in San Luis are proud and industrious and often fiercely dedicated to issues that relate to their language, land, and water.

The attraction base for San Luis includes the Stations of the Cross Shrine and the La Capilla de Todos Los Santos (Chapel of All Saints); the San Luis Museum and Cultural Center; Viego San Acacio (the oldest church in Colorado); various mission churches; and the 600+ acre Vega, one of only two communal pasture areas still in existence in the United States. San Luis is also the site of the state's most senior water right, dating back more than 100 years, as well as numerous fishing areas and much scenic beauty. Tourist services include six eating establishments, a 22-room motel, a B&B, and two gas stations. The locally owned grocery store on Main Street was established in 1857 and is the oldest business in Colorado.

La Capilla de Todos Los Santos (Chapel of All Saints) rises from mesa that is the site of the Stations of the Cross Shrine.
Photo by Wendy L. Oden.

San Luis is Colorado's oldest town and its town center is recognized as a National Historic District. Photo by Cynthia Messer.

San Luis is located on State Highway 159, a major road that runs from Costilla, New Mexico, to Fort Garland, Colorado. This highway is considered a shortcut to Taos, New Mexico, less than two hours away. Highway 159 is also part of the Los Caminos Antiguos Scenic and Historic Byway, which encompasses communities in Costilla, Conejos, and Alamosa counties, as well as the Great Sand Dunes National Monument in the northern part of the San Luis Valley.

San Luis is one of the major tourist communities in Costilla County, in addition to Fort Garland, which is located 16 miles north. Fort Garland is the eastern gateway into the San Luis Valley and home to the Fort Garland Museum and Visitor Information Center. Fort Garland serves as the official welcome center for the entire county.

San Luis has maintained a small, volunteer run visitor center, but as of mid-2010, it had temporarily closed due to lack of staffing. Neither San Luis nor Fort Garland has sufficient attractions to keep visitors long. Both cater primarily to a pass-through market, drawing visitors from Denver (200 miles north) and Colorado Springs (150 miles north), as well as those traveling alternative routes to Santa Fe and Taos, New Mexico.

Background

San Luis was first profiled in the 1991 National Rural Tourism Development project due to its successful creation of the Stations of the Cross Shrine as part of a community-driven effort to develop a tourism attraction reflecting residents' religious heritage. San Luis had been suffering from a steady economic decline and tourism was viewed as a means of saving the town. A group of local citizens got together and formed the Costilla County Economic Development Council (CCEDC) as a nonprofit organization whose main function was to solicit grant funding for specific development projects. It was a grassroots coalition fueled by volunteer efforts, local pride, and enthusiasm, since the county and city had limited means to fund economic development. As of mid-2010, the organization continued to operate with an executive director and one support staff. Several of the original board members still serve.

The CCEDC's initial strategy was to stimulate economic activity with religious and cultural tourism, as well as local arts development. The central project became the development of the Stations of the Cross Shrine, a series of two-thirds life-size bronze sculptures depicting the hours before Christ's death and his resurrection. The shrine is situated along a dirt trail two-thirds of a mile long. The trail runs up to the top of the San Pedro Mesa, inviting visitors to stop, rest, meditate, or take in the breathtaking views of San Luis, the Vega, and other villages on the Culebra River below.

The shrine has put San Luis on the map for tourists and provided the community with a sense of pride and accomplishment. The project began at the direction of the Reverend Pat Valdez, pastor of Sangre De Cristo Parish and one of the initial CCEDC board members. Local families and organizational sponsors raised more than $100,000 for the effort, and local volunteers constructed the trail. City and county governments helped provide access to the site and committed to improvements there, as well as to other public areas in town. The project was dedicated in May 1990 and during that year, San Luis welcomed a record 30,000-plus visitors. From 1990-1999, tourist traffic increased, although no official counts are kept. Today, residents estimate 40,000-50,000 people visit the shrine annually. It is credited for keeping the town alive.

Two scenes from the Stations of the Cross Shrine, which depicts the final hours of the life of Jesus Christ. Photos by Wendy L. Oden (Jesus and Mary) and Cynthia Messer (Jesus carrying the cross).

"I have seen some real excitement in the community because [the residents] are proud of what they have done. They did this," said Felix Romero, local resident and original CCEDC board member. "They put their money, labor, and work into it. There is a real sense of belonging and ownership in this project. During that time, we also made sure that every person got recognized for what they did, even if it was just an hour of volunteer time. We had the governor and his staff come down and issue certificates of appreciation."

In addition to the shrine, the CCEDC's original economic strategy included local arts development. A summer arts network/performing arts series was expanded, and a woodworking production facility was started. A major initiative was creation of El Centro Artesano (the artists center), which was located in a renovated convent building operated by the Sangre de Cristo Parish Church as a B&B. The goal of the center was to preserve folk crafts by training young people and to boost families' incomes by providing workshop space and a sales outlet for indigenous folk arts and crafts. In El Centro Artesano's first year of operation the number of artists involved grew to 60, with total sales of approximately $17,400. This initial growth was not sustained, however, and the center—unable to achieve its hoped-for potential—no longer operates.

Nevertheless, local art continues to be an important part of the community, and El Centro has been replaced by a nonprofit facility on Main Street—Ventero Open Press Fine Art. Opened in 2007 by regional artist Randy Pijoan to support arts and culture in the San Luis Valley, the facility includes printing presses, a fine art gallery featuring regional artists, and a full-service espresso bar. This espresso bar has become a gathering spot for local artists and residents, as well as a stopping point for visitors to San Luis. In 2009, Ventero Open Press hosted the Rio Costilla Studio Tour Emerging Artist Show and is working to develop a new arts/cultural center in San Luis scheduled to open in 2010.

A

Successes and Challenges

San Luis enjoyed some positive effects from tourism following dedication of the shrine in 1990 and subsequently expanded its offerings. In 1992, the Knights of Columbus Education Building was completed on top of San Pedro Mesa as a shelter for the thousands of people a year who come in pilgrimage and prayer to this sacred site. In 1997, the town completed La Capilla de Todos Los Santos at the top of the mesa next to the shrine. The chapel provides a place for residents, visitors, and small groups to pray, meditate, and hold religious services. The shrine is accessible year-round, both by foot from town and via an unmarked dirt road across the mesa.

A renovated convent is the home of the El Convento B&B. The building also once housed the El Centro Artesano (artists center), but the initial growth could not be sustained and the center has since closed. Photos by Cynthia Messer.

While the community was extremely successful in creating and developing a tourist attraction of national renown, it has not been able to sustain the initial economic benefit from tourism. Visitors have little opportunity or incentive to linger in San Luis. Other than a small park with picnic benches and one or two shops catering mostly to locals, there is little to engage visitors. The visitor center and cultural center are closed, although local residents stress that this is temporary.

Main street facades were improved, but the downtown area still needs revitalization, including sidewalk maintenance, landscaping, lighting, and addressing boarded-up storefront properties. There are places to eat, but they do not keep regular hours; in fact, visitors may find a business unexpectedly closed if the owner is on vacation or lacks adequate help. Given the lack of things to do, tourists are not enticed to stay in San Luis once they have walked up to the shrine.

The town also has struggled over the years with a lack of understanding and support among residents and county commissioners regarding tourism. Several local tourism leaders cited many residents' fear that tourism would change their community. Residents are fiercely proud of their heritage and want to protect their culture. Interviews of residents also suggest that few beyond tourism leaders understand the seriousness with which tourism must be pursued in conjunction with other economic strategies if meaningful benefits are to be realized. "You have to be tenacious," said one CCEDC board member.

Despite these issues, there is renewed optimism in San Luis about tourism's potential because of Congressional designation of the Sangre de Cristo National Heritage Area (NHA), under the auspices of the National Park Service, in 2009. The area includes the San Luis Valley counties of Costilla, Alamosa, and Conejos, together with three wildlife refuges and the Great Sand Dunes National Park. Local residents involved in this new project bring a new excitement to the community and stress that the heritage area will help to preserve and promote local heritage, cultural history and traditions. They were quick to point out that this heritage area classification could bring in up to $10 million in federal matching funds over the next 15 years to finance projects with a host of aims. They also recognize that this designation will require collaboration and dedicated effort to be successful.

"There has been a lot of hesitation to bring visitors into this town, but [the heritage area] is a different type of tourism," said Emerita Romero-Anderson, local author and tourism activist. "These people are educated; they are not coming to buy trinkets and tee shirts and trash the place, as one person put it. They will be here to learn from us, to have an experience, and see who we are in the national story. We play a very important part in the national story."

The R&R Market serve guests in San Luis' town center.
Photo by Cynthia Messer.

While tourism is credited with keeping the town alive, it did not bring the economic windfall and jobs that the community had initially hoped for. New business development has been limited to the efforts of a few long-time residents and some newcomers with an entrepreneurial spirit, financial means, and faith to invest in the community. Local service stations and markets have benefited from the increased traffic, but community leaders acknowledge that sustaining a tourism business is challenging. "We aren't visitor ready," said one local leader.

Nevertheless, local residents are optimistic that a renewed focus on regional arts and culture and the new heritage area designation will have positive effects on San Luis. Romero-Anderson said the community plans to manage growth through the economic development council and city and county government and by involving the people. "Helping to incorporate the local voice is key here," she noted. "We need to have local input and local involvement. This is a grass roots effort." The local heritage area board plans to host open community meetings to gain residents' input about the direction and plans for tourism development in the three counties.

Growth Issues

San Luis and Costilla County face challenges in proposed development by outside investors and inadequate infrastructure due to a lack of community planning. As noted, the San Luis Valley is home to the Sangre de Cristo mountain range and abundant fertile agricultural land. Given that it is also one of the poorest and smallest communities, residents find themselves facing one crisis after another to ward off land speculators, developers, and corporations seeking to exploit the area's rich water, mineral, and timber resources and depressed labor pool.

More than 78,000 acres of the Sangre de Cristo range on the east side of San Luis have been purchased by a single developer. Community residents and local leaders are very concerned about timbering practices and development on this range, since it is also the county's watershed. Lack of a long-term, effective land use and zoning plan has resulted in acquisition of a significant portion of the county by outside investors. The county has more than 47,000 lots of undeveloped land owned by outsiders, some of whom want to retire to the area. Costilla County completed a comprehensive plan as a policy tool to help guide land use and zoning in 1999, but concerns remained as of 2010.

Concerns center on the lack of a planning department and a specific community growth plan. The county comprehensive plan called for creation of design standards to protect the integrity of the historic district in San Luis, but this was not seen as an issue until 2009, when a national low-cost retailer came to Main Street—generating concern and controversy. The 8,000 square foot store is located on the historic main street at the northern entrance into town, directly below the mesa.

With no zoning and planning regulations in place, local leaders realized they were unable to guide building and architectural design of new buildings to fit the character of their historic main street. Community leaders acknowledge the benefit of the new retailer to the community, but they are concerned about its location and impact on other businesses. This has prompted a renewed call for planning in San Luis, and a zoning and planning commission has been established.

"What we are trying to do is develop a plan for San Luis and neighboring communities that allows for people to come in and visit all the amenities and want to come back in the future," said Robert Rael, CCEDC Executive Director.

"We are working with the city and the county and discussing the importance of proper zoning rules and laws, so we are not always just playing catch-up. This is a long term thing that is extremely important for San Luis and Costilla County."

Lessons Learned

Local residents acknowledge that although the community was very successful in developing a major tourist attraction, anticipated benefits have not been at the level expected. Reasons cited for this include the perception of tourism as a "quick fix" and fear of change, leading to a lack of overall planning and few tourism services.

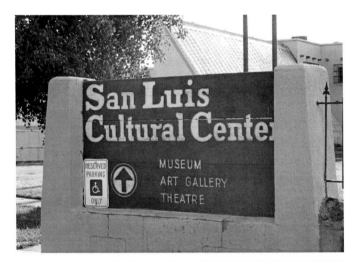

The San Luis Cultural Center and Museum, built in the 1930s, is one of the town's oldest attractions, while Ventero Open Press Fine Art opened in 2007 to support arts and culture in San Luis Valley. Photos by Cynthia Messer.

As noted, however, the new National Heritage Area designation has stimulated renewed optimism and interest in developing tourism. Residents are excited about the potential. Community open house meetings have been held across the three counties to engage residents in planning and build support. The local Heritage Area Board of Directors is also working with the National Park Service on project planning for the Sangre de Cristo NHA.

Local government also is making changes to support efforts related to the NHA designation. In November 2009, Costilla County took a step forward by filling the county administrator's post, which had been cut at the beginning of the decade. Both the new administrator and county commissioners have expressed a desire to develop tourism.

"We have an asset that now we have to take a really hard look at what we want to do with it," said Rick Manzanares, Director of the Fort Garland Museum and Visitor Information Center and member of the local Heritage Area Board. "We want to share [the asset], but how much more do we want to share it? I don't think that has been defined. We are just starting out, and we realize that San Luis and Fort Garland are tourist centers. Our concern is that we can attract tourists here, but how do we get them to stay and spend money in our communities and have those dollars turn over in our general economy?"

Development of the Stations of the Cross Shrine was driven as much by local religious beliefs as it was by a desire to create tourism. Residents interviewed repeatedly voiced the view that "we don't want to become another Taos. We don't want tourism at the expense of losing our community, our heritage, and our entire way of life." They view the Sangre de Cristo National Heritage Area as a way to help preserve and protect their culture and heritage while promoting tourism.

"A lot of people in San Luis are commenting that we have tourists coming to our town, and we are telling people to come, but are we really ready for them? Are little shops and restaurants open, and are there things to do other than walking up to the shrine and coming back down?" said David Garcia, a local community development consultant. "Do boarded-up storefronts help you? There is a feeling by some that the town wasn't ready to invite a bunch of people. So now we are paying the price of asking ourselves, 'what did we get into and how do we serve these tourists who are stopping?' We still have a lot of work to do to make sure that if tourism is going to be a viable part of economic development, we [must be able to] take care of tourists."

Future Vision

The future vision for tourism in San Luis remains firmly focused on cultural heritage tourism and local arts development. Residents and town officials are again optimistic about the community's tourism potential. They are dedicated to revitalizing Main Street, building new leadership, and developing an adequate infrastructure and strong local business base to capture the economic benefits of tourism.

"I think tourism is real important to economic development. Without it, our community will die again," said former San Luis mayor John Apodaca. "Tourism is what will increase our tax base and help revitalize our town. We have a long way to go, but we have a lot of plans to upgrade the city, redo curbs and gutters, do a real facelift to the town to attract new businesses, and make this a better place for people to come and stay."

In the late 1990s, the CCEDC phased out its formal economic development and tourism efforts, with the idea that the county and city would eventually take over these tasks. As noted,

A

the volunteer, nonprofit corporation evolved as an umbrella organization managing grants for specific projects. In 2009, the CCEDC named a new executive director and as of mid-2010, was again addressing tourism as a priority in its strategic plan. Plans include increased tourism marketing efforts and development of a website.

"Something we recognized from the beginning of this project was the need for leadership development," said Felix Romero. "We took people through training to become community leaders." Training has been conducted by the Kellogg and Ford foun-

dations. "A lot of us made the commitment that we were going to focus our energies into acquiring results rather than just making the noises."

The future of tourism in San Luis and the valley is bright if residents can build community support and collaborate to move forward. The National Heritage Area designation has inspired new leaders to step forward and has revived interest in tourism in San Luis. The focus on planning and new efforts to engage the community are expected to build support for cultural heritage tourism in San Luis and sustain it in the future.

Persons Interviewed

Felix Romero
Original CCEDC Chairperson,
Owner R&R Market

Huberto Maestas
Sculptor, Stations of the Cross

Santos Martinez
Land Use Administrator,
Costilla County

Bernadette Lucero
Vice President, CCEDC

Rick Manzaneres
Director
Fort Garland Museum

David Garcia
Community Development
Consultant

John Apodaca
Former Mayor of San Luis

Bob Green
Water Conservancy District &
Editor, La Sierra

Sallie Harper
Local Economic Development
Consultant

The Reverend Pat Valdez
Sangre De Cristo Parish

Robert Rael
Executive Director of the
CCEDC

Emerita Romero-Anderson
Author and Tourism Activist

The Villages of Van Buren, Iowa

Population: 7,679 in Van Buren County
Economy: Tourism, agriculture, retail trade, government, manufacturing
Employment: Durable goods, agriculture, government and service jobs
County: Van Buren
Web site: www.villagesofvanburen.com

An Age Apart

The Villages of Van Buren County, in south-eastern Iowa, are a unique cluster of 12 small towns that have joined together to market the quiet country feel of their region. Located along the Des Moines River, these communities were founded in the mid-1800s when the river was a primary means of transport and riverboats brought visitors, supplies, and settlers to the rich, rolling farmland. Bentonsport, Keosauqua, Bonaparte, and Farmington are perhaps the best-known river villages in Van Buren County. They are within 20 miles of each other. Other villages include Cantril, Milton, Stockport, Birmingham, Pittsburg, Douds-Leando, Iowaville-Selma, and Mt. Sterling. The county seat of Keosauqua, located at the "Horseshoe Bend" of the Des Moines River, is the largest of the villages, with a population of just over 1,000. Unlike many rural areas, Van Buren County's population has remained relatively steady over the past 20 years.

State Highways 1 and 2 run through the county (north/south and east/west, respectively). These two-lane highways are the primary arteries of

travel into the county, with Interstates 80 and 35 located more than 75 miles to the north and west. Van Buren County is about a two-hour drive from Des Moines and Cedar Rapids.

Van Buren County is a rural area with a strong agricultural base. The county has a relatively low cost-of-living index, and residents are happy with the quality of life in their small communities. There is a sense of optimism in the county fueled by several local business expansions, retail sales that are above projections and quality healthcare services with a progressive hospital and clinics. A manufacturing business that employed 65 people in 1991 has grown to employ more than 400. There is a tight housing market, and land values have been driven up by demand.

After years of population decline, the 1990s was the first decade in the 20th century to see an increase, and a portion of this is attributed to tourism. The population has remained relatively stable and today nearly one-fourth is under 18. Individuals came to the county to visit, hunt, or fish, and some returned to settle. Residents welcome the growth, but place great value on the slower pace, the rich history, and the friendliness of small town America in their communities. Residents take tremendous pride in the fact that there are still no stoplights or fast-food chain businesses in the entire county.

The attractions and activities in the Villages of Van Buren are centered on simple pleasures— relaxation, outdoor recreation, historic architecture, and events. In the words of the Bentonsport Web page, "A spirit of dedication to preservation is strongly evident here, and an atmosphere of peace and timelessness prevails. It is the feeling of having stepped back in time that appeals to visitors and keeps them coming back."

Abundant Natural Resources

Most attractions and activities are locally operated and represent the heritage and lifestyles passed down through generations. The natural resources of Van Buren County provide excellent year-round recreational opportunities and are an important draw for visitors. The beautiful Des Moines River meanders 40 miles through the county and is popular for canoeing and kayaking as part of the 54-mile Des Moines Trail, Iowa's longest trail system.

Another natural resource is Lacey-Keosauqua State Park, one of Iowa's biggest state parks. The park's 1,653 acres of hills, bluffs, and valleys provide several recreational opportunities, including hiking, camping, bird watching, and swimming. The park features six family cabins and 113 campsites (45 with electrical hookups), modern rest rooms, shower facilities, and a trailer dump station.

Lacey-Keosauqua State Park is one of Iowa's largest parks and a key natural resource in Van Buren County.
Photos by Cynthia Messer.

Lake Sugema is one of Van Buren County's premier attractions. Set in the 3,000-acre Indian Creek Wildlife Area, Lake Sugema is a high-quality man-made fishing lake. Created in 1992, it is stocked with largemouth bass, bluegill, black crappie, channel catfish, and saugeye. Facilities include boat ramps, a fishing pier for people with disabilities, floating boat docks, and wildlife islands. The Iowa Department of Natural Resources and the Van Buren County Conservation Board manage the lake and area. It is a year-round attraction offering fishing, hunting, trapping, hiking, bird watching, cross country skiing, picnicking, and camping opportunities.

A third key natural resource is Shimek State Forest, which includes nearly 9,000 acres of hills and valleys. The forest is a multipurpose oak and hickory woodland used for forestry demonstrations, research, wildlife management, and recreation. Twenty-six miles of equestrian

trails and quality campgrounds attract outdoor enthusiasts. Hunters find excellent wild turkey and white-tailed deer in season.

Rich History

History figures prominently in Van Buren County tourism. Indians first settled along the river, and 19 burial mounds are still visible today. Pioneer settlement began in the 1830s, when traders, trappers, and settlers came up the Des Moines on riverboats. The Mormons crossed the county in 1846 en route West, and visitors can trace the steps of these early pioneers. At Ely's Ford in Lacey-Keosauqua State Park, visitors to the site can easily imagine wagons crossing the river. Keosauqua was established as the county seat in 1838, and the courthouse, built in 1840, is the second-oldest courthouse in continuous use in the United States.

Keosauqua also played a role in the story of runaway slaves from the South. Its location just north of the Missouri border made it a stop on the famed Underground Railroad, the escape route of many slaves during the mid-1800s. Visitors to the Villages of Van Buren can tour the Pearson House, maintained by the Van Buren County Historical Society and see a hide-away under the floor reached through a trap door.

Many of the sites and buildings in the Villages of Van Buren are on the National Registry of Historic Places. Two villages—Bentonsport and Bonaparte—are National Historic Districts. Bentonsport, with fewer than 40 residents, is a collection of restored brick homes, two churches, a working blacksmith and pottery business, and a two-block-long main street. The Greef General Store is a restored 1840s building complete with wooden sidewalk. It is owned and operated by Van Buren County Conservation as an antique and craft shop. Across the street along the banks of the river is the foundation of an old mill and an English rose garden.

Four miles downriver is Bonaparte, the smallest town in the National Main Street Program. The downtown area, restored through the efforts of local citizens, includes several historic sites. An old gristmill is the home of the Bonaparte Retreat, one of Iowa's finest restaurants. Next door, the old woolen mill is now an antique shop and fudge factory. This facility at one time served as the community hall and includes a 1938 stage with original lights and curtain. The current owners operate this as a dinner theatre and tearoom to serve both visitors and locals. The Aunty Green Hotel, built in 1844, houses the town library and historic museum.

Bill and Betty Printy offer blacksmith and pottery workshops at their shop, Iron & Lace, in Bentonsport.
Photo by Cynthia Messer.

The historic Whiteley Opera House on Main Street currently houses the Bonaparte City Hall, Bonaparte Main Street, Inc., and a community room. One of the newest businesses in town is the Bonaparte Inn B&B in a restored factory building. Most residents firmly believe that the preservation of their heritage is important for community pride, and more and more recognize the role tourism plays in their community.

Bonaparte Main Street, Inc., is a locally-initiated program started in 1987. Over the years it has played a key leadership role in the revitalization of Bonaparte and works closely with the city and business owners in the historic district. Gianna Barrow, chair of Bonaparte Main Street, Inc., said, "In Bonaparte many of us look at the success of tourism in our business retention, business expansion and then creating new business. We have always seemed to have a progressive city council and they seem to have an interest in seeing tourism grow in Bonaparte and they work well with us to that effect."

Visitors to the Villages of Van Buren can stay in one of several historic hotels and inns—the "steamboat Gothic" Hotel Manning in Keosauqua, the Mason House Inn in Bentonsport, built in 1846, or the Bonaparte Inn with 13 rooms and suites, which opened in 2006. Since 2001, lodging options in the county have also been expanded with the addition of the 13-room Bonaparte Inn B&B, several multi-unit cabins or cottages along banks of the river and Lake Sugema, and modern camping facilities. The campgrounds, both public and privately operated, include hook-ups or primitive camping options for campers and RVs.

New Opportunities

History is significant in attracting visitors, but the Villages also have been successful in developing complementary products and services to enhance visitors' experiences in Van Buren County. Stacey Reese, Executive Director of the Villages of Van Buren, Inc., explains. "We have been very fortunate within the last five years in diversifying the products and services that we are offering. We have had four wineries open up in the county, and that is a result of an effort probably about 10 years ago when we did sort of a test market with wine to see if it would be something that visitors would buy. The wineries have definitely been a big boost to our tourism. Also, the Amish and Mennonite communities just recently have become more involved with tourism. We have seen a lot of Amish businesses develop [including] a greenhouse, a furniture store, the Mennonite cheese factory, and the Mennonite general store in Cantril."

Artisans discovered the beauty of the area more than 30 years ago, and they produce and sell ironwork, pottery, paintings, fabric art, woodwork and sculpture. This focus on the arts has created a new opportunity for the Villages. In 2010, a new Folk Art School will welcome students to hands-on learning from artisans in residence across the county. The school is housed in historic buildings across the county. The idea grew from the blacksmith and pottery workshops offered by Bill Printy and his wife Betty at their shop, Iron & Lace, in Bentonsport. "In the last 10 or 11 years we have had over 1,200 people through our workshops just here at Iron & Lace," Bill said. "So we had a little pilot program for this concept that we are going to go after now as a county-wide folk art school."

Tourism in Van Buren County remains primarily seasonal. Winter events draw mostly local or regional visitors, and many shops are closed in the winter. Winter use of outdoor recreation sites, including Shimek State Forest and Keosauqua-Lacey State Park, were described as marginal due to unsteady snow cover.

Background

The Villages of Van Buren were profiled in 1991 because of their successful collaborative approach to marketing the historic villages and rural agricultural lifestyle. In 1991, the Villages were promoting "life as it was 100 years ago." Goals of the collaboration were to develop tourism as an economic diversification strategy by preserving historic buildings and capitalizing on the natural beauty of the area.

In 1991, target audiences were families and retirees from urban areas in the Upper Midwest, as well as motorcoach groups. Advertising and promotion included TV and radio ads, billboards, a visitor guide, FAM tours for media, and a promotional video for the welcome center. Visitor counts in 1991 were estimated at 100,000, but

no systematic tracking methods were in place. An effort was also made to renew local pride through "explore your own back yard" tours, newspaper articles, and hospitality training.

The tourism strategy in 1991 included development and expansion of festivals and events, and lodging based on a B&B concept plus cabins in natural areas. Primary development and promotional efforts were channeled through Villages of Van Buren, Inc., a volunteer membership organization that served as the county economic development entity.

Today, nearly 20 years later, the marketing focus remains much the same, although the Villages increasingly use the Internet to reach their target audiences. The 12 communities are still working in a successful collaboration to market themselves as the Villages of Van Buren. Their strategy remains focused on the history and natural beauty of the county, and visitors are invited to step back in time. The strength of tourism efforts stems from the commitment of individuals and community leaders to authenticity and preservation of attractions.

The historic Wickfield Farm Sales Pavilion near Cantril sits empty, but conversion to a lodging establishment or a historic education site remains a possibility. Photo by Cynthia Messer.

A

The Villages of Van Buren, Inc., has not changed much in function over the past decade. According to its mission statement, "the Villages of Van Buren, Inc., will directly undertake efforts to facilitate community cooperation and initiatives in tourism development, community development, and business development and retention. The ultimate goal of the Villages of Van Buren, Inc., is to maintain and enhance the quality of life of all Van Buren County residents."

The Villages of Van Buren Inc., is a nonprofit organization classified as a 501c4. It is governed by a board of directors; and that board consists of a representative from each community. "I have a huge board—14 people, but that's good," said Stacey Reese. Board members are part of a vital communication link. "They bring me news and information from their communities and I share with them information to take back to their communities and organizations," Reese noted.

A street in Bentonsport includes the restored Greef General Store, which leases space to craft and antique shop vendors. Photo by Cynthia Messer.

The system has worked well, although it took time to evolve. "I think the original board was maybe five people," Reese said. "But as we grew, we knew that we had to unite and get all of our villages together. We knew that we had to have a voice from every single community. We do communicate and we do get things done."

Funding for the organization comes primarily from the Van Buren Foundation and the county board of supervisors. Additional sources are business membership dues, grants and fundraising from hosting events. Since 2001, both Keosaukua and Cantril have implemented a hotel tax, but despite campaigns to educate residents about what a lodging tax is, the other communities have voted down efforts to establish similar taxes.

Planning and inclusion were factors in the early success of the Villages of Van Buren, Inc., with planning initially done in three-year cycles. In 1999 the staff and board of the organization, with the assistance of the University of Northern Iowa, generated a three-year plan of action. This plan guided tourism marketing efforts through 2003, but since then the board has moved away from regular planning. Today the organization does not have a formal written marketing plan. Some feel this will be problematic in the long run.

Despite the current lack of a written marketing plan, the marketing efforts of the organization are highly successful. The Villages of Van Buren is a six-time winner of the Tourism County of the Year award. Their website has been recognized twice and their visitors guide was named the consumer publication of the year by the Iowa Office of Tourism. Much of this can be attributed to the leadership of the staff and board who are willing to try new things.

Successes and Challenges

Van Buren County has seen many positive effects from tourism. Growth has been gradual enough that it has been accepted by residents, and is now fairly well integrated into the county's economy. Community leaders cite tourism as one of their three top economic drivers along with agriculture and light manufacturing. Increased community pride is also widely cited as a positive effect of tourism in the county.

"Today in my restaurant it is a common thing that people drive even up to 100 miles just to come and eat supper," said business owner Ben Hendricks. "The reason that tourism is so important in my business is the fact that probably well over 50 percent of my income is from tourism. It is very important for me for tourism to exist for my livelihood—tourism is the outside dollar coming into your community. I buy as many things as I possibly can locally, and I wouldn't be buying those things if I didn't have the tourism dollars to spend."

The historic Whitely Opera House houses the Bonaparte City Hall, Bonaparte Main Street, Inc., and a community room.
Photo by Cynthia Messer.

Monitoring and evaluating the success of tourism has been a challenge for the Villages of Van Buren, Inc., but it has tried several approaches, including asking business members to collect data.

Villages staff tracks visitor inquiries and brochure distribution, but identifying how many of those inquiries result in visits continues to be a struggle.

In 2009 the Villages implemented visitor survey cards using business reply mail to save responders the cost of stamps. The result has been "surprisingly good" returns," Reese said. "Believe it or not, a 27 cent stamp can make or break a postcard return," she noted.

The survey cards ask questions such as, "Where did you hear about us?" "How much money did you spend on lodging? On gas? On gifts?" The survey yields information on "good things and bad things," Reese said, with negative feedback just as important as positive. Negative feedback "tells us where we can improve," she noted.

Over the years, the Villages of Van Buren, Inc., has successfully capitalized on the county's assets with a strategy of county-wide events to draw visitors. The largest is the Scenic Drive Festival, held the second full weekend of October each year. Formerly known as the Forest Craft and Scenic Drive Festival, this event began in the early 1980s as a partnership between the city of Keosaukua and the Department of Natural Resources (DNR) to promote the state park through a mix of forest-based products and activities.

Over the years, the event became county-wide, took on a new name and underwent full-scale revamping in 2007. Due to budget constraints, the DNR had to pull back its involvement, but this enabled organizers to consider new approaches. Activities were expanded so that each village is tied to the two-day festival with community-organized activities and events, and visitors are encouraged to move throughout the county.

A

This approach allows each community to develop and retain its unique aspects while being part of the larger event. The event has added new elements and today includes an art show, music, parade, antiques, and a car show. County tourism supporters believe the Scenic Drive Festival brings thousands of new dollars into the county, although they cannot quantify its impact.

Bike Van Buren, held the third full weekend in August, has been held annually for nearly 25 years. Participation peaked in the mid-1990s at approximately 500 people. Stacey Reese estimated 2007 participation at about 225 people. The Villages have worked to freshen the event and help boost participation by making changes, such as a poker run. The designated route winds across the county and through the Villages, in part along the new Historic Hills Scenic Byway.

In 2000, the Villages added Canoe Van Buren, a two-day event that starts on the river in one end of the county and floats 41 miles to the other end. The most recent addition is a barn tour that ties the agricultural roots of the county to the event.

An old grist mill is the home of the Bonaparte Retreat, one of Iowa's finest restaraunts. Photo by Cynthia Messer.

Preservation efforts in Van Buren County are driven as much by a desire to preserve heritage and lifestyle as to generate economic gain. Most are collaborations among the county historic preservation commission, individuals, and the county. However, while historic preservation is a major focus in each village, staffing and money continue to be issues—requiring public support. For example, the county owns, manages, and subsidizes the restored Greef General Store in Bentonsport, leasing space to craft and antique shop vendors. The primary audience is visitors to the area.

The historic Wakefield Farm Sales Pavilion near Cantril proved to be another challenge in 2000, when plans to restore and develop it into a B&B fell through. Built in 1912 as an auction and lodging facility, the pavilion saw many uses over the years, including serving as an attraction in the county. Today, the pavilion sits empty and its private owners recently listed it for sale. Its future will depend on the new owners, but a lodging establishment remains a possibility and conversion to a history education site has also been discussed.

On the plus side, Lake Sugema has exceeded expectations of even the most optimistic supporters. "The DNR told us what this was going to do to the economy of our county—and it has had a major impact," said Mary Muir, former director of The Villages of Van Buren, Inc. "Two businesses developed directly because of the lake—a bait and tackle shop and a hunting supply store—and seven log cabins were built at the lake. Then Keosauqua Economic Development built three cabins along the river and the hotel put up a 14-unit building. You know that growth is directly from the lake because boats are parked all over around the hotel. It really has made a difference."

Additional cabins and cottages have been built around the lake, adding to the lodging options. One is the Bonaparte Inn B&B, which opened in 2006. Housed in a former factory, the building was purchased in 2004 and underwent an 18-month renovation. The inn has nine rooms, four suites and an event space. In addition to lodging, the inn's owners have carved out a niche market for special events and weddings. Villages Folk School was started in 2009, based on an idea of local artisans. The school offers learning experiences in traditional arts and crafts, such as pottery, forge iron, quilting, spinning and painting. Participants are invited to relax, create, unplug, and to "return to times when things were simpler and creativity was a way of life."

Bill Printy said the county came up with idea of a folk arts school in about 2007 or 2008. "We have a whole lot of underutilized real estate, and by that I mean old historic empty buildings. It occurred to me at that time, 'Why can't we use this underutilized real estate and make the whole county the campus of this folk school?' It seemed to us a whole new market out there and that was people wanted Bentonsport to be a whole new learning experience."

Growth Issues

Although the evidence is anecdotal, it's clear that tourism has grown since 1991 when we first profiled the county. Both community and tourism leaders value tourism as part of their economy, but they have not sought development that would jeopardize the quiet lifestyle they enjoy and promote.

It's also clear that the infrastructure in Van Buren County has been improved through tourism. Lake Sugema was a key addition to the resource base, and the state invested more than $1 million on improving the infrastructure at both Keosauqua-Lacey State Park and Shimek State Forest

in the 1990s. Tourism on Scenic Drive Festival weekends creates increases in traffic, but the organizers have figured out how to manage this.

"Our population triples in those two days," said Stacey Reese. "The infrastructure we have in place in our communities isn't set for that many people, so we had to get those people spread out. To do that we incorporated the Scenic Drive Festival and the communities have taken it upon themselves to come up with something, some kind of special activity for that weekend. We've gotten good comments from our visitors. Our outlying communities see that it works and that encourages our communities."

Pumpkin and squash create a pretty autumn scene on a street in Bentonsport. Photo by Cynthia Messer.

The lack of county land-use planning and zoning ordinances is a serious potential problem. Resident sentiment has strongly opposed zoning ordinances to date, but many of those interviewed see a glimmer of hope that this is changing. "The county went through a process two or three years ago to try to get a comprehensive plan, but that met with stiff resistance, primarily from our agricultural sector in the county," said County Auditor John Finney. "Lots of folks like to live here because they like to have the freedom to build where they want to build and do what they want to do on their own land. They saw the planning as another step toward zoning. We are not growing that fast, but we must be careful."

Those in the business and tourism sector understand the value of zoning for managed growth and protection of local resources, as well as the need for a comprehensive plan. One county supervisor said, "It will come to pass. There are people who don't like the word 'zoning' who are actually asking for it in a roundabout way. It is an educational process."

Affordable housing is still a major concern. The increase in population and expanded business has filled most vacant housing. A new subdivision helped ease the housing shortage, but demand helped drive up land valuations. Tax abatement is available for commercial, residential, and industrial development, and Keosauqua has established a tax increment financing district for industrial development and the new housing subdivision.

Lessons Learned

Success with marketing efforts has led to further development of new marketing strategies. As noted, the Villages of Van Buren produces a variety of brochures on attractions and hosts a website. The organization also plans to use social media, such as Twitter and Facebook, to reach audiences.

In 1991 we cited community involvement in Van Buren County as vital to the villages' tourism strategy, and 20 years later it continues to be important. Local volunteers are very active in preserving their collective history and providing services for events and festivals. "None of this would really happen without volunteers, because the funds just aren't there to do it any other way," said Mary Muir. "It's the way things get done in small communities—volunteerism.

We are very fortunate. There is a nice mix of people who have lived here all their lives and people who have come in and are involved. Volunteerism has grown since 1991." Volunteers participate individually and through community service groups and clubs.

"There's a dramatic difference in tourism in Van Buren County today as compared to 20 years ago [when] there were chance visitors. Now I think Van Buren County is a destination for tourism," said Bill Printy. "There have been an awful lot of things done that have been factors in that. We are fortunate to have in this county a lot of community-based organizations run by volunteers—Van Buren County Historical Society, the Bentonsport Improvement Association, Bonaparte Main Street, Cantril Grassroots, etc. And all these community-based organizations over the last 10 years especially have been working diligently on things to enhance this as a destination for tourism."

This collaboration has been a critical factor in the success of tourism in Van Buren County and of marketing efforts for the Villages of Van Buren, Inc.

"I think our communities and those community leaders realize their community cannot stand alone," said Reese. "And if they're relying on tourism, it's going to take all the communities, and that's a good thing. We continue to remind people that they are not competing against the community down the road. It's a partnership and we need to cross-promote each other."

The Villages of Van Buren, Inc., is the primary marketing entity for the county. As noted, the board has grown from five to 14 members representing each of the villages. The staff credits this large board for facilitating communication with each of the villages, which in turn, enables continued collaboration. Classified as a 501c4, the organization depends heavily on memberships for part of its funding. The organization is not self-sustaining, and funding also comes from the county government and event fees. The Villages also receives grants from two private foundations in the county, as well as funds from a state foundation created from gambling proceeds. Nevertheless, funding continues to be a challenge for the organization.

Developing B&Bs and emphasizing history and natural attractions have proven a successful combination. The two distinct markets for the county—heritage tourists and outdoor enthusiasts—are complementary. Motorcoach groups, a target audience in 1991, are still identified as an important audience; however, the lack of accommodations for large groups is cited as a drawback. One business owner believes many of the one-day motorcoach visitors return independently, but there is no documentation of this.

Vision of the Future

The benefits from tourism have met or exceeded the expectations of tourism and community leaders in Van Buren County. Tourism continues to play a valued part in the county economy. Strong community pride is a key asset to tourism growth. Cooperation among villages has been a major factor in success and will continue to benefit the greater county. Improved tracking, monitoring, and evaluation methods will help maintain the support of local stakeholders and elected officials. Van Buren County tourism leaders are sensitive to the need to protect their natural and cultural assets, but they seem resistant to comprehensive planning—including land-use planning and zoning.

The vision of the Villages of Van Buren remains focused on heritage tourism and natural attractions. Cultural-heritage tourism and soft adventure trends (as noted in Chapter 7) suggest that the Villages of Van Buren are well positioned to benefit from tourism in the future. The attention to authenticity and quality, the use of events such as the Scenic Drive Festival to both educate and entertain, and the public/private partnership approach to tourism are strong assets.

Most residents want to see tourism continue to grow slowly and remain a part of the economic base of the county. By implementing systems to document growth and impact, tourism leaders will be in a better position to show the value of tourism to the county and encourage compatible development. The Folk Art School will be a complementary attraction—drawing new visitors and creating additional positive economic benefits for local businesses. As Bill Printy said, Van Buren County has become "a destination for tourism."

A

Persons Interviewed

Stacey (Glandon) Reese
Executive Director
Villages of Van Buren, Inc.

Mary Muir
Former Executive Director of
Villages of Van Buren, Inc.

Cheryl Duke
Manager, Greef General Store,
Bentonsport

Ben & Rose Hendricks
Owners, Bonaparte Retreat
Restaurant

Jon Finney
County Auditor

Bill Printy
Owner, Iron & Lace

Gianna Barrows
Chair, Bonaparte Main Street,
Inc.

Rhea Huddleston
Owner, Addie May Fudge
Factory
Bonaparte, IA

Marvin Philips
County Supervisor

Nancy Alexander
Owner, Alexander's Cottage
Bentonsport, IA

Doris Secor
Van Buren County Historical
Society

Source: Smith, W. (2008, March 16). Van Buren villages promote festival fever. *The Hawk Eye,* Burlington, IA. Retrieved July 29, 2010 from http://www.thehawkeye.mobi/Story/PRG08-Villages-031608

Appendix B
Wildlife Tourism

Opportunities and Examples

Introduction

Wildlife tourism is a niche market opportunity that has the potential to serve dual purposes: to generate economic benefit as well as to utilize and protect vital natural resources. With sometimes relatively simple steps, wildlife tourism provides an opportunity to expand attraction offerings and reach new markets. Perhaps the most appealing thing about wildlife tourism is its reach across seasons: wildlife viewing opportunities exist 365 days a year.

Wildlife tourism covers a broad array of experiences, and every state has a wildlife division with resources available to assist. For example, in Minnesota, the Nongame Wildlife Program is the primary source within the Department of Natural Resources. Other sources for information and technical assistance in most states include the state office of tourism and universities and colleges. Nationally, government entities such as the U.S. Fish and Wildlife Service, the U.S. Forest Service, and the National Park Service provide good resources.

The following materials offer an overview of wildlife tourism, a snapshot of the participants, a process to help you develop a strategy to profit from wildlife tourism, and a list of valuable resources.

First, what **IS** wildlife tourism?

> Wildlife tourism can be defined as any form of tourism in which the primary aim of the tourist is to experience the natural environment or the animals and plants that live within it.
>
> Velander & Ladle

Wildlife tourism is related to wildlife recreation such as hunting, fishing, and wildlife viewing. Wildlife viewing activities include observing, feeding, or photographing wildlife. However, the tourism component relates to the distance traveled (100 miles), visit duration (overnight), and motivation (pleasure).

B

Importance

As of 2004, wildlife tourism was a significant growth area. Nearly everybody enjoys seeing wildlife, but more and more enthusiasts are making wildlife viewing a purpose for travel. In the United States, more than **66 million** U.S. residents engage in wildlife viewing and **spend $38 billion annually**. Birdwatchers spend $32 billion dollars annually on travel, food, and equipment. (Source: USFWS, 2001)

According to the 2001 National Survey of Fishing, Hunting and Wildlife Associated Recreation conducted by the U.S. Fish and Wildlife Service, wildlife watchers increased in number by 5 percent from 1996 to 2001. Their expenditures for trips, equipment, and other items increased 16 percent.

> *"If wildlife watching were a company, its sales of $38.4 billion would rank it 33rd in the Forbes 500 list for 2001—placing it just ahead of Motorola and Kmart."*
>
> 2001 National and State Economics of Wildlife Watching, U.S. Fish and Wildlife Service

Nationwide

- 66 million Americans participate in wildlife watching
- Wildlife viewers spent $38.4 billion in 2001
- Produced more than 1 million jobs
- Generated over $4 billion in state and federal income tax
- Generated $2.1 billion in state sales taxes

Figure 1: 2001 U.S. Wildlife Watching Expenditures by Major Category

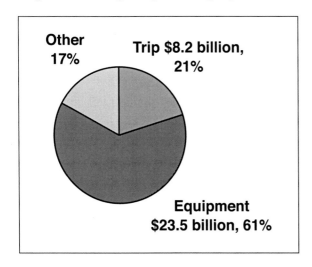

Figure 2: U.S. Trip Expenditures for Wildlife Viewing, 2001

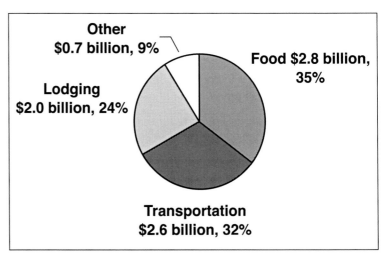

The Market

So, who are wildlife viewers, and what do they want?

Wildlife viewers are categorized in several different ways. For example, the U.S. Fish and Wildlife Service in the 2001 survey used a strict definition of wildlife watching. Participants either had to take a "special interest" in wildlife around their homes or take a trip for the "primary purpose" of watching wildlife. Wildlife watching that occurred while pleasure driving was considered a secondary activity and was not included.

In the most general terms, wildlife viewers range from avid enthusiasts to casual viewers.

Avid Enthusiast	Casual Viewer
Avid enthusiasts not only view wildlife in nature, but often engage in related activities. These may include keeping lists and notes about wildlife, making sketches or spending hours trying to snap the perfect photo, traveling to wildlife viewing sites, growing specialized plants or gardens to attract wildlife, and feeding birds or providing nesting sites.	Casual viewers occasionally feed, photograph, and watch wildlife or birds but don't necessarily consider themselves enthusiasts. These visitors probably don't travel specifically for wildlife viewing, but may take advantage when an opportunity presents itself. They may be attracted by a brochure, an event, or interest in a particular type of wildlife.

Additionally, other wildlife viewing frameworks exist that serve as simple foundations for planning a spectrum of viewing. Shackley modeled wildlife-watching experiences into a continuum from observation to participation and captive to free (Figure 3). Although a somewhat simplistic model, it is useful for comparing and further segmenting those who view wildlife. The addition of captive observational and participatory opportunities adjacent to free observation areas may enhance wildlife viewing experiences.

Figure 3: Characterization of wildlife tourist activity from Shackley (1996).

Nature of tourist activity	Nature of animal captivity	
	Captive	Free
Observation	Zoo Aquarium	Safari Game drives Diving Whale watching
Participation	Feed zoo animal Interactive exhibits	Gorilla watching Swim with dolphins Hunting

Shackley, M. (1996). *Wildlife tourism*. London, England: International Thomson Business Press.

B

Market Interests Beyond Wildlife Viewing

Wildlife viewers are also interested in outdoor activities and experiences that may expand opportunities for a community or region. Combining wildlife viewing with other activities can keep these visitors in the area longer, or bring them back.

Research indicates that people are primarily motivated to watch wildlife to be close to nature and because of a fascination with wildlife. A key factor to viewing wildlife is the wildlife experience: viewing, seeing, and hearing wildlife in a quiet atmosphere.

A combination of additional nature-based activities and cultural/historic opportunities are likely to enhance experiences and extend wildlife viewing trips. Studies in the past 20 years suggest that nature tourists may enjoy visiting cultural sites and a variety of nature-based activities.

Several national studies have identified activities and features that wildlife viewers desire. For example, in one study (Cordell et al., 1999), birders indicated they are active in a variety of outdoor recreation pursuits including walking, visiting nature and historic centers, cross-country skiing, orienteering, and nature study. In a similar study from Colorado (Manfredo & Larson, 1993), wildlife viewers indicated interest in combining camping, picnicking, and auto sightseeing with wildlife viewing.

In addition to activities, seven key features associated with an ideal nature-oriented vacation were identified in a study by Meric and Hunt (1998). These seven features include: uncrowded, experiencing nature, inexpensive, historic, educational, friendly, and hospitable.

Communities and tourism businesses that can create wildlife tourism experiences that combine features, activities, and opportunities can maximize the benefit of wildlife tourism and create positive experiences for wildlife tourists.

MINNESOTA

A study of Minnesota wildlife viewers found that similar to wildlife viewers across the U.S., wildlife viewers are mature, Anglo, and possess relatively high income and education levels. Respondents' gender was balanced—male (50.7%) and female (49.3%). The mean age was 55.9 years. Most reported an annual income of more than $75,000 (41.6%) and 75 percent of respondents had at least a college degree. When asked about day and overnight travel to view wildlife in Minnesota, participants indicated more day trips than overnights. The majority (50.3%) took between one and 20 day trips in a one-year period, but 11.8 percent took 50 or more day trips.

Those traveling overnight for wildlife viewing took an average of nearly two trips in a year. The average length of stay was 2.7 nights and the majority traveled in groups of one or two people. Average travel expenditures for overnight wildlife viewing trips in Minnesota were $184.78.

According to the Minnesota Department of Natural Resources, Nongame Wildlife Program, the key species in Minnesota for wildlife tourism are:

Loons	Greater Prairie Chickens
Bald Eagles	Tundra Swans
Peregrine Falcons	Trumpeter Swans
Fall Hawk Migration	Warblers
Northern Wintering Owls	Moose
Sharp-tailed Grouse	Timber Wolves

In the study of Minnesota wildlife viewers, the interest in each of these species was assessed. Survey respondents ranked warblers, bald eagles, hawk migrations, and loons as the top species of interest. (See Tables 1 & 2)

Table 1: Species of interest among Minnesota wildlife viewing mail survey respondents, 2002.

	Mean[1]	S.D.
Warblers (n=1077)	4.3	1.0
Bald eagles (n=1087)	4.2	1.1
Hawk migrations (n=1074)	4.1	1.1
Loon (n=1085)	4.1	1.1
Northern wintering owls (n=1067)	4.1	1.1
Peregrine falcons (n=1070)	4.1	1.1
Trumpeter swans (n=1073)	3.9	1.1
Tundra swans (n=1066)	3.9	1.1
Moose (n=1071)	3.8	1.2
Timberwolves (n=1069)	3.8	1.3
Greater prairie chickens (n=1065)	3.6	1.2
Sharp-tailed grouse (n=1061)	3.6	1.2

[1] Rated on a scale from 1 to 5, where 1=very uninterested, 3=unsure, and 5=very interested.

Table 2: Type of wildlife most viewed or enjoyed among Minnesota wildlife viewing mail survey respondents, 2002.

	Frequency	Percent*
Type of wildlife most frequently watched, fed, or photographed		
Birds	1039	95.4
Large mammals	20	1.8
Small mammals	21	1.9
Other	9	0.8
Total	1089	100.0
Type of wildlife most enjoyable to watch, feed, or photograph		
Birds	962	89.9
Large mammals	64	5.9
Small mammals	36	3.3
Other	20	1.8
Total	1082	99.9

* Percent may not total 100 due to rounding.

Schneider, I and Salk, R. (2002). *Information needs and experience preferences of birders and watchable wildlife participants*. St. Paul, MN: University of Minnesota.

B

Planning for Success

Developing a plan for your wildlife tourism effort will help you create a niche market opportunity that is beneficial and sustainable. Wildlife tourism engages the visitor in an encounter with nature, and care should be taken from the earliest stage of the development process to ensure that the encounter is positive for the visitor, the community, and the natural resources upon which it depends. A well-crafted plan will help!

Four key elements of the planning process include understanding the market, assessing your resources, developing what you have, and marketing. The previous overview of wildlife viewers provides initial insight into the market. The following information will help you to assess your resources, and consider strategies for developing and marketing what you have to offer.

Resource Assessment

Once you have identified and understand something about the potential market for wildlife viewing, a comprehensive resource assessment is needed.

> ...natural beauty is not limited to mammals and birds. There is a living collage of butterflies, moths, dragonflies, frogs, toads, turtles, and other hopping, flying, crawling, and swimming creatures that offer the potential for endless hours of observation, photography and enjoyment.
>
> (Henderson, Lambrecht et al., 1997)

Step 1: *Determine the "Area"*

- Is it your community, county, multiple counties, or a single site?
- Who else in the region is already promoting wildlife tourism?

Step 2: *Identify Area Experts*

Identify local and regional contacts with specific knowledge of your area.

- Local, state and federal officials
- Tourism or wildlife promotion groups
- Local organizations or clubs (e.g., birders, photography, natural history, historical society, etc.)
- Nature centers and environmental learning centers
- Academics—local teachers, college professors, Extension educators, etc.
- Residents with a special interest
- Local specialty store owners often have knowledge or network

Many of these experts may also be potential partners. However, they may be motivated by different reasons to participate in the effort. One of the first steps in the process of developing a community wildlife tourism effort is to discuss the idea and gauge interest. Schedule a formal meeting and invite all of these experts and partners. This will help gain their support and interest in developing a plan for wildlife tourism development in your area. Determining what role each might serve will help the success of your wildlife tourism effort.

POTENTIAL PARTNERS
FOR WILDLIFE TOURISM EFFORTS

City, County, Government Officials

Natural Resource/Public Land Managers
Local Parks & Recreation Director
County Extension Educators
State Tourism Office
State Natural Resource Offices

Local Planning & Zoning Department
Transportation Dept. & Public Utilities
Mayor/City Council/City Manager
County Commissioners
Other Local Political Leaders

Civic, Business, Nonprofit Organizations

Birding, Garden, Photography or Other Civic Clubs
Sports Clubs – Hunting, Ski, Snowmobile, etc.
Convention and Visitors Bureau
Economic Development Officer
Environmental/Conservation Groups
Nature or Environmental Learning Centers
Chamber of Commerce

Historical Society/Preservation Groups
Cultural Organizations
Minority Groups/Indigenous Populations
Business/Professional Clubs
Event & Festival Organizations
Rotary/Lions/Optimist/Kiwanis Civic Clubs

Local Businesses

B&Bs/Resorts/Motels/Hotels/Campgrounds
Tourist Attraction Operators
Outdoor Recreation Outfitters
Retail/Specialty Shop Owners

Travel Agents
Newspaper Editor or Columnist
Radio/TV Station Managers
Banks or Financial Institutions

Other Community Decision Influencers

College & University Professors/Researchers
Local School Teachers /Principals

Local farmers/Ranchers/Land Owners
Other Decision Influencers

SAMPLE ROLES FOR PARTNERS

- Develop & manage facility
- Protect resources
- Protect the wildlife
- Fund wildlife tourism development
- Provide access
- Provide lodging
- Provide tourist services

- Guides (train, schedule, etc.)
- Create & produce interpretive signs, maps, literature
- Create, produce & distribute marketing & promotion
- Package wildlife tourism experiences
- Evaluate marketing efforts
- Evaluate customer satisfaction

Step 3: *Create an Inventory*

One of the first questions a community or business needs to answer is, *What type of wildlife and natural features do we have?* Although we see nature around us every day, it can be amazing how much we miss or take for granted. What is commonplace to you may in fact be a potential attraction for someone else!

In order to answer this question, a complete inventory of the resources you have in the area should be completed. Consider wildlife and the natural features that attract wildlife.

Ten Top Features or Species for Wildlife Tourism

1) **Bald Eagles.** The first rule of wildlife tourism is that people can't get enough of bald eagles.

2) **Large conspicuous mammals** like bison, deer, elk, mountain sheep, mountain goats, moose, or pronghorns.

3) **Wildlife breeding grounds** or display (lek) sites. Bison in rut, elk bugling, prairie chickens booming, sharptail grouse displaying.

4) **Migratory concentration** sites or wintering sites. The spectacle of migration is a natural attraction for people. This can include shorebirds, geese, cranes, bald eagles, fish, butterflies, songbirds, etc. (Note: observation needs to be done in a controlled manner to avoid disrupting natural feeding or resting patterns.)

5) **Native biomes.** For example, Minnesota's four major biomes are tallgrass prairie, eastern hardwood forest, aspen parkland, and boreal forest. Learn the special features and major plants of your local biome(s).

6) **Lakes, swamps, wetlands, and rivers.** The edges and adjacent lands are natural concentration for many species. Interpretative opportunities exist from trails, boardwalks, viewing platforms, and boats.

7) **Wildflower concentrations** including associated butterflies, moths, and other insects. Butterfly gardens, night lights, and natural settings can provide opportunities at resorts and lodging establishments.

8) **Rare or unusual species** that can be viewed without endangering or disturbing their natural behavior.

9) **Places where families,** children, and those with disabilities can view and experience common wildlife easily. The opportunity to view deer, ducks, foxes, beaver, squirrels, butterflies, turtles, and other common wildlife is an attraction for many casual viewers. Local parks, resorts, or wildlife sanctuaries can provide these opportunities using simple techniques such as ponds, feeders, and natural areas with protected wildlife populations.

10) **Nocturnal viewing** and listening for wolves, bats, etc.; observing nesting sea turtles or penguins with a guide; or just stargazing!

Adapted from Henderson, C. (2004). Minnesota Department of Natural Resources.

Contact local and regional experts prior to conducting the inventory, as they may already have inventories that can be integrated into your information. They also will be important partners in developing and promoting opportunities.

- Wildlife
  - Large mammals like deer, moose, bison, bear
  - Small mammals such as fox, wolf, squirrel, beaver
  - Birds, including migratory and year-round species
  - Wildflower concentrations or native grass/prairies

- Natural features that attract wildlife
  - Lakes, rivers, wetlands, bogs
  - Unusual forest stands, etc.
  - Easily accessible viewing sites—for families, and those with general interest
  - Migration sites, breeding grounds, etc.
  - Nocturnal viewing sites
- Public lands that are accessible (e.g., parks, refuges, campuses, trails, or rights-of-way, etc.)
- Private lands identified as potential wildlife tourism sites

Where Is Wildlife Found?

As you create an inventory of wildlife in your area, you will need to consider where the best viewing is located. Is the best viewing site on private or public lands? If you don't know, you will need to check city, county, or state records to identify ownership. This is an opportunity to build collaboration on wildlife tourism efforts with key partners. Key questions regarding access:

- Do you have permission of the landowner or public body to actively promote and encourage visitors to go there? This must be done before marketing begins, and signage should guide visitors to the viewing site.

- Is access open or controlled? Is there a fee to enter?
  - Fees or controlled access may be used to protect the wildlife and visitors, minimize negative impact on critical resources or fragile eco-systems, and generate revenue.
  - Fees will require careful consideration of pricing and management. How will fees be collected and managed? Who will do it?

See Worksheet B.1, Inventory of Wildlife, at the end of this appendix.

Step 4: *Create a Phenology Chart*

In simple terms, phenology is tracking nature through the seasons. It is the relationship between climate and the plant and animal world. Phenology documents change in the natural world—changes we can see, hear, smell, feel, and taste. Local experts and public agencies may already have phenologies for the region, or be interested in helping to develop one for your area. For example, see if your state has a calendar—check with your Department of Natural Resources.

Become aware of the changes in nature. Changes can occur day to day, week to week, season to season or year to year.

Create a phenology. Simply make note of any observation or indication of the constant change going on in the natural world. For instance: When did you hear the first loon yodel or see a returning robin? When did you watch a flight of Canada geese head north, observe the peak fall colors or taste the first ripe wild blueberry? Record these observations and sounds in a notebook. Include the date, time, and location. Over time, you can compare these events and begin to draw connections between plant and animal life and the climate or weather associated with them. For comparison purposes, the

B

best observations are those that are made from the same location year after year. A specific site may not be possible for some animal observations, but for comparison purposes, observations made from approximately the same area are the best. This information can be set up in a simple chart to share with visitors about when and where the best viewing for different wildlife occurs.

Commonly monitored events for animals include:

- Mammals — dates of hibernation, courting rituals, birth of young
- Birds — migration, courting rituals, or nesting dates
- Amphibians (frogs & toads) — first singing, egg laying, life stages
- Insects — dates of appearance/emergence or life stage cycles

There are many examples of phenologies available.
See Worksheet B.2 at the end of this appendix.

Developing What You Have

Once you have identified key potential partners and inventoried your resources you are set to look at developing your options. You can begin with the opportunities that will require minimal effort to implement, and leave until later others that will require significant effort and broad collaborations plus funding and time to develop. Start with the easy ones, and build from there. Consider developing activities that extend your current tourism offering and create opportunities to package wildlife tourism activities with lodging, entertainment, or transportation. Focus on what is important to the potential wildlife tourist.

For example, according to the research previously cited, wildlife viewing visitors seek an experience that offers good viewing at an uncrowded site and is educational. Can you create a wildlife viewing opportunity by expanding the use of existing resources such as a walking or biking trail? With a few relatively quick additions, such as creating a brochure that provides information on the types of wildlife that can be viewed here, providing interpretive signage, and adding occasional benches, you may extend the potential use of the trail to a new audience.

For an example, see the case study of the Paul Bunyan Scenic Byway at the end of this section. For opportunities that require greater development, you will need to create a more comprehensive development plan and team. Review the chapters in this manual related to planning and development. Wildlife tourism should be considered as you develop or review your tourism development strategy.

When wildlife tourism visitors do come, are you prepared to meet their needs? This involves both the local infrastructure and the visitor experience. Some changes may be required, but these changes can enhance the tourist experience for other visitors and benefit local residents as well.

Infrastructure

A primary consideration for creating a positive wildlife experience is the development or maintenance of quality facilities, clear signage, and good roads. Employ universal design concepts that consider the diverse needs of as many people as possible.

- Facilities
  - Roads/access
  - Parking
  - Restrooms
  - Drinking fountains
  - Entrances
  - Assembly area
  - Signs
  - Exhibits & interpretation
  - Viewing/rest areas: seating, telescopes, interpretation

- Programs
  - Information systems
  - Displays/exhibits
  - Self-discovery program: Individuals use maps, handouts and interpretive signage to guide themselves on a self-discovery walk or viewing experience
  - Audiovisual programs—videos, audio guide, etc.
  - Guide/ranger-led programs
  - Handouts: brochures, maps, etc.

- Liability Issues
  - Insurance
  - Fencing

Use Worksheet B.3 at the end of this appendix to begin documenting information about your site.

The Visitor Experience

Visitors place value on their experiences beyond their expenditures. Travelers today are often experienced consumers, and their expectations are formed by a number of factors including their past experiences, their needs, and what they have heard or read. By seeking to understand the needs and expectations of wildlife viewers, you are more likely to help create positive experiences for them that bring them back and get them telling others about the experience.

One of the key attributes that wildlife viewers seek is a hospitable welcome. This is more than just a friendly greeting. It is providing service that meets or exceeds their expectations and making sure that they have a positive experience. Consider hosting customer service/hospitality training for your staff and for others in the community to develop or enhance service in your region. This can have a positive impact on residents as well.

B

You cannot guarantee that wildlife viewers will see wildlife, but you can make them feel welcomed and work to meet their unique needs. Provide services and products that address their specific needs and interests.

Examples _____

Hours:	Extend hours of service beyond 9:00 a.m. to 5:00 p.m. Include weekend service hours
Food:	Provide hearty meal options Offer earlier breakfast hours (before dawn) Box lunches
Information:	Have information available about the wildlife in the area including books and field guides, detailed maps, checklists, contacts for local guides, etc.
Equipment:	Provide opportunities to rent and/or purchase wildlife equipment such as binoculars, or items like hats, t-shirts, and postcards. Consider partnering with local suppliers or retailers for rental items

---

Marketing

Marketing your wildlife tourism opportunity is like marketing any tourism experience. You need to set realistic goals and develop a marketing plan that includes research of the market, matching market and "product" pricing, promotion, and evaluation of both the marketing effort and customer satisfaction.

- Market Research
  - Who is your current market, and will this appeal to them?
  - What is the potential new market and what information is available about them? (e.g., demographics, likes/dislikes, etc.)
  - Where are they located? (regional, within state, national, international?)
  - What is the competition?

- Pricing
  - Will you charge a fee for wildlife viewing experiences?

- Promotion and Advertising
  In the 2002 study (Schneider and Salk, 2002) of wildlife viewers in Minnesota, respondents indicated that the information sources most used were birding books (88.5 percent), magazines (83.2 percent) and brochures or pamphlets (78.1 percent). Other frequently used sources included the Minnesota Ornithological Union hotline (1-800-657-3700), Internet, and friends or family.
  - How will you reach the target market?
  - What is the best mix of advertising and promotion?
  - Can wildlife viewing be packaged with lodging, transportation, or other tourism components?
  - Who are potential partners: local convention and visitor bureaus, chambers, tour operators, travel agencies, etc.

- Evaluation
  - How will you track the response to advertising?
  - How will you evaluate the effectiveness of your marketing?
  - How will you evaluate customer satisfaction?

Conclusion

Wildlife tourism provides a niche market opportunity that reaches across seasons with potential for wildlife viewing 365 days a year. It includes a broad array of wildlife tourism experiences. A good plan with sometimes relatively simple steps will help you create experiences that are beneficial and sustainable.

Twelve Quick Actions to Increase Wildlife Tourism

1. Purchase field guides and related books and make these available to guests.

2. Start a phenology notebook about your site.

3. Add wildlife or bird posters and information in your lobby.

4. Put up bird and/or wildlife feeders, birdbaths, etc.

5. Obtain a supply of wildlife and bird checklists, brochures, and maps of the area.

6. Contact local birding and wildlife clubs or groups.

7. Obtain and maintain a list of events by local parks, DNR, nature center, etc.

8. Develop landscaping improvements designed to appeal to wildlife.

9. Enhance walking trails in the immediate area—through forest, lakeshore, or fields.

10. Order magazine subscriptions to birding and wildlife/nature magazines.

11. Network with local Convention & Visitors Bureau, Chamber of Commerce, and other tourism promotion groups to promote wildlife tourism in your area.

12. Promote your wildlife tourism directly to potential participants through targeted efforts.

B

Selected Resources

National Park Service, www.nps.gov

Bureau of Land Management, www.blm.gov

U.S. Forest Service, www.fs.fed.us

The U.S. Forest Service Nature Watch has created a useful CD-ROM (2004) entitled *"D.I.Y. – Do It Yourself."* It includes numerous examples, samples, and models.

U.S. Department of Agriculture, www.usda.gov or www.recreation.gov

U.S. Fish and Wildlife Service, www.fws.gov

National Interpreters' Association, http://interpnet.com/

American Birding Association, www.americanbirding.org

Watchable Wildlife, www.watchablewildlife.org

Survey information

National Survey of Fishing, Hunting and Wildlife Associated Recreation, http://federalaid.fws.gov/ or http://fa.r9.fws.gov/surveys/surveys.html

National Survey on Recreation and the Environment, www.srs.fs.fed.us/trends/nsre2.html

Minnesota State Resources

Minnesota Department of Natural Resources, www.dnr.state.mn.us

MN Ornithologists' Union, www.mou.mn.org

Explore Minnesota Tourism, www.exploreminnesota.com

University of Minnesota Forestry Library, including a searchable database on trails, http://forestry.lib.umn.edu/

University of Minnesota Tourism Center, www.tourism.umn.edu

References

Adams, C.E., Leifester, J.A., & S.C., Herron, J. (1997). Understanding wildlife constituents: Birders and waterfowl hunters. *Wildlife Society Bulletin, 25(3)*, 653-660.

Cordell, H.K., Herbert, N.G., & Pandolfi, F. (1999). *Birding, 31(2),* 168-176.

Duda, M.D. (1995). *Watching wildlife*. Helena, MT: Falcon Publishers.

Henderson, C., Lambrecht, A.L., et al. (1997). *Traveler's guide to wildlife in Minnesota*. St. Paul, MN: Minnesota Department of Natural Resources.

Hunter, C. (2002). *Everyone's nature*. Cambridge, MN: Adventure Publications, Inc.

Manfredo, M.J. (2002). *Wildlife viewing: A management handbook*. Corvallis, OR: Oregon State University Press.

Meric, H.J., & Hunt, J. (1998). Ecotourists' motivational and demographic characteristics: A case study of North Carolina travelers. *Journal of Travel Research, 36,* 57-61.

Oberbillig, D.R. (2001). *Providing positive wildlife viewing experiences*. Denver, CO: Colorado Division of Wildlife and Watchable Wildlife, Inc.

Schneider, I., & Salk, R. (2002). *Information needs and experience preferences of birders and Watchable Wildlife participants*. St. Paul, MN: University of Minnesota. (College of Food, Agricultural and Natural Resource Sciences Staff Paper 165)

U.S. Department of the Interior, Fish and Wildlife Service, U.S. Department of Commerce, U.S. Census Bureau. (2002). *2001 national survey of fishing, hunting and wildlife-associated recreation*. Washington, D.C.: Federal agencies named above.

B

Birds of the Byway

The Paul Bunyan Scenic Byway is one of 20 designated Scenic Byways in Minnesota. The Byway was developed in the year 2000 to promote the scenic, historic, cultural, and natural resources of the area, which is located approximately 25 miles north of Brainerd.

The Birds of the Byway project was one of the very first initiatives completed by the Byway group. Members of the byway group saw opportunity in a program offered by the Minnesota Department of Natural Resources and the Minnesota Office of Tourism (MOT) to help communities develop watchable wildlife attractions in their areas. This program included workshops and financial assistance for developing marketing materials.

In March 2000, the Paul Bunyan Scenic Byway group applied for and received a grant for $2,000 from MOT for development of a birding brochure. Another $2,000 of matching funds was raised from local partners.

A brochure and checklist were developed to attract visitors to the area and guide them along the Byway. The Birds of the Byway brochure and checklist are also available for download from the Scenic Byway website: www.paulbunyanscenicbyway.org

This project incorporated two important regional tourism opportunities—a scenic byway and wildlife watching. Although the primary use of the Byway was recreation, as the group was identifying points of interest along the Byway, they found that there were a great number of sites for quality bird watching along the Byway. One of the key attractions is the Upgaard Wildlife Management area, managed by the Department of Natural Resources.

Partners

This is a good example of private-public partnership to bring together expertise and funding to develop a tourism opportunity.

> *"Just because you are not the expert, it doesn't mean you can't do the project.*
> *Find the local experts in your area and work with them."* Lynn Scharonbroich

Minnesota DNR Non-game Wildlife Program

Minnesota Office of Tourism

Steve and Jo Blanich – well-known local birding authorities

University Minnesota Extension

The Bird Feeder – local bird store

Local photographers

Funders (for brochure and checklist)

Minnesota DNR Non-game Wildlife Program

Minnesota Office of Tourism

Whitefish Area Lodging Association

Ideal Township

The Bird Feeder – local bird store

Ideal Township Community Service

Marketing

The group works with the local chambers of commerce and the area resorts to market the Byway in addition to a Byway newsletter, radio interviews, and newspaper articles. The Byway group also uses public relations efforts such as:

- **Local bus tours** to develop awareness of the Byway including the wildlife watching opportunities.
- **Guided tours** for media representatives at the 2001 Governor's Fishing Opener event at Breezy Point Resort.

Successes & Challenges

The birding brochure was the first major project completed by the Paul Bunyan Scenic Byway organization. It provided credibility and developed community support for the organization in the local area. Some of the contributors to the Birds of the Byway project became members of the Byway association. It also developed awareness of Byway among locals and visitors.

The original printing of the Birds of the Byway brochure included a coupon incentive to encourage reporting of bird sightings. Those receiving the brochure could return the coupon to receive a gift. It was thought that this would help track users: however, very few coupons were returned. The group does keep track of distribution of the brochure.

The Byway group continues to enhance natural resource opportunities for residents and visitors in the area through grants and community support. The Birds of the Byway project highlighted a valuable asset for residents and visitors.

Contact:

Lynn Scharonbroich
Paul Bunyan Scenic Byway
PO Box 401
Pequot Lakes, MN 56472

www.paulbunyanscenicbyway.org

Make sure you have written permission for all uses of any photographs that you may use in your promotional materials. You may have permission to use a photograph on a brochure, but it may not mean you have permission to use it in other materials or on your website.

B

Worksheet B.1: *Inventory of Wildlife*

ATTRACTION CATEGORY (list each species)	Location	Availability and Abundance *(see codes at bottom)												Comments
		Jan	Feb	Mar	Apr	May	Jun	Jul	Aug	Sep	Oct	Nov	Dec	
BIRDS														
MAMMALS														
REPTILES														
AMPHIBIANS														
INDIGENOUS TREES/PLANTS														

X = Present   R = Rare   C= Common   A= Abundant

Worksheet B.2: Phenology

COMMON NAME	SPECIES	DATE / TIME	EVENT	LOCATION	COMMENTS

Worksheet B.3: Information Checklist
for Wildlife Viewing Destination

Directions: Use this checklist to help you plan and gather the information needed about each wildlife viewing site. This detailed information will help you develop marketing materials and service guides.

Name of Site _____

INFORMATION	COMMENTS
Owner/Manager:	
Phone:	
TTY:	
After hours contact & phone number:	
Mailing address:	
Location & driving directions:	
Seasons/Hours of operation:	
Admission/Usage fees:	
Weather information: (phone and/or website)	

Over ⊃

INFORMATION	COMMENTS
Services Available: ☐ Parking ☐ Public rest rooms ☐ Public telephones ☐ Campground ☐ Picnic area ☐ Swim area ☐ Fishing access ☐ Boat ramp and/or dock ☐ Boat gas dock ☐ Marina ☐ Interpretive areas ☐ Hiking trails ☐ Gift shop ☐ General store ☐ Other: ☐ _____ ☐ _____ ☐ _____ ☐ _____	
Services available for visitors with mobility, visual, hearing, or learning impairments?	
Map(s) of the area detailing the services and indicating other nearby services such as lodging, dining, equipment rentals, medical services, shopping.	
Other information:	